ONE CHRIST
ONE GOSPEL

Library of Congress Control Number: 2019920305

Contact: OneChristOneGospel@gmail.com

Cover Design and Layout:
Raelynn Cramer

Special Thanks:
Dawn J.
Linda A.
Jenny B.

ONE CHRIST ONE GOSPEL

A Reader's Harmony of the Life of Jesus

Aaron Delisio

Table Rock Press

CONTENTS

Appendices

The beginning of the Good News of Jesus Christ the Son of God

In the beginning was the Word, and the Word was with God, and the Word was God. He was in the beginning with God. All things came to be through him, and without him not one thing came to be that has come to be. In him was life, and the life was the light of men. And the light shines in the darkness, and the darkness has not recognized it.

There came a man, sent from God, whose name was John. He came as a witness, that he might bear witness of the light, that all might believe through him. He was not the light, but came that he might bear witness of the light.

There was the true light, which illuminates everyone, coming into the world. In the world he was, and the world came to be through him, and the world did not know him. To his own he came, and those who were his own did not receive him. But as many as received him, to them he gave the right to become children of God, to those who believe in his name, who were born not of blood, nor of the will of the flesh, nor of the will of man, but of God.

And the Word became flesh, and pitched his tent among us, and we gazed upon his glory, glory as of the only begotten from the Father, full of grace and truth. John bears witness about him and has cried out, saying, "This was he of whom I said, 'The one who comes after me has come before me, for he was first before me.' " For of his fullness we all received, and grace for grace. For the Law was given through Moses; grace and truth came through Jesus Christ. No one ever has watched God; the only begotten Son, who is in the heart of the Father, he has disclosed him.

There was in the days of Herod, the king of Judea, a certain priest named Zacharias, of the priestly division of Abijah, and he had a wife of the daughters of Aaron, and her name was Elizabeth. Now they were both righteous before God, walking in all the commandments and ordinances of the Lord blamelessly. And they had no child, because Elizabeth was barren, and both were advanced in their days.

Now it came to pass, while he executed the priest's office before God in the order of his division, according to the custom of the priest's office, his lot was to enter into the temple of the Lord and burn incense. And the whole multitude of the people were praying outside at the hour of incense.

Now there appeared to him an angel of the Lord standing on the right side of the altar of incense. And Zacharias was troubled when he saw him and fear fell upon him. But the angel said to him, "Fear not, Zacharias, because your supplication has been heard, and your wife Elizabeth shall bear you a son, and you shall call his name John. And there shall be joy to you and exultation, and many shall rejoice at his birth for he shall be great before the Lord, and he shall drink no wine nor strong drink, and he shall be filled with the Holy Spirit, even from his mother's womb. And many of the sons of Israel he shall turn to the Lord their God. And he shall go before his face in the spirit and power of Elijah, to turn the hearts of the fathers to the children, and the disobedient to the wisdom of the just, to prepare for the Lord a people made ready."

And Zacharias said to the angel, "On what basis will I know this? For I am an old man, and my wife is advanced in her days."

And answering the angel said to him, "I am Gabriel, who stands before God, and I was sent to speak to you and to announce to you this Good News. And behold, you shall be silent and not able to speak till the day that these things shall come to pass because you did not believe my words which shall be fulfilled in their time."

And the people were expecting Zacharias, and they marveled that he delayed in the temple. But when he came out, he could not speak to them, and they realized that he had seen a vision in the temple, and he kept making signs to them and remained mute.

And it came to pass, when the days of his service were fulfilled, he went to his house. And after these days Elizabeth his wife conceived, and she hid herself five months, saying, "Thus has the Lord done to me in the days in which he looked upon me, to take away my disgrace among men."

Now in the sixth month the angel Gabriel was sent from God to a town of Galilee named Nazareth, to a virgin betrothed to a man whose name was Joseph, of the house of David; and the virgin's name was Mary. And having come to her he said, "Rejoice, you who are favored with grace! The Lord is with you."

But she was greatly troubled by this word and reasoned what kind of greeting this might be. And the angel said to her, "Fear not, Mary, for you have found grace with God. And behold, you shall conceive in your womb and bring forth a son and shall name him Jesus. He shall be great and shall be called the Son of the Most High. And the Lord God shall give to him the throne of his father David and he shall reign over the house of Jacob forever, and of his kingdom there shall be no end."

So Mary said to the angel, "How will this be, since I know no man?"

And answering the angel said to her, "The Holy Spirit shall come upon you, and the power of the Most High shall overshadow you. Therefore also that which is begotten shall be called holy, the Son of God. And behold, Elizabeth your relative, she also has conceived a son in her old age; and this is the sixth month with her who was called barren, for nothing shall be impossible with God."

So Mary said, "Behold, the bondmaid of the Lord; let it be to me according to your pronouncement."

And the angel went from her.

Now having risen up in those days, Mary went into the hill country with haste, into a town of Judah, and entered into the house of Zacharias and greeted Elizabeth. And it came to pass, when Elizabeth heard Mary's greeting, the baby leapt in her womb; and Elizabeth was filled with the Holy Spirit, and she exclaimed with a loud voice and said, "Blessed are you among women, and blessed is the fruit of your womb!

And why is this granted to me that the mother of my Lord should come to me? For behold, when the voice of your greeting came into my ears, the baby leapt in my womb in exultation! And blessed is she who believed that there will be a fulfillment of the things which have been spoken to her from the Lord!"

And Mary said,

"My soul magnifies the Lord,
    my spirit is jubilant in God my Savior;
for he has looked at the lowliness of his bondmaid,
    for behold, from now on all generations will call me blessed,
    for the mighty one has done for me great things.
And holy is his name,
    and his mercy is to generations and generations
    upon those who fear him.
He has shown strength with his arm,
    he has scattered the proud in the thought of their heart;
he has put down princes from thrones,
    and has exalted the lowly;
the hungry he has filled with good things,
    and the rich he has sent away empty.
He has given help to Israel his servant,
    that he might remember mercy;
as he spoke to our fathers,
    to Abraham and his seed forever."

And Mary stayed with her about three months, and returned to her house.

Now Elizabeth's time was fulfilled that she should give birth, and she bore a son. And her neighbors and her relatives heard that the Lord had magnified his mercy toward her, and they rejoiced with her.

And it came to pass, on the eighth day, that they came to circumcise the child, and they were calling him Zacharias after the name of his father. And responding his mother said, "Not so; but he will be called John."

And they said to her, "There's no one among your relatives who's called by this name."

So they made signs to his father, what he would have him called. And requesting a writing tablet, he wrote, saying, "His name is John." And they all marveled.

Now his mouth was opened instantly and his tongue freed and he spoke, blessing God. And fear came on all who dwelt around them, and all these sayings were talked about throughout all the hill country of Judea. And all who heard them laid them up in their heart, saying, "What then will this child be?" For the hand of the Lord was with him.

And his father Zacharias was filled with the Holy Spirit and prophesied, saying,

"Blessed be the Lord, the God of Israel,
for he has visited and made redemption for his people,
and has raised up a horn of salvation for us
in the house of his servant David;
as he spoke by the mouth of his holy prophets of old,
salvation from our enemies,
and from the hand of all who hate us;
to show mercy toward our fathers;
and to remember his holy covenant,
the oath which he swore to Abraham our father;
to grant to us without fear,
having been delivered out of the hand of our enemies;
to serve him in holiness and righteousness
before him all the days of our life.

"And now you, child,
prophet of the Most High you will be called;
for you will go before the face of the Lord,
to prepare his ways;
to give knowledge of salvation to his people
in the forgiveness of their sins,
because of the tender mercy of our God;
in which the sunrise from on high will visit us,
to shine on those sitting in darkness and the shadow of death,
to guide our feet into the way of peace."

And the child grew and was strengthened in spirit, and was in the desert until the day of his appearance to Israel.

Now the birth of Jesus Christ was thus: When his mother Mary was betrothed to Joseph, before they came together, she was found with child by the Holy Spirit. So Joseph her husband, being a righteous man and not wishing to make her a public example, was minded to divorce her privately. But when he thought on these things, behold, an angel of the Lord appeared to him in a dream, saying, "Joseph, Son of David, fear not to take Mary as your wife, for that which is begotten in her is of the Holy Spirit. So she shall bring forth a son, and you are to call his name Jesus, for it is he who shall save his people from their sins."

Now all this has come to pass that it might be fulfilled which was spoken by the Lord through the prophet, saying, "Behold, the virgin shall be with child, and shall bring forth a son, and they shall call his name Immanuel," which is, being interpreted, "God with us."

So arising from his sleep, Joseph did as the angel of the Lord decreed him and took his wife; and did not know her until she had brought forth a son.

Now it came to pass, in those days, there went out a decree from Caesar Augustus that all the world be registered. This was the first registration made when Quirinius was governor of Syria. And all went to register themselves, each to his own town. So Joseph also went up from Galilee, out of the town of Nazareth into Judea, to the city of David, which is called Bethlehem, because he was of the house and family of David, to register himself with Mary, who was betrothed to him, being pregnant.

Now it came to pass, while they were there, the days were fulfilled for her to give birth. And she brought forth her firstborn son, and she wrapped him in swaddling clothes and laid him in a manger, because there was no room for them in the guest room.

And there were shepherds in the same region living in the field and keeping watch by night over their flock. And an angel of the Lord stood by them, and the glory of the Lord shone round about them, and they were frightfully afraid. And the angel said to them, "Fear not, for behold, I announce Good News of great joy which shall be to all the people. For there is born to you this day, in the city of David, a Savior who is Christ the Lord. And this is the sign to you: You shall find a baby wrapped in swaddling clothes and lying in a manger."

And suddenly there was with the angel a multitude of the heavenly army, praising God and saying,

"Glory to God in the highest,
and on earth peace among men whom he favors!"

And it came to pass, when the angels went away from them into heaven, the shepherds said one to another, "Let's now go to Bethlehem and see this thing that has happened which the Lord has made known to us!"

And hurrying they came and found both Mary and Joseph, and the baby who was lying in the manger. So seeing him, they made known the pronouncement which was spoken to them about this child. And all who heard it marveled at the things which were spoken to them by the shepherds. But Mary treasured all these pronouncements, pondering them in her heart.

And the shepherds returned, glorifying and praising God for all the things that they had heard and seen, just as it was spoken to them.

And when eight days were fulfilled for the circumcising of him, his name was called Jesus, which was so called by the angel before he was conceived in the womb.

When the days of their purification according to the Law of Moses were fulfilled, they brought him up to Jerusalem, to present him to the Lord, as it is written in the Law of the Lord, "Every male who opens the womb shall be called holy to the Lord"; and to offer a sacrifice according to that which is said in the Law of the Lord, "A pair of turtledoves, or two young pigeons."

And behold, there was a man in Jerusalem whose name was Simeon, and this man was righteous and devout, waiting for the consolation of Israel, and the Holy Spirit was upon him. And it had been unveiled to him by the Holy Spirit that he should not see death before he had seen the Lord's Christ. And he came in the Spirit into the temple, and when the parents brought in the child Jesus, that they might do for him according to the custom of the Law, then he received him into his arms and blessed God and said,

"Now you dismiss your bondservant, Master,
according to your pronouncement, in peace;
for my eyes have seen your salvation,
which you have prepared before the face of all peoples;
a light for revelation to the Gentiles,
and the glory of your people Israel."

And his father and mother were marveling at the things which were spoken concerning him. And Simeon blessed them and said to Mary his mother, "Behold, this child is set for the falling and the rising of many in Israel, and for a sign which is spoken against. So also a sword will go through your own soul, that the thoughts of many hearts may be revealed."

And there was one, Anna, a prophetess, the daughter of Phanuel, of the tribe of Asher—she was of a great age, having lived with a husband seven years from her virginity, and she had been a widow until she was eighty-four—who did not leave the temple, serving with fastings and supplications night and day. And coming up at that very hour, she gave thanks to the Lord and spoke of him to all those who were waiting for redemption in Jerusalem.

Now when Jesus was born in Bethlehem of Judea in the days of Herod the king, behold, magi from the east came to Jerusalem, saying, "Where is the one who is born King of the Jews? For we have seen his star in the east and have come to worship him."

So when King Herod heard it, he was troubled, and all Jerusalem with him. And gathering together all the chief priests and scribes of the people, he inquired of them where the Christ should be born. So they said to him, "In Bethlehem of Judea, for thus it is written through the prophet:

'And you, Bethlehem, land of Judah,
are by no means least among the leaders of Judah;
for out of you shall come forth one leading,
who shall be shepherd of my people Israel.' "

Then Herod, having secretly called the magi, learned exactly from them the time of the appearing star. And sending them to Bethlehem, he said, "Go and search out precisely concerning the young child, and when you have found him, report to me, that I also may come and worship him."

So having heard the king, they went their way. And behold, the star, which they saw in the east, went before them until it came and stood over where the young child was.

Now when they saw the star, they rejoiced with exceedingly great joy. And coming into the house, they saw the young child with Mary his mother, and falling down, they worshiped him; and opening their treasures, they offered to him gifts: gold and frankincense and myrrh. And being forewarned in a dream that they should not go back to Herod, they withdrew to their own country another way.

Now when they had withdrawn, behold, an angel of the Lord appeared to Joseph in a dream, saying, "Arise, take the young child and his mother and flee into Egypt, and be there till I tell you, for Herod is about to seek the young child to destroy him."

So arising, he took the young child and his mother by night and withdrew into Egypt, and was there until the death of Herod, that it might be fulfilled which was spoken by the Lord through the prophet, saying, "Out of Egypt I called my son."

Then Herod, seeing that he was made a fool by the magi, was extremely furious and dispatched and slaughtered all the male children who were in Bethlehem and in all its borders, from two years old and under, according to the time he exactly learned from the magi. Then was fulfilled that which was spoken through Jeremiah the prophet, saying,

"A voice was heard in Ramah, weeping and great mourning;
Rachel weeping for her children;
And she would not be comforted,
because they are no more."

Now when Herod had died, behold, an angel of the Lord appeared in a dream to Joseph in Egypt, saying, "Arise, take the young child and his mother and go into the land of Israel, for they are dead who sought the young child's life."

So arising, he took the young child and his mother and entered into the land of Israel. But when he heard that Archelaus was reigning over Judea in place of his father Herod, he was afraid to go there; and being forewarned in a dream, he withdrew into the district of Galilee and came and dwelt in a town called Nazareth, that it might be fulfilled which was spoken through the prophets that a Nazarene shall he be called.

And the child grew and became strong, being filled with wisdom, and the grace of God was upon him.

Jesus' parents went every year to Jerusalem at the feast of the Passover. And when he was twelve years old, they went up to Jerusalem according to the custom of the feast; and when they had completed the days, as they were returning the boy Jesus stayed behind in Jerusalem, and his parents did not know it. But supposing him to be in the group, they went a day's travel; and they searched for him among their relatives and acquaintances, and when they did not find him, they returned to Jerusalem, searching for him.

And it came to pass, after three days, they found him in the temple, sitting in the midst of the teachers, both hearing them and questioning them; so all who heard him were amazed at his understanding and his answers. And when they saw him they were astonished, and his mother said to him, "Child, why have you treated us this way? Behold, your father and I were anguished looking for you!"

And he said to them, "Why were you looking for me? Didn't you know that I must be in my Father's house?" And they did not understand the saying that he spoke to them. And he went down with them and came to Nazareth, and he was subject to them. And his mother treasured all these sayings in her heart.

And Jesus advanced in wisdom and stature, and in grace with God and men.

Now in the fifteenth year of the reign of Tiberius Caesar, Pontius Pilate being governor of Judea, and Herod being tetrarch of Galilee, and his brother Philip tetrarch of the region of Ituraea and Trachonitis, and Lysanias tetrarch of Abilene, in the high priesthood of Annas and Caiaphas, the pronouncement of God came to John the son of Zacharias in the wilderness. And he came into all the region around the Jordan proclaiming in the wilderness of Judea a baptism of repentance for the forgiveness of sins and saying, "Repent! For the Kingdom of Heaven has drawn near!" For this is the one who was spoken of through the book of Isaiah the prophet, saying,

"Behold, I send my messenger before your face,
who shall make ready your way;
The voice of one calling out in the wilderness,
'Prepare the way of the Lord,
make his paths straight!
Every valley shall be filled,
and every mountain and hill shall be brought low;
and the crooked shall become straight,
and the rough ways smooth;
and all flesh shall see the salvation of God.' "

Now John himself had his clothing of camel's hair and a belt of leather about his waist, and his food was locusts and wild honey. Then went out to him Jerusalem and all of Judea and all the region round about the Jordan, and they were baptized by him in the river Jordan, confessing their sins. He said therefore to the crowds going out to be baptized by him and many of the Pharisees and Sadducees, "You offspring of vipers, who warned you to flee from the coming wrath? Therefore bring forth fruit worthy of repentance. And think not to say within yourselves, 'We have Abraham for a father,' for I say to you that from these stones God is able to raise up children to Abraham. And already the ax lies at the root of the trees; therefore every tree that does not bring forth good fruit is cut down and cast into the fire."

And the crowds asked him, saying, "What then should we do?"

So answering he said to them, "The one who has two coats, let him give to him who has none; and the one who has food, let him do likewise."

Now there also came tax collectors to be baptized, and they said to him, "Teacher, what should we do?"

So he said to them, "Collect no more than that which is instructed for you."

Now soldiers also asked him, saying, "And what should we do?"

And he said to them, "Extort from no one by violence, nor accuse anyone wrongfully, and be content with your wages."

Now as the people were in expectation, and all men reasoned in their hearts concerning John whether perhaps he was the Christ, John responded, saying to them all, "I indeed baptize you with water, but after me comes the one who is mightier than I, the strap of whose sandals I am not worthy to stoop down and untie. I baptized you with water, but he will baptize you in the Holy Spirit and in fire. His winnowing fork is in his hand, and he will thoroughly clear his threshing floor, and he will gather his wheat into the barn, but the chaff he will burn up with unquenchable fire."

Then with many other exhortations he announced Good News to the people.

Now it came to pass, in those days, when all the people were baptized, that Jesus came from Nazareth of Galilee to the Jordan, to John, to be baptized by him. But John hindered him, saying, "I need to be baptized by you, and you come to me?"

But answering Jesus said to him, "Allow it now, for thus it is fitting for us to fulfill all righteousness." Then he allowed him.

And when he was baptized, Jesus went up straightaway from the water, and behold, he saw the heavens tearing open and the Holy Spirit descending in a bodily form as a dove upon him, and behold, a voice came out of the heavens, saying, YOU ARE MY BELOVED SON, IN WHOM I AM WELL PLEASED.

And Jesus himself, when he began to teach, was about thirty years old, being the son—as was supposed—of Joseph, a descendant of David and a descendant of Abraham and a descendant of Noah and a descendant of Adam the son of God.

Now Jesus, full of the Holy Spirit, returned from the Jordan, and straightaway the Spirit expelled him into the wilderness to be tempted by Satan the devil. And he was in the wilderness with the wild animals forty days and forty nights. And he ate nothing in those days, and when they were completed, he hungered.

And the tempter coming to him said, "If you are the Son of God, tell these stones to become bread."

But answering Jesus said, "It is written, 'Man shall not live by bread alone, but by every saying that proceeds out of the mouth of God.' "

Then the devil took him into Jerusalem, the holy city, and he set him on the pinnacle of the temple and said to him, "If you are the Son of God, cast yourself down from here, for it is written,

> 'He shall give his angels command concerning you, to protect you;'
> and,
> 'On their hands they shall bear you up,
> lest perhaps you dash your foot against a stone.' "

And answering Jesus declared to him, "Again it is written, 'You shall not test the Lord your God.' "

Again the devil took him to an extremely high mountain and showed him all the kingdoms of the world in an instant and the glory of them, and the devil said to him, "To you will I give all this authority and the glory of it, for it has been delivered to me; and to whomever I desire, I give it. Therefore if you will fall down and worship before me, it will all be yours."

Then responding Jesus said to him, "Be gone, Satan, for it is written, 'You shall worship the Lord your God, and him only shall you serve.' "

And when the devil had completed every temptation, he left from him until another time. And behold, angels came and were serving him.

This is the witness of John, when the Jews sent to him from Jerusalem priests and Levites to ask him, "Who are you?"

He confessed and did not deny, but he confessed, "I am not the Christ."

And they asked him, "What then? Are you Elijah?"

He said, "I am not."

"Are you the Prophet?"

And he answered, "No."

Therefore they said to him, "Who are you, that we may give an answer to those who sent us? What do you say about yourself?"

He declared, "I am the voice of one calling out in the wilderness, 'Make straight the way of the Lord,' as said Isaiah the prophet."

And some who had been sent belonged to the Pharisees, and they asked him and said to him, "Why then do you baptize if you are not the Christ nor Elijah nor the Prophet?"

John answered them, saying, "I baptize in water, but in the midst of you stands one whom you do not know, the one who comes after me, whose sandal strap I am not worthy to untie."

These things were done in Bethany beyond the Jordan, where John was baptizing.

The next day he saw Jesus coming to him and said, "Look! The Lamb of God, who takes away the sin of the world! This is he of whom I said, 'After me comes a man who has come before me, for he was first before me.' And I did not know him; but that he would be made visible to Israel, for this reason I came baptizing in water."

And John bore witness, saying, "I have gazed upon the Spirit descending like a dove out of heaven, and it remained upon him. And I did not know him; but the one who sent me to baptize in water, he said to me, 'Upon whomever you shall see the Spirit descending and remaining upon him, this is the one who baptizes with the Holy Spirit.' And I have watched and have borne witness that this is the Son of God."

Again the next day John was standing with two of his disciples, and peering at Jesus as he walked by he said, "Look! The Lamb of God!"

And the two disciples heard him speak, and they followed Jesus. So Jesus, having turned, and having gazed upon them following, said to them, "What do you seek?"

And they said to him, "Rabbi, where are you staying?"

He said to them, "Come and you shall see."

They came and saw where he was staying. And they stayed with him that day; it was about the tenth hour. Andrew, Simon Peter's brother, was one of the two who heard John and followed him. He first found his own brother Simon and said to him, "We have found the Messiah!"

He brought him to Jesus. Peering at him Jesus said, "You are Simon the son of John. You shall be called Cephas"—which means Peter.

The next day he desired to go forth into Galilee, and he found Philip, and Jesus said to him, "Follow me."

Now Philip was of Bethsaida, from the town of Andrew and Peter. Philip found Nathanael and said to him, "We have found him of whom Moses in the Law and the Prophets wrote: Jesus of Nazareth, the son of Joseph!"

And Nathanael said to him, "Can anything good come out of Nazareth?"

Philip said to him, "Come and see."

Jesus saw Nathanael coming to him and said of him, "Look! Surely an Israelite in whom is no deceit!"

Nathanael said to him, "How do you know me?"

Jesus answered and said to him, "Before Philip called you, when you were under the fig tree, I saw you."

Nathanael answered him, "Rabbi, you are the Son of God! You are King of Israel!"

Jesus answered and said to him, "Because I said to you, 'I saw you underneath the fig tree,' do you believe? You shall see greater things than these." And he said to him, "Truly, truly, I say to you, you shall see heaven opened, and the angels of God ascending and descending upon the Son of Man."

And the third day there was a wedding in Cana of Galilee, and the mother of Jesus was there. So Jesus also was invited, and his disciples, to the wedding. And when the wine ran out, the mother of Jesus said to him, "They have no wine."

And Jesus said to her, "What does this have to do with me, woman? My hour has not yet arrived."

His mother said to the servants, "Whatever he says to you, do it."

Now there were six water jars of stone set there after the Jews' way of purifying, containing twenty or thirty gallons apiece. Jesus said to them, "Fill the jars with water."

And they filled them up to the brim. And he said to them, "Now draw some out, and take it to the master of the banquet." So they took it.

Now when the master of the banquet tasted the water now become wine and did not know where it came from—but the servants who had drawn the water knew—the master of the banquet called the bridegroom and said to him, "Every man sets forth the good wine first, and when the guests have drunk freely, the inferior. You have kept the good wine until now!"

This beginning of his signs Jesus did in Cana of Galilee, and made visible his glory; and his disciples believed in him.

After this, he went down to Capernaum, he and his mother and his brothers and his disciples. And they stayed there a few days.

The Passover of the Jews was at hand, and Jesus went up to Jerusalem. And he found in the temple those who sold oxen and sheep and doves, and the money changers sitting. And making a whip of cords, he expelled all out of the temple, both the sheep and the oxen; and he poured out the changers' money and overturned their tables; and to those selling the doves he said, "Take these things from here! Do not make the house of my Father a house of business!"

His disciples remembered that it was written, "Zeal for your house will consume me."

The Jews therefore responded and said to him, "What sign do you show to us, seeing that you do these things?"

Jesus answered and said to them, "Destroy this temple and in three days I shall raise it up."

The Jews therefore said, "In forty-six years was this temple built, yet in three days you will raise it up?"

But he spoke of the temple of his body. Therefore when he was raised from the dead, his disciples remembered that he said this; and they believed the Scripture, and the word which Jesus had said.

So when he was in Jerusalem at the Passover during the feast, many believed in his name, observing his signs which he did. But Jesus did not entrust himself to them, for he knew all men and because he had no need for anyone to bear witness about man, for he himself knew what was in man.

Now there was a man of the Pharisees named Nicodemus, a ruler of the Jews. This one came to him by night and said to him, "Rabbi, we know that you come from God as a teacher, for no one can do these signs that you do unless God is with him."

Jesus answered and said to him, "Truly, truly, I say to you, unless one is born from above, he cannot see the Kingdom of God."

Nicodemus said to him, "How can a man be born when he is old? Can he enter a second time into his mother's womb and be born?"

Jesus answered, "Truly, truly, I say to you, unless one is born of water and spirit, he cannot enter into the Kingdom of God. That which is born of the flesh is flesh, and that which is born of the Spirit is spirit. Marvel not that I said to you, 'You must be born from above.' The wind blows where it desires, and you hear its sound, but do not know from where it comes and where it goes; so is everyone who is born of the Spirit."

Nicodemus answered and said to him, "How can this happen?"

Jesus answered and said to him, "Are you the teacher of Israel and do not know these things? Truly, truly, I say to you, that which we know, we speak, and that which we have watched, we bear witness of; and you do not receive our witness. If I told you earthly things and you do not believe, how shall you believe if I tell you heavenly things? And no one has ascended into heaven but the one who out of heaven descended: the Son of Man. And as Moses lifted up the serpent in the wilderness, thus must the Son of Man be lifted up, that whoever believes may have eternal life in him."

For God so loved the world that he gave his only begotten Son, that whoever believes in him should not perish, but have eternal life. For God did not send his Son into the world to judge the world, but that the world might be saved through him. The one believing in him is not judged; but the one not believing has been judged already, because he has not believed in the name of the only begotten Son of God. So this is the judgment: that the light has come into the world, and men loved the darkness rather than the light, for their works were evil. For everyone doing vice hates the light, and does not come to the light, lest his works be exposed. But the one doing the truth comes to the light, that his works may be made visible that have been worked in God.

After these things Jesus and his disciples came into the Judean countryside, and there he lingered with them and baptized. Now John also was baptizing in Aenon near Salim, because there was much water there. And they were coming and being baptized, for John was not yet cast into prison. Then a question arose on the part of John's disciples with a Jew about purification. And they came to John and said to him, "Rabbi, he who was with you beyond the Jordan, to whom you have borne witness, look, he baptizes, and all come to him!"

John answered and said, "A man cannot receive anything unless it has been given him from heaven. You yourselves bear witness to me that I said, 'I am not the Christ, but I have been sent before him.' The one who has the bride is the bridegroom. But the friend of the bridegroom, the one standing and hearing him, rejoices greatly because of the bridegroom's voice. Therefore my joy is filled. He must increase, but I must decrease."

The one who comes from above is over all. The one from the earth, from the earth is he, and from the earth he speaks. The one who comes from heaven is over all. What he has watched and heard, of that he bears witness; and no one receives his witness. The one receiving his witness has set his seal to this, that God is true. For he whom God has sent speaks the sayings of God, for he gives the Spirit without measure. The Father loves the Son and has given all things into his hand. The one believing in the Son has eternal life, and the one disobeying the Son will not see life, but the wrath of God remains upon him.

Now Herod the tetrarch, being admonished by John for Herodias, his brother's wife, and for all the evil things which Herod had done, also added this to them all: He shut up John in prison.

So when the Lord heard that John was delivered up, and when he knew that the Pharisees had heard that Jesus was making and baptizing more disciples than John—although Jesus himself did not baptize, but his disciples—he left Judea and withdrew again into Galilee; but he had to pass through Samaria.

So he came to a town of Samaria called Sychar near the plot of ground that Jacob gave to his son Joseph, and Jacob's spring was there. Therefore Jesus, being wearied from his journey, sat thus by the spring; it was about the sixth hour.

There came a woman of Samaria to draw water. Jesus said to her, "Give me a drink," for his disciples had gone away into the town to buy food.

Therefore the Samaritan woman said to him, "How is it that you, being a Jew, ask a drink from me, a Samaritan woman?"—for Jews have no dealings with Samaritans.

Jesus answered and said to her, "If you knew the gift of God and who it is that says to you, 'Give me a drink,' you would have requested of him, and he would have given you living water."

The woman said to him, "Sir, you have nothing to draw with, and the well is deep. Where then do you have that living water? Are you greater than our father Jacob, who gave us the well and drank from it himself, and his sons and his livestock?"

Jesus answered and said to her, "Everyone drinking of this water shall thirst again, but whoever drinks of the water that I shall give him shall forever not thirst. But the water that I shall give him shall become in him a spring of water gushing up to eternal life."

The woman said to him, "Sir, give me this water, that I may not thirst, nor come here to draw."

Jesus said to her, "Go, call your husband and come here."

The woman answered and said to him, "I have no husband."

Jesus said to her, "You have said well, 'I have no husband,' for you have had five husbands, and he whom you now have is not your husband. This you have said truly."

The woman said to him, "Sir, I observe that you are a prophet. Our fathers worshiped on this mountain, and you say that in Jerusalem is the place where people need to worship."

Jesus said to her, "Believe me, woman, that an hour is coming when neither on this mountain nor in Jerusalem shall you worship the Father. You worship that which you do not know. We worship that which we know, for salvation is from the Jews. But an hour is coming, and now is here, when the true worshipers shall worship the Father in spirit and truth, for the Father seeks such to worship him. God is spirit, and those worshiping him must worship in spirit and truth."

The woman said to him, "I know that Messiah is coming. When he comes, he will report to us all things."

Jesus said to her, "I am he, the one speaking to you."

And upon this came his disciples, and they marveled that he was speaking with a woman. Yet no one said, "What do you want?" or "Why do you speak with her?"

Now the woman left her water pot and went away into the town and said to the people, "Come, see a man who told me everything that I ever did! Can this be the Christ?"

They went out of the town and came to him. In the meantime the disciples urged him, saying, "Rabbi, eat."

But he said to them, "I have food to eat that you do not know."

Therefore the disciples said to one another, "Has anyone brought him something to eat?"

Jesus said to them, "My food is to do the will of him who sent me and to accomplish his work. Say not, 'There are yet four months, and then comes the harvest?' Behold, I say to you, lift up your eyes and gaze upon the fields, that they are white for harvest. Already the one reaping receives wages and gathers fruit to eternal life, that the one who sows and the one who reaps may rejoice together. For in this the words are true: 'One sows and another reaps.' I sent you to reap that for which you have not labored. Others have labored, and you have entered into their labor."

Now from that town many of the Samaritans believed in him because of the word of the woman witnessing, "He told me everything that I ever did!"

So when the Samaritans came to him, they urged him to stay with them, and he stayed there two days. And many more believed because of his word, and they said to the woman, "No longer because of your speaking do we believe, for we have heard for ourselves and know that this is surely the Savior of the world."

Now after the two days he went forth from there into Galilee. For Jesus himself bore witness that a prophet has no honor in his hometown.

Jesus returned in the power of the Spirit into Galilee, and the Galileans received him, having watched all the things that he did in Jerusalem at the feast, for they also had gone to the feast. From that time, Jesus began to proclaim and to say, "The time is fulfilled and the Kingdom of God has drawn near! Repent and believe in the Good News." And fame about him went out through all the surrounding region. And he taught in their synagogues, being glorified by all.

Then he came again to Cana of Galilee, where he made the water into wine. And there was a certain royal official whose son was sick at Capernaum. Hearing that Jesus had arrived from Judea into Galilee, he went to him and urged that he would come down and cure his son, for he was about to die. Jesus therefore said to him, "Unless you see signs and wonders, you will not believe."

The royal official said to him, "Sir, come down before my little boy dies!"

Jesus said to him, "Go. Your son lives."

The man believed the word that Jesus spoke to him, and he went his way. And already, as he was going down, his slaves met him saying that his child was alive. So he inquired of them the hour in which he got well. Therefore they said to him, "Yesterday at the seventh hour the fever left him."

So the father knew that it was at that hour in which Jesus said to him, "Your son lives." And he himself believed, and his whole household.

This is again the second sign that Jesus did, having come out of Judea into Galilee.

And he came to Nazareth, where he had been brought up. And he entered, as was his custom, into the synagogue on the Sabbath day and stood up to read. And there was given to him the scroll of the prophet Isaiah; and unrolling the scroll, he found the place where it was written,

"The Spirit of the Lord is upon me,
because he has anointed me to announce good news to the poor.
He has sent me to proclaim to the captives forgiveness,
and to the blind recovery of sight;
to send forth the oppressed in forgiveness,
to proclaim the acceptable year of the Lord."

And rolling up the scroll, giving it back to the attendant, he sat down. And the eyes of all in the synagogue were fixed upon him.

Now he began to say to them, "Today this Scripture has been fulfilled in your ears."

And all bore witness and marveled at the words of grace which proceeded out of his mouth, and they said, "Isn't this Joseph's son?"

And he said to them, "No doubt you will tell me this parable, 'Doctor, heal yourself! Whatever we have heard done at Capernaum, do also here in your hometown.' " But he said, "Truly I say to you, no prophet is acceptable in his hometown. But in truth I say to you, there were many widows in Israel in the days of Elijah, when the sky was shut up three years and six months, when there came a great famine over all the land; and to none of them was sent Elijah except to Zarephath, in the land of Sidon, to a woman who was a widow. And there were many lepers in Israel in the time of Elisha the prophet, and none of them was cleansed except Naaman the Syrian."

And they were all filled with wrath in the synagogue hearing these things, and getting up they expelled him from the town and led him to the brow of the hill that their town was built on in order to throw him off the cliff. But he, passing through the midst of them, went away.

And leaving Nazareth, he came and dwelt in Capernaum, a town of Galilee, which is by the sea, in the borders of Zebulun and Naphtali, that it might be fulfilled which was spoken through Isaiah the prophet, saying,

"The land of Zebulun and the land of Naphtali,
by the way of the sea, beyond the Jordan, Galilee of the Gentiles;
the people sitting in darkness saw a great light;
and to those sitting in the region and shadow of death,
light arose to them."

Now walking by the Sea of Galilee, he saw two brethren, Simon, who is called Peter, and Andrew his brother, casting a net into the sea, for they were fishermen. And Jesus said to them, "Come after me, and I shall make you become fishers of men."

So straightaway leaving their nets, they followed him.

And going on a little further, he saw two other brethren, James the son of Zebedee and John his brother, and they were in the boat mending the nets. And straightaway he called them; and leaving their father Zebedee in the boat with the hired servants, they went after him.

And Jesus went about in all Galilee, teaching in their synagogues and proclaiming the Good News of the kingdom and healing all manner of disease and all manner of sickness among the people. And his fame went forth into all Syria, and they brought to him all who were sick, afflicted with various diseases and torments, possessed with demons, and epileptics and paralytics; and he healed them. And there followed him great crowds from Galilee and Decapolis and Jerusalem and Judea and from beyond the Jordan.

So seeing the crowds, he went up on the mountain. And sitting down, his disciples came to him; and opening his mouth, he taught them, saying,

"Blessed are the poor in spirit, for theirs is the Kingdom of Heaven.

Blessed are those who mourn, for they shall be comforted.

Blessed are the gentle, for they shall inherit the earth.

Blessed are those who hunger and thirst for righteousness, for they shall be filled.

Blessed are the merciful, for they shall receive mercy.

Blessed are the pure in heart, for they shall watch God.

Blessed are the peacemakers, for they shall be called sons of God.

Blessed are those who have been persecuted for the sake of righteousness, for theirs is the Kingdom of Heaven. Blessed are you when they shall revile you and persecute you and say every evil statement against you falsely for my sake. Rejoice and be jubilant, for your reward is great in heaven, for thus did they persecute the prophets who were before you.

"You are the salt of the earth, but if the salt becomes tasteless, with what shall it be salted? It is no longer good for anything but to be cast out and trodden underfoot by men.

"You are the light of the world. A city set on a hill cannot be hidden. Nor do they light a lamp and place it under a basket, but upon the lampstand, and it shines to all those in the house. Thus let your light shine before men, that they may see your good works and glorify your Father who is in heaven.

"Think not that I came to destroy the Law or the Prophets. I came not to destroy, but to fulfill. For truly I say to you, till heaven and earth pass away, one letter or one dot shall not pass away from the Law till all things are accomplished. Therefore whoever shall break one of the least of these commandments, and shall teach men so, shall be called least in the Kingdom of Heaven; but whoever shall do and teach them, this one shall be called great in the Kingdom of Heaven. For I say to you that unless your righteousness shall exceed that of the scribes and Pharisees, you shall not enter into the Kingdom of Heaven.

"You have heard that it was said to the ancients, 'You shall not murder;' and 'Whoever murders shall be liable to judgment.' But I say to you that everyone who is angry with his brother shall be liable to judgment; and whoever shall say to his brother, 'You brainless' shall be liable to the tribunal, and whoever says, 'You dullard' shall be liable to the hell of fire. Therefore if you are offering your gift at the altar, and there remember that your brother has anything against you, leave there your gift before the altar and go your way; first be reconciled to your brother, and then come and offer your gift. Agree with your adversary quickly while you are with him on the way, lest the adversary deliver you to the judge, and the judge deliver you to the guard, and you be cast into prison. Truly I say to you, you shall not come out of there till you have paid the last cent.

"You have heard that it was said, 'You shall not commit adultery;' but I say to you that everyone who looks on a woman to lust after her has committed adultery with her already in his heart. And if your right eye causes you to stumble, tear it out and cast it from you, for it is better for you that one of your members should be destroyed and not your whole body to be cast into hell. And if your right hand causes you to stumble, cut it off and cast it from you, for it is better for you that one of your members should be destroyed and not your whole body go into hell.

"It was also said, 'Whoever shall divorce his wife, let him give her a note of divorce,' but I say to you that whoever divorces his wife, save for the cause of fornication, makes her an adulteress; and whoever shall marry her when she is put away commits adultery.

"Again you have heard that it was said to the ancients, 'You shall not swear falsely, but shall perform to the Lord your vows,' but I say to you, swear not at all, neither by heaven, for it is the throne of God, nor by the earth, for it is the footstool of his feet, nor toward Jerusalem, for it is the city of the great King; nor shall you swear by your head, for you cannot make one hair white or black. But let your word be 'Yes, yes; No, no,' so whatever is more than these is of the evil one.

"You have heard that it was said, 'An eye for an eye and a tooth for a tooth,' but I say to you, resist not him who is evil; but whoever slaps you on your right cheek, turn to him the other also. And if any man would take you to law and take your shirt, let him have your cloak also. And whoever shall compel you to go one mile, go with him two. Give to him that requests of you, and from him who would borrow of you, do not turn away.

"You have heard that it was said, 'You shall love your neighbor and hate your enemy.' But I say to you, love your enemies and pray for those who persecute you, that you may become sons of your Father who is in heaven, for he makes his sun to rise on the evil and the good and sends rain on the righteous and the unrighteous. For if you love those who love you, what reward have you? Do not even the tax collectors do the same? And if you greet your brethren only, what are you doing more than others? Do not even the Gentiles do the same? Therefore you shall be perfect, just as your heavenly Father is perfect.

"Beware that you do not do your righteousness before men, to be gazed upon by them, else you have no reward with your Father who is in heaven. Therefore when you do alms, sound not a trumpet before you, as the hypocrites do in the synagogues and in the streets, that they may have glory of men. Truly I say to you, they have received their reward. But when you do alms, let not your left hand know what your right hand is doing, that your alms may be in secret; and your Father, who looks in secret, shall repay you.

"And when you pray, you shall not be as the hypocrites, for they love to stand and pray in the synagogues and in the corners of the streets, that they may be seen by men. Truly I say to you, they have received their reward. But you, when you pray, enter into your inner chamber, and having shut your door, pray to your Father, who is in secret; and your Father, who looks in secret, shall repay you. And in praying use not empty repetitions as the Gentiles do, for they think that they shall be heard in their many words. Therefore do not become like them, for your Father knows what things you have need of before you request of him. Therefore in this way you are to pray:

"Our Father who is in heaven,
  hallowed be your name,
your kingdom come,
  your will be done on earth as it is in heaven.
Give us this day our ceaseless bread;
and forgive us our debts,
  as we also have forgiven our debtors;
and bring us not into temptation,
  but deliver us from the evil one.

For if you forgive men their trespasses, your heavenly Father shall also forgive you. But if you do not forgive men their trespasses, neither shall your Father forgive your trespasses.

"Moreover when you fast, be not, as the hypocrites, of a sad countenance, for they disfigure their faces that they may be seen by men to fast. Truly I say to you, they have received their reward. But you, when you fast, anoint your head and wash your face, that you may not be seen by men to fast, but by your Father, who is in secret; and your Father, who looks in secret, shall repay you.

"Do not store up for yourselves treasures on the earth, where moth and rust consume and where thieves break through and steal, but store up for yourselves treasures in heaven, where neither moth nor rust consume and where thieves do not break through and steal. For where your treasure is, there your heart will be also.

"The lamp of the body is the eye. Therefore if your eye is sincere, your whole body shall be full of light, but if your eye is evil, your whole body shall be full of darkness. Therefore if the light that is in you is darkness, how great is the darkness?

"No man can serve two masters; for either he shall hate the one and love the other, or else he shall hold to one and despise the other. You cannot serve both God and wealth. For this reason I say to you, be not anxious for your life, what you shall eat or what you shall drink, nor yet for your body, what you shall wear. Is not the life more than the food, and the body more than the clothing? Peer at the birds of the air, that they do not sow nor reap nor gather into barns, and your heavenly Father feeds them. Are you not of much more value than they?

"And which of you by being anxious can add a single foot to his height? And why are you anxious concerning clothing? Consider the lilies of the field, how they grow; they do not toil nor spin. But I say to you that even Solomon in all his glory was not clothed like one of these. So if God clothes in this way the grass of the field, which is here today and tomorrow is cast into the oven, shall he not much more clothe you, you of little faith?

"Therefore be not anxious, saying, 'What shall we eat?' or 'What shall we drink?' or 'With what shall we be clothed?' For after all these things the Gentiles seek; for your heavenly Father knows that you have need of all these things. But seek first his kingdom and his righteousness, and all these things shall be added to you. Therefore be not anxious for tomorrow, for tomorrow will be anxious for itself; sufficient to the day is its own misfortune.

"Judge not, that you not be judged. For with what judgment you judge, you shall be judged, and with what measure you measure, it shall be measured to you. So why do you look at the speck that is in your brother's eye, but do not perceive the beam that is in your own eye? Or how shall you say to your brother, 'Let me remove the speck from your eye,' and behold, the beam is in your own eye? Hypocrite, first remove the beam out of your own eye, and then you shall see clearly to remove the speck out of your brother's eye.

"Give not that which is holy to the dogs, nor cast your pearls before the pigs, lest they trample them underfoot and turn and rend you.

"Request, and it shall be given to you; seek, and you shall find; knock, and it shall be opened to you. For everyone requesting receives, and the one seeking finds, and to the one knocking it shall be opened. Or what man is there of you who, if his son requests of him bread, will give him a stone, or if he requests a fish, will give him a serpent? If you then, being evil, know how to give good gifts to your children, how much more shall your Father who is in heaven give good things to those who request of him?

"All things then, whatever you desire that men should do unto you, thus also you do unto them, for this is the Law and the Prophets.

"Enter in by the narrow gate; for wide is the gate and broad the way that leads to destruction, and many are those who enter in through it.

For narrow is the gate and constricted the way that leads to life, and few are those who find it.

"Beware of false prophets, who come to you in sheep's clothing but inwardly are ravening wolves. By their fruits you shall recognize them. Do men gather grapes from thorns, or figs from thistles? Thus every good tree brings forth good fruit, but the corrupt tree brings forth evil fruit. A good tree cannot bring forth evil fruit, neither can a corrupt tree bring forth good fruit. Every tree that does not bring forth good fruit is cut down and cast into the fire. Therefore by their fruits you shall recognize them.

"Not everyone who is saying to me, 'Lord, Lord,' shall enter into the Kingdom of Heaven, but the one doing the will of my Father who is in heaven. Many shall say to me in that day, 'Lord, Lord, did we not prophesy by your name, and by your name expel demons, and by your name do many mighty works?' And then I shall profess to them, 'I never knew you. Get away from me, you who work lawlessness.'

"Therefore everyone who hears these words of mine and does them shall become like a wise man who built his house upon the rock. And the rain descended, and the floods came, and the winds blew and beat upon that house, and it did not fall, for it was founded upon the rock. And everyone who hears these words of mine and does not do them shall become like a foolish man who built his house upon the sand. And the rain descended, and the floods came, and the winds blew and beat upon that house, and it fell, and great was its fall."

And it came to pass, when Jesus had finished these words, the crowds were astonished at his teaching, for he taught them as one having authority, and not as their scribes.

Now when he had come down from the mountain, great crowds followed him. And he came down to Capernaum; and straightaway on the Sabbath day he entered into the synagogue and taught. And in the synagogue there was a man who had a spirit of an unclean demon, and he screamed with a loud voice, saying, "Ah! What do we have to do with you, Jesus of Nazareth? Have you come to destroy us? I know you, who you are: the Holy One of God!"

And Jesus rebuked him, saying, "Be silent and come out of him!"

And the unclean spirit, throwing him down in their midst, convulsing him and calling out with a loud voice, came out of him. And amazement came upon all, so that they discussed among themselves, saying, "What is this word? A new teaching with authority! Even the unclean spirits he commands and they obey him!"

And the fame of him went out straightaway everywhere into all the surrounding region of Galilee.

Now arising from the synagogue, Jesus came into the house of Simon and Andrew, with James and John. He saw Simon's mother-in-law lying sick, gripped by a great fever, and they urged him for her. And standing over her, he touched her hand and rebuked the fever, and it left her; and instantly getting up, she served them.

Now when evening had come, when the sun had set, they brought to him all who were sick with various diseases and those who were possessed by demons; and all the town was gathered together at the door. So laying his hands on each one of them, he healed them; and he expelled the demons out of many with a word and the demons were shouting out and saying, "You are the Christ, the Son of God!" So rebuking them, he did not allow them to speak, because they knew that he was the Christ.

Now early in the morning, while it was still dark, getting up, he went forth and went into a deserted place, and was praying there. And Simon and those with him pursued him, and they found him and said to him, "Everyone is looking for you!"

And the crowds sought him and came to him and were restraining him to prevent him from going from them. But he said to them, "I must announce the Good News of the Kingdom of God to the other towns also, because for this was I sent."

And he was going, proclaiming in their synagogues in all Galilee, and expelling demons.

Now it came to pass, while the crowd pressed upon him and heard the word of God, that he was standing by the lake of Gennesaret. And he saw two boats lying by the lake, but the fishermen had gone out of them and were washing their nets. So entering into one of the boats, which was Simon's, he asked him to put out a little from the land. And sitting down, he taught the crowds from the boat.

Now when he had stopped speaking, he said to Simon, "Put out into the deep, and let down your nets for a catch."

And responding Simon said, "Master, through the night we toiled and took nothing, but at your saying I will let down the nets."

And doing this they enclosed a great multitude of fish, so their nets were breaking, and they beckoned to their partners in the other boat that they should come and help them. And they came and filled both boats so that they began to sink.

Now having seen it, Simon Peter fell down at the knees of Jesus, saying, "Go from me for I am a sinful man, Lord!" For he was amazed, and all who were with him, at the catch of fish that they had caught, and so also were James and John, sons of Zebedee, who were partners with Simon.

And Jesus said to Simon, "Fear not. From now on you shall be catching men."

And when they had brought their boats to land, leaving all, they followed him.

And it came to pass, while he was in one of the towns, behold, there was a man full of leprosy. So seeing Jesus, falling on his face, he pleaded with him, saying, "Lord, if you desire, you can cleanse me!"

And being moved with compassion, reaching out his hand, he touched him and said to him, "I desire. Be cleansed."

And straightaway the leprosy went from him and he was cleansed. And sternly warning him, straightaway he expelled him and said to him, "But go your way and watch that you say nothing to anyone; and go show yourself to the priest, and offer for your cleansing the gift that Moses decreed, for a testimony to them."

But going forth, he began to proclaim it widely and to spread abroad the word, so that Jesus could no more openly enter into a town, but was out in deserted places; and they came to him from every quarter. And great crowds came together to hear and to be healed of their infirmities. So he retired himself into the desert, and prayed.

And it came to pass, when he entered again into Capernaum after some days, that he was teaching, and there were Pharisees and teachers of the Law sitting by who had come out of every village of Galilee and Judea and Jerusalem. And it was heard that he was in the house, and many were gathered together, so that there was no more room, not even around the door; and the power of the Lord was with him to cure them, and he was speaking to them the word.

And behold, four men carrying upon a mat a man who was paralyzed, and they sought to bring him in to lay before him. And not finding a way to bring him in because of the crowd, they removed the roof where he was; and having broken it up, they let down the mat into the midst before Jesus. And Jesus, seeing their faith, said to the paralytic, "Take courage, child; your sins are forgiven."

But behold, the scribes and the Pharisees began to reason in their hearts, "Who is this who speaks blasphemies? Who can forgive sins but one—God?"

Now seeing their thoughts in his spirit, Jesus said, "Why do you reason these things in your hearts? Which is easier: to say to the paralytic, 'Your sins are forgiven;' or to say, 'Arise, and take up your mat and walk?' But that you may know that the Son of Man has authority on earth to forgive sins…"—he said to the paralytic— "I say to you, arise, take up your mat and go to your house."

And instantly he got up; and straightaway, taking up the mat, he went out before them all, and went to his house, glorifying God.

So the crowds, seeing it, marveled and glorified God, who had given such authority to men. And they were filled with fear, saying, "We've never seen anything like this!"

And after these things he went forth again by the seaside. And all the crowd came to him, and he taught them. And passing by, he gazed upon a tax collector named Levi the son of Alphaeus, called Matthew, sitting at the tax booth, and said to him, "Follow me." And leaving everything, getting up, he followed him.

And it came to pass that Levi made a great feast for him in his house, and there was a great crowd of tax collectors and other sinners who were reclining with them, for there were many, and they followed him. And the scribes and the Pharisees, seeing him eating with the sinners and tax collectors, said to his disciples, "Why does your teacher eat with tax collectors and sinners?"

But hearing this he said, "Those who are strong have no need of a doctor, but those who are sick. So go and learn what this means: 'I desire mercy, and not sacrifice.' For I came not to call the righteous, but sinners to repentance."

And John's disciples and the Pharisees were fasting, and they came and said to him, "John's disciples fast often and offer supplications, likewise also those of the Pharisees, but yours eat and drink."

So Jesus said to them, "Can you make the guests of the wedding fast while the bridegroom is with them? As long as they have the bridegroom with them, they cannot fast. But the days shall come when the bridegroom shall be taken away from them, and then they shall fast in that day.

Now he also spoke a parable to them: "No one tears a piece from a new garment and puts it on an old garment, or else he will tear the new, and also the piece from the new will not match the old. And no one sews a piece of unshrunk cloth on an old garment, or else the patch pulls away from it, the new from the old, and a worse tear is made.

"And no one puts new wine into old wineskins, or else the new wine will burst the skins and it will be spilled and the skins will be destroyed. But new wine must be put into fresh wine skins, and both are preserved. And no one having drunk old wine immediately desires new, for he says, 'The old is good.' "

Now it came to pass that on the Sabbath day Jesus was passing through the grain fields, and his disciples were hungry and were plucking and eating the heads of grain, rubbing them in their hands. But some of the Pharisees, when they saw it, said to him, "Look! Why are they doing what is not lawful to do on the Sabbath day?"

But answering them Jesus said, "Have you not read what David did when he was in need and was hungry, he and those who were with him, how he entered into the house of God and took and ate the bread of the Presence, which it is not lawful to eat except for the priests, and gave also to those who were with him? Or have you not read in the Law that on the Sabbath day the priests in the temple profane the Sabbath and are guiltless? But I say to you that something greater than the temple is here. So if you had known what this means, 'I desire mercy and not sacrifice,' you would not have condemned the guiltless. The Sabbath was made for man, not man for the Sabbath. So then the Son of Man is Lord even of the Sabbath."

Now it came to pass, on another Sabbath, that he entered into the synagogue and taught. And behold, there was a man there, and his right hand was withered. So the scribes and the Pharisees were monitoring him, whether he would heal on the Sabbath, and they asked him, saying, "Is it lawful to heal on the Sabbath day?"—so that they might find how to accuse against him.

But he knew their thoughts, so he said to the man who had the withered hand, "Arise and stand in the midst." And getting up, he stood.

So Jesus said to them, "I ask you, is it lawful on the Sabbath to do good, or to do harm? To save a life, or to destroy? What man shall there be of you who shall have one sheep, and if this falls into a pit on the Sabbath day, will he not take hold of it and raise it out? How much more value then is a man than a sheep! Therefore it is lawful to do good on the Sabbath day."

And looking around at them all with anger, being grieved at the hardness of their heart, he said to him, "Reach out your hand."

So he reached it out, and his hand was restored.

But they were filled with madness and discussed with one another what they should do to Jesus. And going out, the Pharisees straightaway with the Herodians took counsel against him, how they might destroy him.

Now knowing this, Jesus with his disciples withdrew from there to the sea. And a great multitude from Galilee followed; and from Judea and from Jerusalem and from Idumaea and beyond the Jordan and around Tyre and Sidon, a great multitude, hearing what things he was doing, came to him.

And he spoke to his disciples, that a small boat should wait for him because of the crowd, lest they constrict him; for he had healed many, so that they pressed upon him that they might touch him, as many as had afflictions. And the unclean spirits, whenever they observed him, fell down before him and cried out, saying, "You are the Son of God!" And he strictly rebuked them that they should not make him known, that it might be fulfilled which was spoken through Isaiah the prophet, saying,

"Behold, my servant whom I have chosen,
    my beloved in whom my soul is well pleased;
I will place my Spirit upon him,
    and he shall report justice to the Gentiles.
He shall not quarrel nor shout,
    neither shall anyone hear his voice in the streets;
a bruised reed he shall not break,
    and smoldering wick he shall not quench,
till he thrusts forth justice to victory,
    and in his name shall the Gentiles hope."

Now it came to pass, in these days, that he went out to the mountain to pray, and he continued all night in prayer with God. And when it was day, he called his disciples, and he summoned to himself those whom he wanted, and they went to him. And he chose from them twelve, whom he also named apostles, that they might be with him and that he might send them to proclaim and to have authority to expel demons. And he appointed the Twelve: Simon whom he gave the name Peter; and James the son of Zebedee and John the brother of James, and he gave to them the name Boanerges, which means Sons of Thunder; and Andrew and Philip and Bartholomew and Matthew and Thomas and James the son of Alphaeus and Thaddaeus and Simon the Zealot and Judas Iscariot, who also became a traitor.

And having come down with them, he stood on a level place, and there was a great crowd of his disciples and a great multitude of people from all Judea and Jerusalem and the sea coast of Tyre and Sidon who came to hear him and to be healed of their diseases; and those who were troubled by unclean spirits were being cured. And all the crowds sought to touch him, for power came forth from him and cured all.

And lifting up his eyes to his disciples he said,

"Blessed are the poor, for yours is the Kingdom of God.

Blessed are those who hunger now, for you shall be filled.

Blessed are those who weep now, for you shall laugh.

Blessed are you when men shall hate you and when they exclude you and revile you and expel your name as evil for the sake of the Son of Man. Rejoice in that day and leap for joy, for behold, your reward is great in heaven, for in the same way their fathers did to the prophets.

"But woe to you who are rich, for you have received your consolation.

Woe to you, you who are full now, for you shall hunger.

Woe to you who laugh now, for you shall mourn and weep.

Woe to you when all men speak well of you, for in the same way their fathers did to the false prophets.

"But I say to you who hear: love your enemies, do good to those who hate you, bless those who curse you, pray for those who mistreat you. To him who strikes you on the cheek, also offer the other; and from him who takes away your cloak, do not withhold your shirt also. To everyone who requests of you, give; and of the one who takes away what is yours, do not demand it back.

"And as you desire that men would do to you, do to them likewise. And if you love those who love you, what grace is that to you? For even sinners love those who love them. And if you do good to those who do good to you, what grace is that to you? For even sinners do the same. And if you lend to those of whom you hope to receive, what grace is that to you? Even sinners lend to sinners, to receive back as much. Yet love your enemies and do good, and lend hoping for nothing back, and your reward shall be great and you shall be sons of the Most High; for he is kind toward the ungrateful and evil. Be merciful, just as your Father is also merciful.

"And judge not, and you shall not be judged. And condemn not, and you shall not be condemned. Pardon, and you shall be pardoned. Give, and it shall be given to you; good measure, pressed down, shaken together, running over, they shall put it in your lap. For with the same measure you measure it shall be measured back to you."

Now he also spoke a parable to them: "Can the blind guide the blind? Shall they not both fall into a pit? A disciple is not above the teacher, but everyone fully trained shall be like his teacher. So why do you look at the speck that is in your brother's eye, but do not perceive the beam that is in your own eye? Or how can you say to your brother, 'Brother, let me remove the speck that is in your eye,' when you yourself do not look at the beam that is in your own eye? Hypocrite, first remove the beam from your own eye, and then shall you see clearly to remove the speck that is in your brother's eye. For there is no good tree that brings forth corrupt fruit, nor again a corrupt tree that brings forth good fruit, for each tree is known by its own fruit. For from thorns they do not gather figs, nor from a bramble bush do they gather grapes. The good man out of the good treasure of his heart brings forth that which is good, and the evil man out of the evil treasure brings out that which is evil, for out of the abundance of the heart his mouth speaks.

"And why do you call me, 'Lord, Lord,' and do not do the things that I say? Everyone who is coming to me and hearing my words and doing them, I shall show you whom he is like: He is like a man building a house who dug and went deep and laid a foundation upon the rock. Now when a flood came, the stream broke against that house and could not shake it, because it had been well built. But the one hearing and not doing is like a man who built a house upon the earth without a foundation, against which the stream broke and straightaway it fell, and the ruin of that house was great."

After he had completed all his sayings in the ears of the people, he entered into Capernaum.

Now a certain centurion's slave, who was dear to him, was lying in his house paralyzed, grievously tormented and about to die. So when he heard about Jesus, he sent to him elders of the Jews, urging him that he come and save his slave. So coming to Jesus, they begged him earnestly, saying, "He is worthy for you to do this for him, for he loves our nation and he built our synagogue for us." So Jesus went with them.

But when he was now not far from the house, the centurion sent friends, saying to him, "Lord, don't trouble yourself, for I am not worthy for you to come under my roof, therefore I didn't even think myself worthy to come to you. But say with a word, and my servant will be cured. For I also am a man set under authority, having under myself soldiers; and I say to this one, 'Go!' and he goes; and to another, 'Come!' and he comes; and to my slave, 'Do this,' and he does it."

Now when he heard this, Jesus marveled, and turning to the crowd following him, said "Truly I say to you, not even in Israel have I found such great faith. So I say to you that many shall arrive from east and west and shall recline with Abraham and Isaac and Jacob in the Kingdom of Heaven. But the sons of the kingdom shall be expelled into the darkness outside where there shall be weeping and gnashing of teeth." And Jesus said concerning the centurion, "Go your way; as you have believed, be it done unto you."

And those who were sent, returning to the house, found that the slave who had been sick was in good health.

And it came to pass, soon afterward, that he went to a town called Nain, and his disciples went with him, and a great crowd. Now when he drew near to the gate of the town, behold, there was carried out one who was dead, the only son of his mother, and she was a widow; and a considerable crowd of the town were with her.

And when the Lord saw her, he was moved with compassion for her and said to her, "Don't cry."

And having come near, he touched the coffin, so the bearers stood still. And he said, "Young man, I say to you, arise!"

And the dead man sat up and began to speak. And he gave him to his mother.

So fear took hold of all, and they glorified God, saying, "A great prophet has arisen among us!" and, "God has visited his people!" And this word went out about him in the whole of Judea and in all the surrounding region.

Now when the disciples of John informed him in the prison about the works of the Christ, calling a certain two of his disciples, John sent them to the Lord, saying, "Are you the one who comes, or should we expect another?"

So coming to Jesus, the men said, "John the Baptist has sent us to you, saying, 'Are you the one who comes, or should we expect another?' "

In that hour he cured many of diseases and afflictions and evil spirits, and to many who were blind he gave sight. And answering he said to them, "Go and report to John the things that you hear and see: the blind receive sight and the lame walk, the lepers are cleansed and the deaf hear, and the dead are raised and the poor have Good News announced to them. And blessed is the one who shall not be stumbled by me."

Now when John's messengers had gone, Jesus began to say to the crowds about John, "What did you go out into the wilderness to gaze upon? A reed shaken with the wind? But what did you go out to see? A man dressed in fine clothing? Behold, those in glorious apparel and living in luxury are in kings' courts. But what did you go out to see? A prophet? Yes, I say to you, and much more than a prophet. For this is he of whom it is written,

'Behold, I send my messenger before your face,
who shall make ready your way before you.'

Truly I say to you, among those who are born of women there has not arisen one greater than John the Baptist; yet the least in the Kingdom of Heaven is greater than he. But from the days of John the Baptist till now the Kingdom of Heaven suffers violence, and the violent plunder it. For all the Prophets and the Law prophesied till John. And if you are willing to receive it, this is Elijah, the one who is to come. He who has ears to hear, let him hear!"

And all the people and the tax collectors hearing this justified God, having been baptized with the baptism of John. But the Pharisees and the experts on the Law of Moses rejected for themselves the plan of God, not having been baptized by him.

"What then shall the people of this generation become like, and what are they like? They are like children who sit in the marketplace, and call one to another, saying,

> 'We played the flute for you,
> and you did not dance;
> we sang a lament,
> and you did not weep.'

For John the Baptist came neither eating nor drinking and they say, 'He has a demon!' The Son of Man came eating and drinking and they say, 'Behold, a gluttonous man and a drunkard, a friend of tax collectors and sinners!' But wisdom is justified by her works and all her children."

Then he began to chastise the towns in which most of his mighty works had been done, because they did not repent. "Woe to you, Chorazin! Woe to you, Bethsaida! For if the mighty works had been done in Tyre and Sidon that were done in you, they would have repented long ago in sackcloth and ashes. Even so I say to you, it shall be more tolerable for Tyre and Sidon on the day of judgment than for you. And you, Capernaum, shall you be exalted to heaven? You shall go down to Hades. For if the mighty works had been done in Sodom that were done in you, it would have remained till today. Even so I say to you that it shall be more tolerable for the land of Sodom in the day of judgment than for you."

At that time responding Jesus said, "I thank you, Father, Lord of heaven and earth, that you hid these things from the wise and knowledgeable and revealed them to infants; yes, Father, for so it was well-pleasing in your sight. All things have been delivered to me by my Father; and no one recognizes the Son, except the Father, nor does anyone recognize the Father, except the Son, and he to whom the Son wishes to reveal him.

"Come to me, all you who toil and are overburdened, and I shall give you rest. Take my yoke upon you and learn from me, for I am gentle and lowly in heart, and you shall find rest for your souls. For my yoke is easy and my burden is light."

Now one of the Pharisees asked him to eat with him. And having entered into the Pharisee's house, he reclined at the table. And behold, a woman who was in the town, a sinner. And having learned that he was reclining in the Pharisee's house, bringing an alabaster jar of fragrant oil and standing behind at his feet weeping, she began to wet his feet with her tears; and she was wiping them with the hair of her head and kissing his feet and anointing them with the fragrant oil.

Now seeing it, the Pharisee who had invited him said within himself, saying, "This one, if he were a prophet, would know who and what kind of woman this is who touches him, that she is a sinner."

And responding Jesus said to him, "Simon, I have something to say to you."

"Teacher, say it," he declared.

"There were two debtors to a certain lender. The one owed five hundred denarii, but the other fifty. They not having means to repay, he forgave both. Which of them therefore shall love him more?"

Answering Simon said, "I suppose the one he forgave more."

So he said to him, "You have judged correctly." And turning to the woman, he declared to Simon, "Do you see this woman? I entered into your house; you gave me no water for my feet, but she has wet my feet with her tears and wiped them with her hair. You gave me no kiss, but she, from the time I entered, has not stopped kissing my feet. You did not anoint my head with oil, but she has anointed my feet with fragrant oil. Therefore I say to you, her sins, which are many, are forgiven, for she loved much. But the one who is forgiven little, loves little."

Now he said to her, "Your sins are forgiven."

And those reclining at the table with him began to say to themselves, "Who is this who even forgives sins?"

So he said to the woman, "Your faith has saved you. Go in peace."

And it came to pass, soon afterward, that he went about through towns and villages, preaching and announcing the Good News of the Kingdom of God, and with him were the Twelve and certain women who had been healed of evil spirits and infirmities: Mary who was called Magdalene, from whom seven demons had gone out, and Joanna the wife of Chuzas, administrator of Herod, and Susanna, and many others who were serving them from their means.

And he came into a house. And the crowd came together again, so that they could not so much as eat bread. And hearing it, his family went out to seize him, for they said, "He is out of his mind!"

Then was brought to him one possessed with a demon, blind and mute, and he healed him, so that the mute man both spoke and saw. And all the crowds were amazed and said, "Can this be the Son of David?"

But hearing this, the scribes and Pharisees who came down from Jerusalem said, "He has Beelzebul, the ruler of the demons!" and, "By the prince of the demons he expels the demons!"

Now seeing their thoughts, having summoned them, in parables he said to them, "Every kingdom divided against itself is brought to desolation, and every city or house divided against itself shall not stand. And if Satan expels Satan, he is divided against himself; how then shall his kingdom stand? If Satan has risen up against himself and is divided, he cannot stand, but has an end. And if I by Beelzebul expel demons, by whom do your sons expel them? Therefore they shall be your judges. But if I by the Spirit of God expel demons, then has the Kingdom of God come upon you. Or how can one enter into the house of the strong man and loot his goods unless he first binds the strong man? And then he shall loot his house. The one not with me is against me, and the one not gathering with me scatters.

"For this reason I say to you, that all shall be forgiven the sons of men, the sins and the blasphemies, as many as they have blasphemed; but whoever shall blaspheme against the Holy Spirit has no forgiveness forever, but is guilty of eternal sin. And whoever shall speak a word against the Son of Man, it shall be forgiven him; but whoever shall speak against the Holy Spirit, it shall not be forgiven him, neither in this age nor in that which is to come."

"Either make the tree good and its fruit good, or make the tree corrupt and its fruit corrupt; for the tree is known by its fruit. You offspring of vipers, how can you, being evil, speak good things? For out of the abundance of the heart the mouth speaks. The good man out of his good treasure brings forth good things, and the evil man out of his evil treasure brings forth evil things. So I say to you that every careless saying that men shall speak, they shall give account for it in the day of judgment. For by your words you shall be justified, and by your words you shall be condemned."—because they said, "He has an unclean spirit."

Then some of the scribes and Pharisees responded, saying, "Teacher, we desire to see a sign from you."

But answering he said to them, "An evil and adulterous generation seeks after a sign, and a sign shall not be given to it but the sign of Jonah the prophet. For as Jonah was three days and three nights in the belly of the great fish, so shall the Son of Man be three days and three nights in the heart of the earth. The men of Nineveh shall stand up in the judgment with this generation and shall condemn it; for they repented at the preaching of Jonah, and behold, something greater than Jonah is here. The Queen of the South shall rise up in the judgment with this generation and shall condemn it; for she came from the ends of the earth to hear the wisdom of Solomon, and behold, something greater than Solomon is here.

"But the impure spirit, when it has gone out of the man, passes through arid places seeking rest and does not find it. Then it says, 'I will return into my house from which I came out.' And when it has come, it finds it empty, swept, and put in order. Then it goes and takes with itself seven other spirits more evil than itself, and entering in, they dwell there; and the last state of that man becomes worse than the first. Thus shall it be also to this evil generation."

Now there came to him his mother and brothers, and they were not able get to him because of the crowd. So standing outside, they sent to him, calling him. And a crowd was sitting around him, and they said to him, "Behold, your mother and your brothers and your sisters are outside wanting to see you."

But responding he said to them, "Who is my mother? And who are my brothers?" And looking around at those who sat about him, and stretching forth his hand over his disciples, he said, "Look! My mother and my brothers! For whoever shall hear the word of God and do the will of my Father who is in heaven, they are my brother and sister and mother."

Now on that day, having come out of the house, Jesus sat by the seaside and began to teach. And when a great crowd came together, and those from every town were traveling to him, he entered into a boat in the sea and sat down; and all the crowd were on the land by the sea.

And he taught them many things in parables, and said to them in his teaching, "Listen! Behold, the sower went forth to sow; and as he sowed some seeds fell along the path, and they were trampled under foot, and the birds came and devoured them. Now others fell upon rocky places, where they had not much earth, and straightaway they sprang up because they had no depth of earth; so when the sun rose, they were scorched, and because they had no root, they withered away. Now others fell upon the thorns, and the thorns grew up and choked them, and they yielded no fruit. But others fell upon good earth and yielded fruit, growing up and increasing, some indeed brought forth a hundredfold, some sixty, and some thirty. He who has ears, let him hear!"

And when he was alone, those who were around him with the Twelve asked him, "Why do you speak to them in parables?"

And answering he said to them, "To you it is given to know the mysteries of the Kingdom of Heaven, but to those who are outside it is not given. For whoever has, to him shall be given, and he shall have abundance; but whoever does not have, from him shall be taken away even that which he has. For this reason I speak to them in parables, because looking they do not look, and hearing they do not hear, nor do they understand. And to them is fulfilled the prophecy of Isaiah, which says,

> 'By hearing you shall hear and shall not understand;
>   and looking you shall look and shall not see.
> For this people's heart has become callused,
>   and their ears are dull of hearing,
>   and their eyes they have closed;
> lest they should see with their eyes,
>   and hear with their ears,
>   and understand with their heart,
> and should return,
>   and I should cure them.'

But blessed are your eyes, for they look, and your ears, for they hear. For truly I say to you, that many prophets and righteous men desired to see the things that you look upon and did not see them, and to hear the things which you hear and did not hear them."

And he said to them, "Do you not know this parable? And how shall you understand all the parables? The seed is the word of God.

When anyone hears the word of the kingdom and does not understand it, then Satan comes and plunders that which has been sown in his heart, that he may not believe and be saved. This is that which was sown along the path. Now that which was sown on the rocky places, this is the one who hears the word and straightaway with joy receives it, but he does not have root in himself yet endures for a while; but when tribulation or persecution arises because of the word, straightaway he stumbles. Now that which was sown among the thorns, this is the one who hears the word, but the cares of this age and the deceitfulness of riches and pleasures of life choke the word, and he becomes unfruitful. Now that which was sown on the good earth, this is the one with a good and noble heart, hearing and understanding the word, holds it, and who truly bears fruit and brings forth fruit by perseverance, some indeed a hundredfold, some sixty, and some thirty."

And he said to them, "No one, having lit a lamp, covers it with a container or puts it under a bed, but places it upon a lampstand, that those who enter in may see the light. For nothing is hidden that shall not become evident, nor secret that shall not be known and come to light. If anyone has ears to hear, let him hear!

"Therefore take heed of what you hear. With whatever measure you measure, it shall be measured to you, and more shall be added to you. For whoever has, to him shall be given; and whoever does not have, from him shall be taken away even that which he thinks he has."

And he said, "Thus is the Kingdom of God, as if a man should cast seed upon the earth, and should sleep and rise night and day, and the seed should sprout and grow; how he does not know. The earth bears fruit by itself: first the blade, then the ear, then the full grain in the ear. But when the fruit is ripe, straightaway he sends the sickle, because the harvest has come."

Another parable he set before them, saying, "The Kingdom of Heaven has become like a man who sowed good seed in his field. But while men slept, his enemy came and sowed weeds also among the wheat and went away. So when the blade sprouted and brought forth grain, then also appeared the weeds.

"Now the slaves of the master of the house, having come, said to him, 'Sir, did you not sow good seed in your field? How then has it weeds?' So he declared to them, 'A man, an enemy, has done this.'

"So the slaves said to him, 'Do you desire us, then, to go and gather them up?' But he declared, 'No, lest perhaps while you gather up the weeds, you root up the wheat with them. Let both grow together until the harvest, and in the time of the harvest I will say to the reapers: Gather up first the weeds, and bind them in bundles to burn them, but gather the wheat into my barn.' "

Another parable he set before them, saying, "What has the kingdom of God become like, or with what parable shall we present it? As to a grain of mustard, which having taken, a man sowed in his field, which indeed is least of all seeds, but when it is grown, it is greater than the herbs and puts out great branches and becomes a tree, so that the birds of the sky come and nest in its branches and under its shadow."

Another parable he spoke to them: "The Kingdom of Heaven is like yeast, which having taken, a woman hid in three measures of dough, till it was all leavened."

All these things Jesus spoke in parables to the crowds, and without a parable he spoke nothing to them, that it might be fulfilled which was spoken through the prophet, saying,

"I will open my mouth in parables,
I will utter things hidden from the foundation of the world."

Then having sent away the crowds, he went into the house and his disciples came to him, saying, "Explain in detail to us the parable of the weeds of the field."

So answering he said, "The one who sows the good seed is the Son of Man; and the field is the world; and the good seed, these are the sons of the kingdom; and the weeds are the sons of the evil one; and the enemy who sowed them is the devil; and the harvest is the end of the age; and the reapers are angels. Therefore as the weeds are gathered up and burned with fire, so shall it be at the end of the age. The Son of Man shall send his angels, and they shall gather out of his kingdom all that cause stumbling and those who commit lawlessness, and shall cast them into the furnace of fire where there shall be weeping and gnashing of teeth. Then shall the righteous shine forth like the sun in the kingdom of their Father. He who has ears, let him hear!

"The Kingdom of Heaven is like a treasure hidden in the field that a man, having found, he hid; and in his joy he went and sold all, whatever he had, and bought that field.

"Again, the Kingdom of Heaven is like a man, a merchant, seeking beautiful pearls; now having found one precious pearl, he went and sold all, whatever he had, and bought it.

"Again, the Kingdom of Heaven is like a net that was cast into the sea and gathered of every kind, which, when it was filled, having drawn up on the beach, and having sat down, they gathered the good into containers but the bad they cast away. So shall it be in the end of the age: The angels shall come forth and separate the evil from among the righteous, and shall cast them into the furnace of fire where there shall be weeping and gnashing of teeth.

"Have you understood all these things?"

They said to him, "Yes."

So he said to them, "For this reason every scribe who has been discipled regarding the Kingdom of Heaven is like a man, a master of a house, who brings forth out of his treasure things new and old."

Now it came to pass, when Jesus had finished these parables, when evening came, Jesus said to his disciples, "Let's go over to the other side of the lake."

And having sent the crowd away, they launched out and they took him with them, just as he was, in the boat; and other boats were with him. But as they sailed, he fell asleep. And behold, there came a great tempest in the sea, so that the boat was covered with the waves and they were being swamped and they were in jeopardy. And he was in the stern, asleep on the cushion, so the disciples woke him up and said to him, "Master, master, we're dying! Save us, Lord!"

And awakening, he said to them, "Why are you fearful, you of little faith?"

Then arising, he rebuked the winds and the raging of the water, and they ceased, and there came a great calm.

So he said to them, "Where is your faith?"

But being frightfully afraid, the men marveled and said to one another, "Who is this then that he commands even the winds and the water and they obey him?"

Then they sailed to the other side of the sea, into the region of the Gerasenes, which is opposite Galilee. And having come out of the boat, straightaway there met him out of the tombs a man with an unclean spirit, extremely fierce, so that no one could pass by that way. For a long time he had worn no clothes, and he did not live in a house but in the tombs. And not even with a chain was anyone able to bind him anymore, because he had been often bound with shackles and chains, and the chains had been torn asunder by him and the shackles broken in pieces, and no one had the strength to subdue him. And always, night and day, in the tombs and in the hills, he was crying out and cutting himself with stones.

Now behold, seeing Jesus from afar, screaming, he ran and fell down before him, and crying out with a loud voice, he said, "What do I have to do with you, Jesus, Son of the Most High God? I adjure you by God, don't torment me before the time!"—for Jesus said to him, "Come forth out of the man unclean spirit!"

Now Jesus asked him, "What is your name?"

So he said to him, "My name is Legion, for we are many." And he begged him greatly that he would not command them to go into the Abyss. Now there was afar off from them on the mountainside a great herd of pigs feeding. And they begged him, saying, "If you expel us, send us into the pigs, that we may enter into them."

And he said to them, "Go!"

So coming out of the man, the unclean spirits entered into the pigs, and behold, the whole herd of about two thousand rushed down the slope into the lake and they perished in the waters.

Now having seen what had happened, those who fed the pigs fled and reported it in the town and in the countryside. So the people went out to see what it was that had happened. And behold, they came to Jesus, and observed the one who had been possessed by demons sitting, clothed and in his right mind, even him who had the legion; and they were afraid. So those who saw it described to them what happened to him who was possessed by demons, how he was saved, and about the pigs. And all the multitudes of the surrounding region of the Gerasenes began to beg him to go from their borders, for they were seized with great fear.

Now entering into the boat, the one who had been possessed by demons begged him that he might be with him. And he did not allow him, but said to him, "Go to your house, to your own people, and report to them how much the Lord has done for you, and how he had mercy on you."

And he went away, and began to proclaim in Decapolis how much Jesus had done for him; and all marveled.

Now when Jesus had crossed over again in the boat to the other side, a great crowd welcomed him, for they were all expecting him; and he was by the sea.

And behold, there came a man named Jairus, and he was a ruler of the synagogue. And seeing him, he fell at his feet and begged him greatly, saying, "My little daughter is at the point of death! Please come and lay your hands on her, that she may be saved and live."

And he went with him, and a great crowd followed him, and they pressed against him.

And behold, a woman having suffered of bleeding twelve years, and who had suffered many things by many doctors, and had spent all that she had and was no better but rather grew worse, hearing the things concerning Jesus, coming in the crowd behind him, touched his clothes. For she said within herself, "If I just touch his clothes I will be saved." And instantly her bleeding stopped, and she knew in her body that she was cured of her affliction.

And straightaway Jesus, discerning in himself that the power had gone out from him, turning in the crowd, said, "Who touched my clothes?"

But when all denied it, Peter and his disciples said to him, "Master, the crowds press and squeeze you, and you say, 'Who touched me?' "

But Jesus said, "Someone touched me, for I know that power has gone out from me." And he looked around to see the one who had done this.

Now the woman, fearing and trembling, knowing what had been done to her, came and fell down before him and informed him before all the people the reason why she had touched him, and how she was cured instantly.

So Jesus said to her, "Take courage, daughter; your faith has saved you. Go in peace, and be made well of your affliction."

While he was still speaking, there came one from the synagogue ruler's house, saying, "Your daughter is dead. Don't trouble the teacher anymore."

But Jesus, not heeding the word spoken, straightaway said to the ruler of the synagogue, "Fear not; only believe and she will be saved."

Now he did not allow anyone to follow with him, except Peter and John and James. So they came to the synagogue ruler's house, and he observed the flute players, and the crowd making an uproar and weeping and wailing greatly. And entering in, he said to them, "Why do you make an uproar and weep? The child is not dead, but is asleep."

And they laughed at him, knowing that she was dead. But he, having expelled all, took the father of the child and her mother and those who were with him and went in where the child was. And taking the child by the hand, he said to her, "Talitha cumi!" which is, being interpreted, "Girl, I say to you, arise!"

And straightaway her spirit returned and she got up instantly and walked, for she was twelve years old. And her parents were astounded with great amazement. And he instructed that something should be given to her to eat, and he strictly charged them that no one should know this. But the fame of this went out into all that land.

And as Jesus passed by from there, two blind men followed him, crying out and saying, "Have mercy on us, Son of David!"

Now when he had come into the house, the blind men came to him, and Jesus said to them, "Do you believe that I am able to do this?"

They said to him, "Yes, Lord."

Then he touched their eyes, saying, "According to your faith be it done unto you." And their eyes were opened. And Jesus sternly warned them, saying, "Watch that no one knows it." But they went forth and spread abroad his fame in all that land.

Now as they went forth, behold, there was brought to him a mute man possessed by a demon. And when the demon was expelled, the mute man spoke, and the crowds marveled, saying, "Never was anything like this seen in Israel!"

But the Pharisees said, "By the ruler of the demons he expels demons!"

Jesus went out from there, and he came into his hometown, and his disciples followed him. And when the Sabbath had come, he began to teach in the synagogue, and many hearing him were astonished, saying, "Where did this man get all these things?" and, "What is the wisdom that is given to this man, that such mighty works are done by his hands? Isn't this the carpenter, the son of Mary, and brother of James and Joses and Judas and Simon? And aren't his sisters here with us?" And they took offense at him.

So Jesus said to them, "A prophet is not without honor, except in his hometown and among his own relatives and in his own house."

And he could do there no mighty work, except that laying his hands on a few sick people, he healed them. And he marveled because of their unbelief.

After these things, there was a feast of the Jews, and Jesus went up to Jerusalem. Now there is in Jerusalem by the Sheep Gate a pool, which is called in Aramaic Bethesda, having five colonnades. In these used to lie a large multitude of those who were sick, blind, lame, withered. And a certain man was there, being thirty-eight years in his infirmity.

Jesus, seeing him lying there, and knowing that he had been so a long time already, said to him, "Do you desire to be made well?"

The sick man answered him, "Sir, I have no man to put me into the pool when the water is stirred up, but while I'm coming, another steps down before me."

Jesus said to him, "Arise. Take up your mat and walk."

And straightaway, the man was made well and took up his mat and walked.

Now it was the Sabbath on that day. So the Jews said to him who was healed, "It's the Sabbath and it's not lawful for you to take up your mat."

But he answered them, "The one who made me well, that one said to me, 'Take up your mat and walk.'"

They asked him, "Who is the man who said to you, 'Take up and walk'?"

But the one who was cured did not know who it was, for Jesus had withdrawn, a crowd being in the place.

Afterward Jesus found him in the temple and said to him, "Look! You are made well. Sin no more, lest something worse happens to you."

The man went away and informed the Jews that it was Jesus who had made him well. And for this cause the Jews persecuted Jesus, because he did these things on the Sabbath.

But Jesus responded to them, "My Father is working till now, and I am working."

For this cause therefore the Jews sought all the more to kill him, because he not only broke the Sabbath, but also called God his own Father, making himself equal with God.

Therefore Jesus responded and said to them, "Truly, truly, I say to you, the Son cannot do anything of himself but what he sees the Father doing, for whatever things he does, these the Son also does in like manner. For the Father loves the Son and shows him all things that he himself does. And greater works than these shall he show him, that you may marvel. For as the Father raises the dead and gives them life, thus the Son also gives life to whom he desires. For neither does the Father judge any one, but he has given all judgment to the Son, that all may honor the Son, even as they honor the Father. The one who is not honoring the Son does not honor the Father who sent him.

"Truly, truly, I say to you, the one who hears my word and believes him who sent me has eternal life and does not come into judgment, but has passed from death into life. Truly, truly, I say to you, an hour is coming, and now is here, when the dead shall hear the voice of the Son of God, and those hearing shall live. For as the Father has life in himself, thus he also gave to the Son to have life in himself, and he gave him authority to execute judgment, because he is the Son of Man. Marvel not at this, for the hour is coming in which all who are in the tombs shall hear his voice and shall come forth: those who have done good, to the resurrection of life, but those who have done vice, to the resurrection of judgment.

"I cannot do anything of myself. As I hear, I judge, and my judgment is righteous because I do not seek my own will, but the will of him who sent me. If I bear witness about myself, my witness is not true. It is another who bears witness about me, and I know that the witness which he witnesses about me is true. You have sent to John, and he has borne witness to the truth. But the witness that I receive is not from man, but I say these things that you may be saved. He was the burning and shining lamp, so you were willing to be jubilant for an hour in his light. But the witness that I have is greater than that of John, for the works which the Father gave me to accomplish, the very works that I do, bear witness about me, that the Father has sent me. And the one who has sent me, the Father himself, has borne witness about me. You have neither heard his voice ever, nor seen his form. And you do not have his word remaining in you because whom he sent, him you do not believe.

"You search the Scriptures because you think that in them you have eternal life, and these are the ones bearing witness about me; and you are not willing to come to me, that you may have life. I do not receive glory from men. But I know you, that you do not have the love of God in yourselves. I have come in my Father's name, and you do not receive me. If another shall come in his own name, him you will receive. How can you believe when you receive glory from one another and you do not seek the glory that comes from the only God?

"Think not that I shall accuse you to the Father. There is one accusing you: Moses, on whom you have set your hope. For if you were believing Moses, you would believe me, for he wrote of me. But if you do not believe his writings, how shall you believe my sayings?"

Jesus went about all the towns and the villages, teaching in their synagogues and proclaiming the Good News of the kingdom and healing all manner of disease and all manner of sickness. But seeing the crowds, he was moved with compassion for them because they were harassed and tossed aside, as sheep not having a shepherd. Then he said to his disciples, "The harvest indeed is plentiful, but the laborers are few. Therefore pray to the Lord of the harvest, that he send forth laborers into his harvest."

Now having summoned his twelve disciples, he gave them power and authority over impure spirits, to expel them, and to heal all manner of disease and all manner of sickness. Now the names of the twelve apostles are these: the first, Simon, who is called Peter, and Andrew his brother; James the son of Zebedee, and John his brother; Philip and Bartholomew; Thomas and Matthew the tax collector; James the son of Alphaeus, and Thaddaeus; Simon the Zealot, and Judas Iscariot, who also betrayed him.

These twelve Jesus sent, having directed them, saying, "Go not down the road of the Gentiles, and enter not into a town of the Samaritans, but rather go to the lost sheep of the house of Israel. Now as you go, proclaim, saying, 'The Kingdom of Heaven has drawn near!' Heal the sick, raise the dead, cleanse the lepers, expel demons. Freely you received, freely give. Acquire no gold nor silver nor copper for your pouch, no bag for the travel, nor extra cloaks nor sandals nor staffs, for the laborer is worthy of his food. So into whatever town or village you shall enter, search out who in it is worthy, and stay there till you go forth. And entering into the household, greet it. And if the household is worthy, let your peace come upon it, but if it is not worthy, let your peace return to you. And whoever shall not receive you nor hear your words, as you go forth out of that house or that town, shake off the dust that is under your feet for a testimony to them. Truly I say to you, it shall be more tolerable for the land of Sodom and Gomorrah in the day of judgment than for that town.

"Behold, I send you as sheep in the midst of wolves; therefore be wise as serpents and harmless as doves. So beware of men, for they shall deliver you up to tribunals, and in their synagogues they shall scourge you, and before governors and even kings shall you be brought for my sake, for a testimony to them and to the Gentiles. But when they deliver you up, be not anxious how or what you shall speak, for it shall be given you in that hour what you shall speak; for it is not you who speak, but the Spirit of your Father who speaks in you.

"And brother shall deliver up brother to death, and the father his child; and children shall rise up against parents and cause them to be put to death. And you shall be hated by all men for my name's sake, but the one enduring to the end, this one shall be saved. So when they persecute you in this town, flee into the next, for truly I say to you, you shall not have finished going to the cities of Israel till the Son of Man comes.

"A disciple is not above his teacher, nor a slave above his lord. It is sufficient for the disciple that he be as his teacher, and the servant as his lord. If they have called the master of the house Beelzebul, how much more those of his household? Therefore fear them not, for there is nothing covered that shall not be revealed, and hidden that will not be known. What I say to you in the darkness, speak in the light, and what you hear whispered, proclaim upon the housetops. And be not afraid of those who kill the body but are not able to kill the soul, but rather fear him who is able to destroy both soul and body in hell.

"Are not two sparrows sold for a cent? And not one of them shall fall to the ground apart from your Father; but the very hairs of your head are all numbered. Therefore fear not; you are of more value than many sparrows. Therefore everyone who shall profess me before men, in him shall I also profess before my Father who is in heaven. But whoever shall deny me before men, him shall I also deny before my Father who is in heaven.

"Think not that I came to thrust peace upon the earth. I came not to thrust peace, but a sword. For I came to set a man at odds against his father, and a daughter against her mother, and a daughter-in-law against her mother-in-law; and a man's foes shall be those of his own household. The one who loves father or mother more than me is not worthy of me, and the one who loves son or daughter more than me is not worthy of me. And whoever does not take his cross and follow after me is not worthy of me; the one who finds his life shall lose it, and the one who loses his life for my sake shall find it.

"The one receiving you receives me, and the one receiving me receives him who sent me. The one receiving a prophet in the name of a prophet shall get a prophet's reward, and the one receiving a righteous man in the name of a righteous man shall get a righteous man's reward. And whoever shall give to drink to one of these little ones a cup of cold water only, in the name of a disciple, truly I say to you, he shall not lose his reward."

And it came to pass, when Jesus had finished instructing his twelve disciples, he departed from there to proclaim and announce in their towns.

Now going forth two by two, the Twelve went throughout the villages announcing the Good News everywhere; and they proclaimed that people should repent; and they expelled many demons, and anointed with oil many who were sick and healed them.

Now at that time, Herod the tetrarch heard the fame about Jesus and of all that was happening. And he was perplexed because some were saying, "John the Baptist has risen from the dead, and therefore these powers work in him." But others said, "He is Elijah." And others said, "He is a prophet, like one of the prophets."

But hearing this, Herod said, "John, whom I beheaded, he has risen." For Herod himself had sent and seized John, and bound him in prison for the sake of Herodias, his brother Philip's wife, for he had married her. For John said to Herod, "It is not lawful for you to have your brother's wife."

And Herodias held it against him and desired to kill him, and she was not able for Herod feared John, knowing that he was a righteous and holy man, and kept him safe. And having heard him, he was greatly perplexed, and he gladly listened to him.

But an opportune day came when Herod on his birthday made a banquet for his nobles and the high officers and the chief men of Galilee; and when the daughter of Herodias herself came in and danced in the midst, she pleased Herod and those reclining at the table with him, and the king said to the girl, "Request of me whatever you want, and I will give it to you." And he swore to her, "Whatever you request of me, I will give you, up to half of my kingdom."

And having gone out, she said to her mother, "What should I request?"

So she said, "The head of John the Baptist."

And entering straightaway with haste to the king, she requested, saying, "I want you to give me right now on a platter the head of John the Baptist."

And the king was grieved exceedingly, but on account of his oaths and those reclining at the table, he did not desire to refuse her. And straightaway sending an executioner, the king commanded his head to be brought; and having gone, he beheaded him in the prison, and brought his head on a platter and gave it to the girl, and the girl gave it to her mother.

And having heard this, his disciples came and took up his corpse, and laid it in a tomb, and they went and informed Jesus.

Having returned, the apostles gathered themselves together to Jesus, and they reported to him all things, whatever they had done and whatever they had taught.

So having heard this, Jesus said to them, "Come you yourselves apart into a deserted place and rest awhile." For there were many coming and going, and they did not even have a chance to eat.

And taking them, Jesus withdrew from there in a boat to the other side of the sea of Galilee of Tiberias, and they retired to a deserted place by themselves near a town called Bethsaida. And people saw them going, and many recognized him and ran together there on foot from all the towns and went ahead of them because they observed his signs which he did on those who were sick. And having gone forth, he saw a great crowd, and was moved with compassion toward them, because they were as sheep without a shepherd; and welcoming them, he spoke to them of the Kingdom of God, and those who needed healing he cured.

Now Jesus went up on the mountain, and there he sat with his disciples. Now the Passover, the feast of the Jews, was at hand.

Then Jesus, lifting up his eyes and gazing that a great crowd was coming to him, said to Philip, "Where are we to buy bread, that these may eat?" But this he said, testing him, for he himself knew what he was about to do.

Philip answered him, "Two hundred denarii worth of bread isn't enough for them, that every one of them may receive a little."

Now the day began to wear away, so the Twelve came and said to him, "This place is desolate and the hour is already late; dismiss the crowds so that they may go into the villages and buy for themselves something to eat."

But Jesus said to them, "They have no need to go away; you give to them to eat."

And they said to him, "Should we go and buy two hundred denarii worth of loaves and give them to eat?"

But he said to them, "How many loaves do you have? Go see."

One of his disciples, Andrew, Simon Peter's brother, said to him, "There is a boy here who has five barley loaves and two fish, but what are these among so many?" For they were about five thousand men, besides women and children.

But he said, "Bring them here to me." And he said to his disciples, "Make them sit down in groups of about fifty each."

Now there was much grass in that place, and they sat down group by group, by hundreds and by fifties.

Now having taken the five loaves and the two fish, having looked up to heaven, he gave a blessing; and having broken the loaves, he gave them to the disciples, and the disciples gave to the crowds, and the two fish he divided to all, as much as they desired. And all ate and were filled.

Now he said to his disciples, "Gather up the left over pieces, so that not anything be lost."

So they gathered them up and filled twelve handbaskets with pieces from the five barley loaves and of the fish which were left over from those that had eaten.

Therefore the people, seeing the sign that he did, said, "This is surely the Prophet, the one who comes to the world!"

Therefore Jesus, knowing that they were about to come and take him, that they may make him king, straightaway compelled his disciples to get into the boat and go ahead of him to the other side, while he himself dismissed the crowd. And having bid them farewell, he withdrew again to the mountain. So when evening came, he was there alone.

Having entered into the boat, his disciples were going over the sea to Capernaum. Now when evening came, having rowed about three or four miles, the boat was in the middle of the sea, a long distance from the land, battered by the waves, for the sea was roiled by a great wind blowing. And it was already dark, and Jesus had not come to them.

And seeing them distressed in rowing, for the wind was against them, about the fourth watch of the night he came to them, walking upon the sea and coming near the boat, and he desired to pass by them.

So when the disciples saw him walking upon the sea, they were troubled, saying, "It's a ghost!" and they cried out for fear.

But straightaway Jesus spoke to them, saying, "Take courage, it's me! Don't be afraid."

So responding to him Peter said, "Lord, if it's you, order me to come to you on the waters."

So he said, "Come!"

And having come down from the boat, Peter walked upon the waters to come to Jesus. But seeing the mighty wind, he was afraid, and beginning to sink he cried out, saying, "Lord, save me!"

So straightaway reaching out his hand, Jesus took hold of him and said to him, "You of little faith, why did you doubt?"

Then they were willing to receive him into the boat, and when they had gone up into the boat, the wind ceased. So those who were in the boat worshiped him, saying, "Surely you are the Son of God!" And they were extremely amazed in themselves beyond measure, for they did not understand about the loaves, but their heart was hardened.

When they had crossed over, they came to land at Gennesaret and moored to the shore. And when they had come out of the boat, straightaway the people recognized him, and ran through that whole region and began to carry about on their mats those who were sick to where they heard he was. And wherever he entered, into villages or into towns or into the countryside, they laid the sick in the marketplaces and begged him that they might just touch the fringe of his clothes; and as many as touched him were saved.

On the next day the crowd that stood on the other side of the sea saw that there was no other boat there save one, and that Jesus had not entered with his disciples into the boat, but his disciples had gone away alone. However boats from Tiberias came near to the place where they ate the bread after the Lord had given thanks. Therefore when the crowd saw that Jesus was not there, nor his disciples, they themselves got into the boats and came to Capernaum seeking Jesus. And finding him on the other side of the sea they said to him, "Rabbi, when did you come here?"

Jesus answered them and said, "Truly, truly, I say to you, you seek me not because you saw signs, but because you ate of the loaves, and were filled. Do not be working for the food which perishes, but for the food which remains for eternal life, which the Son of Man shall give to you; for on him God the Father has set his seal."

Therefore they said to him, "What must we do that we may be working the works of God?"

Jesus answered and said to them, "This is the work of God, that you believe in him whom he has sent."

Therefore they said to him, "What then do you do for a sign, that we may see and believe you? What work do you do? Our fathers ate the manna in the wilderness; as it is written, 'He gave them bread out of heaven to eat.' "

Jesus therefore said to them, "Truly, truly, I say to you, it was not Moses who gave you the bread out of heaven, but my Father gives you the true bread out of heaven. For the bread of God is the one who comes down out of heaven and gives life to the world."

Therefore they said to him, "Lord, always give us this bread."

Jesus said to them, "I am the Bread of Life. The one who comes to me shall not hunger, and the one believing in me shall not ever thirst. But I said to you that you have watched me and yet you do not believe. All that the Father gives me shall arrive to me, and the one who comes to me I shall not expel. For I have come down out of heaven not to do my own will, but the will of him who sent me. So this is the will of him who sent me, that of all he has given to me I should lose none, but should raise him up at the last day. For this is the will of my Father, that everyone observing the Son and believing in him should have eternal life; and I shall raise him up at the last day."

Therefore the Jews murmured about him, because he said, "I am the bread which came down out of heaven." And they said, "Isn't this Jesus, the son of Joseph, whose father and mother we know? How does he now say, 'I have come down out of heaven?' "

Jesus answered and said to them, "Do not murmur with one another. No one can come to me unless the Father who sent me draws him, and I shall raise him up in the last day. It is written in the Prophets, 'And they shall all be taught by God.' Everyone who has heard from the Father and has learned comes to me. Not that anyone has watched the Father, except the one who is from God; he has watched the Father.

"Truly, truly, I say to you, the one who believes has eternal life. I am the Bread of Life. Your fathers ate the manna in the wilderness, and they died. This is the bread which comes down out of heaven, that anyone may eat of it and not die. I am the living bread which came down out of heaven. If anyone eats of this bread, he shall live forever; and also the bread that I shall give is my flesh, for the life of the world."

The Jews therefore argued with one another, saying, "How can this man give us his flesh to eat?"

Jesus therefore said to them, "Truly, truly, I say to you, unless you eat the flesh of the Son of Man and drink his blood, you do not have life in yourselves. The one feeding on my flesh and drinking my blood has eternal life, and I shall raise him up at the last day. For my flesh is true food, and my blood is true drink. The one feeding on my flesh and drinking my blood remains in me, and I in him. As the living Father sent me, and I live because of the Father, so the one feeding on me, he also shall live because of me. This is the bread which came down out of heaven, not as the fathers ate and died. The one feeding on this bread shall live forever."

These things he said in the synagogue, teaching in Capernaum. Therefore hearing this, many of his disciples said, "These are harsh words! Who can listen to them?"

But Jesus, knowing in himself that his disciples murmured at this, said to them, "Does this cause you to stumble? What if then you would observe the Son of Man ascending to where he was before? It is the Spirit giving life; the flesh provides nothing. The sayings that I have spoken to you are spirit and are life. But there are some of you who did not believe." For Jesus knew from the beginning who they were who were not believing, and who it was who would betray him. And he said, "For this reason I have said to you that no one can come to me unless it is given to him from the Father."

At this many of his disciples went back and walked no more with him. Jesus therefore said to the Twelve, "Do you not also desire to go away?"

Simon Peter answered him, "Lord, to whom will we go? You have the sayings of eternal life, and we have believed and have known that you are the Holy One of God."

Jesus answered them, "Did I not choose you, the Twelve, and one of you is the devil?" Now he spoke of Judas son of Simon Iscariot, for it was he who was about to betray him, one of the Twelve.

After these things Jesus walked in Galilee, for he did not desire to walk in Judea because the Jews sought to kill him. And there were gathered together to him the Pharisees and some of the scribes who had come from Jerusalem and had seen some of his disciples eating bread with defiled hands, that is unwashed. For the Pharisees and all the Jews do not eat unless they ritually wash their hands, holding to the tradition of the elders; and when they come from the marketplace, unless they baptize themselves, do not eat, and many other things there are which they have received to hold: baptizing of cups and pitchers and copper utensils. And the Pharisees and the scribes asked him, "Why don't your disciples walk according to the tradition of the elders, but eat their bread with defiled hands? For they do not wash their hands when they eat bread."

But answering he said to them, "Well did Isaiah prophesy of you hypocrites, as it is written,

> 'This people honors me with their lips,
> but their heart is far from me.
> So in vain do they worship me,
> teaching as doctrines the commandments of men.'

You leave the commandment of God and hold to the tradition of men." And he said to them, "Full well do you reject the commandment of God, that you may keep your tradition. For Moses said, 'Honor your father and your mother;' and, 'The one who speaks evil of father or mother must die the death.' But you say, 'If a man tells his father or his mother, "Whatever might have benefitted you is Corban" '—that is, given as an offering—then you no longer let him do anything for his father or his mother, making void the word of God by your tradition which you have handed down. And many such things like this you do."

And summoning to him the crowd again he said to them, "Hear me, all of you, and understand: There is nothing from outside of the man that going into him can defile him, but the things which proceed out of the man are those that defile the man."

Then when he had entered into the house away from the crowd, the disciples said to him, "Do you know that the Pharisees were offended when they heard these words?"

But answering he said, "Every plant which my heavenly Father did not plant shall be uprooted. Leave them be; they are blind guides of the blind. And if the blind guide the blind, both shall fall into a pit."

So responding Peter said to him, "Interpret the parable for us."

But he said to them, "Are you also still ignorant? Do you not comprehend that whatever goes into the man from outside can not defile him because it does not go into his heart, but into the stomach and into the latrine?"—thus he declared all foods clean.

So he said, "That which proceeds out of the man, that defiles the man. For from within, out of the hearts of men, the wretched thoughts proceed: sexual immoralities, thefts, murders, adulteries, covetings, wickednesses, deceit, debauchery, an evil eye, slander, pride, foolishness. All these evil things proceed from within and defile the man, but to eat with unwashed hands does not defile the man."

Now having gone forth from there, Jesus withdrew into the region of Tyre.

And entering into a house, he desired none to know it, yet he could not escape notice. So straightaway having heard, behold, a Canaanite woman whose little daughter had an unclean spirit came and fell down at his feet. Now the woman was a Greek, a Syrophoenician by race, and she urged him and cried out, saying, "Have mercy on me, Lord, Son of David! My daughter is grievously possessed by a demon."

But he answered her not a word.

And having come, his disciples urged him, saying, "Dismiss her, for she is crying out after us."

So answering he said, "I was not sent but to the lost sheep of the house of Israel."

But coming near, she bowed to him, saying, "Lord, help me!"

So responding he said, "Let the children be filled first, for it is not good to take the children's bread and cast it to the dogs."

But she said, "Yes, Lord, for even the dogs eat of the crumbs which fall from their masters' table."

Then answering Jesus said to her, "O woman, great is your faith! Be it to you as you desire. Because of this word, go your way. The demon has gone out of your daughter."

And her daughter was cured from that hour, and going away to her house, she found the child lying on the bed and the demon gone out.

Departing from the region of Tyre, he came through Sidon to the sea of Galilee, through the midst of the region of Decapolis. And they brought to him one who was deaf and had an impediment in his speech, and they begged him to lay his hand upon him. And taking him aside from the crowd privately, he put his fingers into his ears; and having spat, he touched his tongue; and looking up to heaven, he sighed and said to him, "Ephphatha!" that is, "Be opened!"

And immediately his ears were opened and the restriction of his tongue was released and he spoke clearly. And he charged them that they should tell no one, but the more he charged them, so much the more abundantly they proclaimed it. And they were astonished beyond measure, saying, "He has done all things well; he makes even the deaf hear and the mute speak!"

And he went up on the mountain and sat there. And great crowds came to him, having with them the lame, blind, mute, crippled, and many others, and they put them down at his feet. And he healed them, so the crowd marveled when they saw the mute speaking, the crippled made well, and the lame walking, and the blind seeing. And they glorified the God of Israel.

In those days, when there was again a great crowd and they had nothing to eat, summoning his disciples to himself, Jesus said to them, "I am moved with compassion toward the crowd because they already have continued with me three days and have nothing to eat, and if I dismiss them fasting to their home, they will faint on the way, and some of them have come from afar."

And the disciples said to him, "Where could we get so many loaves in a solitary place as to feed so great a crowd?"

And Jesus asked them, "How many loaves do you have?"

So they said, "Seven, and a few small fish."

And he directed the crowd to sit down on the ground. And having taken the seven loaves, and having given thanks, he broke them, and he gave to the disciples, and the disciples gave to the crowds. And having blessed the few small fish, he said to also set these before them. And all ate and were filled.

And they took up the left over pieces, seven large baskets full. Now those eating were four thousand men, besides women and children.

And having dismissed the crowds, he got into the boat with his disciples, and came into the region of Magadan.

And the Pharisees and Sadducees came out and began to contend with him, seeking from him a sign from heaven, testing him. But responding he said to them, "When it is evening you say, 'Fair weather, for the sky is red.' And in the morning, 'A downpour today, for the sky is red and gloomy.' Hypocrites! The appearance of the sky you know how to discern, but the signs of the times you cannot."

And sighing deeply in his spirit, he said, "Why does this generation seek a sign? Truly I say to you, an evil and adulterous generation seeks after a sign, and a sign shall not be given to it but the sign of Jonah. "

And leaving them, again entering into the boat, he went to the other side.

And having come to the other side, the disciples forgot to take bread, and they did not have more than one loaf with them in the boat. Now Jesus charged them, saying, "Watch, look out for the yeast of the Pharisees and Sadducees and the yeast of Herod."

So they reasoned among themselves, saying, "It's because we have no bread."

But knowing this Jesus said, "You of little faith, why do you reason among yourselves because you hold no bread? Do you not yet comprehend nor understand? Is your heart hardened? Having eyes, do you not look? And having ears, do you not hear? And do you not remember? When I broke the five loaves among the five thousand, how many handbaskets full of broken pieces did you take up?"

They said to him, "Twelve."

"And the seven among the four thousand, how many large baskets full of broken pieces did you take up?"

And they said to him, "Seven."

And he said to them, "Do you not yet understand? How is it that you do not comprehend that I did not speak to you about bread? But beware of the yeast of the Pharisees and Sadducees."

Then they understood that he did not say to beware of the yeast of bread, but of the teaching of the Pharisees and Sadducees.

And he came to Bethsaida. And they brought to him a blind man, and begged him to touch him. And taking the blind man by the hand, he brought him out of the village. And having spat upon his eyes, having laid his hands upon him, he asked him, "Do you see anything?"

And looking up he said, "I see men; for like trees I watch them walking."

Then again he laid his hands upon his eyes, and he saw clearly, and was restored, and peered all things with clarity. And he sent him to his house, saying, "Do not even enter into the village."

Now the feast of the Jews, the Feast of Tabernacles, was at hand. His brothers therefore said to him, "Depart from here and go into Judea, that your disciples may also observe your works which you do. For no one does anything in secret when he seeks to be known openly. If you do these things, make yourself visible to the world." For even his brethren did not believe in him.

Jesus therefore said to them, "My time has not yet come, but your time is always ready. The world cannot hate you; but it hates me because I bear witness about it, that its works are evil. You go up to the feast. I am not going up to this feast, because my time is not yet fulfilled." And having said these things to them, he remained in Galilee.

But when his brothers had gone up to the feast, then he also went up, not publicly, but in secret. The Jews therefore sought him at the feast and said, "Where is he?" And there was much murmuring among the crowds concerning him. Some said, "He is a good man." Others said, "No, on the contrary, he leads the crowds astray." Yet no one spoke openly of him for fear of the Jews.

But when it was now the middle of the feast, Jesus went up into the temple and taught. The Jews therefore marveled, saying, "How does this man know the Scriptures, having never been educated?"

Jesus therefore answered them and said, "My teaching is not mine, but his who sent me. If anyone desires to do his will, he shall know about the teaching, whether it is from God or whether I speak from myself. The one speaking from himself seeks his own glory; but the one seeking the glory of him who sent him, this one is true, and no unrighteousness is in him. Did not Moses give you the Law, and yet none of you keeps the Law? Why do you seek to kill me?"

The crowd answered, "You have a demon! Who seeks to kill you?"

Jesus answered and said to them, "I did one work and you all marvel. On account of this Moses has given you circumcision, and on the Sabbath you circumcise a boy. If a boy receives circumcision on the Sabbath, that the Law of Moses may not be broken, are you angry with me because I made a man entirely well on the Sabbath? Cease judging according to appearance, but judge righteous judgment."

Therefore some of those of Jerusalem said, "Isn't this he whom they seek to kill? Look! He speaks openly, and they say nothing to him. Could it be that the rulers really know that this is the Christ? Yet we know where this one is from, but when the Christ comes, no one will know where he is from."

Jesus therefore cried out in the temple, teaching and saying, "You both know me and know where I am from; yet I have not come of myself, but the one who sent me is true, whom you do not know. I know him, because I am from him, and he sent me."

They sought therefore to arrest him; but no one laid a hand on him, because his hour had not yet come. But of the crowd many believed in him, and they said, "When the Christ comes, will he do more signs than those that this man has done?" The Pharisees heard the crowd murmuring these things concerning him, and the chief priests and the Pharisees sent guards to arrest him.

Therefore Jesus said, "I am with you a little time yet, then I go to him who sent me. You shall seek me and shall not find me; and where I am, you cannot come."

The Jews therefore said among themselves, "Where is this man about to go that we won't find him? Is he about to go to the Dispersion among the Greeks and teach the Greeks? What is this word that he said, 'You shall seek me and shall not find me; and where I am, you cannot come'?"

Now on the last day, the great day of the feast, Jesus stood and cried out, saying, "If anyone thirsts, let him come to me and drink! The one believing in me, as the Scripture has said, out of his heart shall flow rivers of living water." But he said this concerning the Spirit, whom those believing in him were about to receive. For the Spirit was not yet given, because Jesus was not yet glorified.

Some of the crowd therefore, when they heard these words, said, "This is surely the Prophet." Others said, "This is the Christ." But some said, "What, does the Christ come out of Galilee? Hasn't the Scripture said that the Christ comes from the seed of David, and from Bethlehem, the village where David was?" Therefore a schism ensued among the crowd because of him. And some of them would have arrested him, but no one laid hands on him.

The guards therefore came to the chief priests and Pharisees, and they said to them, "Why didn't you bring him?"

The guards answered, "Never has a man spoken like this as this man speaks!"

The Pharisees therefore answered them, "Are you also led astray? Have any of the rulers believed in him, or of the Pharisees? But this crowd that doesn't know the Law is cursed!"

Nicodemus, who came to him before, being one of them, said to them, "Does our Law judge a man unless it first hears from him and knows what he does?"

They answered and said to him, "Are you also from Galilee? Search and see that no prophet arises out of Galilee."

Then again Jesus spoke to them, saying, "I am the Light of the World. The one following me shall not walk in the darkness, but shall have the light of life."

The Pharisees therefore said to him, "You bear witness about yourself; your witness is not true."

Jesus answered and said to them, "Even if I bear witness about myself, my witness is true, for I know from where I came, and where I go. But you do not know from where I come, or where I go. You judge according to the flesh; I judge no one. But even if I do judge, my judgment is true; for I am not alone in it, but I and the Father who sent me. Now even in your Law it is written that the witness of two men is true. I am one bearing witness about myself, and the Father who sent me bears witness about me."

Therefore they said to him, "Where is your father?"

Jesus answered, "You know neither me nor my Father. If you knew me, you would know my Father also."

These sayings he spoke in the treasury, teaching in the temple. Yet no one arrested him, because his hour had not yet come. Therefore he said again to them, "I shall go away, and you shall seek me, and you shall die in your sin. Where I go, you cannot come."

The Jews therefore said, "Will he kill himself, that he says, 'Where I go, you cannot come'?"

And he said to them, "You are from below; I am from above. You are of this world; I am not of this world. I therefore said to you that you shall die in your sins, for unless you believe that I am he, you shall die in your sins."

They therefore said to him, "Who are you?"

Jesus said to them, "Just what I spoke to you at the beginning. I have many things to speak and to judge concerning you. But the one who sent me is true, and the things that I heard from him, these I speak to the world."

They did not know that he talked to them about the Father. Jesus therefore said to them, "When you have lifted up the Son of Man, then you shall know that I am he. And I do nothing from myself, but as the Father taught me, I speak these things. And the one who sent me is with me; he has not left me alone, for I always do the things that are pleasing to him."

As he spoke these things, many believed in him. Jesus therefore said to those Jews who believed him, "If you remain in my word, then you are surely my disciples, and you shall know the truth, and the truth shall set you free."

They answered to him, "We are Abraham's seed and have been in bondage to no one ever. How do you say, 'You shall become free'?"

Jesus answered them, "Truly, truly, I say to you, the one committing sin is the slave of sin. But a slave does not remain in the house forever; the son remains forever. Therefore if the Son shall set you free, you shall be free indeed. I know that you are Abraham's seed, yet you seek to kill me because my word has no place in you. That which I have watched my Father do, I speak; therefore you also do the things which you have heard from your father."

They answered and said to him, "Our father is Abraham!"

Jesus said to them, "If you were the children of Abraham, you would do the works of Abraham. But now you seek to kill me, a man who has spoken to you the truth which I heard from God; this Abraham did not. You do the works of your father."

They said to him, "We were not born of fornication. We have one father: God."

Jesus said to them, "If God were your father, you would love me, for I came forth from God and am here. For neither have I come of myself, but he sent me. Why do you not know my speech? Because you cannot hear my word. You are of your father the devil, and the lusts of your father you desire to do. He was a murderer from the beginning, and has not stood in the truth because there is no truth in him. When he speaks a lie, he speaks from his own nature; for he is a liar, and the father of it. But because I say the truth, you do not believe me. Which of you convicts me of sin? If I say the truth, why do you not believe me? The one who is of God hears the sayings of God. For this cause you do not hear, because you are not of God."

The Jews answered and said to him, "Don't we rightly say that you are a Samaritan and have a demon?"

Jesus answered, "I do not have a demon, but I honor my Father and you disgrace me. But I do not seek my own glory. There is one seeking and judging. Truly, truly, I say to you, if anyone keeps my word, he shall forever not see death."

Then the Jews said to him, "Now we know that you have a demon! Abraham died, and the prophets, and you say, 'If anyone keeps my word, he shall forever not taste death.' Are you greater than our father Abraham who died? The prophets died. Whom do you make yourself?"

Jesus answered, "If I glorify myself, my glory is nothing. It is my Father who glorifies me, of whom you say 'He is our God'; and you have not known him. But I know him, and if I say that I do not know him, I shall be like you, a liar. But I know him and keep his word. Your father Abraham was jubilant that he would see my day; and he saw it and rejoiced."

The Jews therefore said to him, "You are not yet fifty years old, and you have watched Abraham?"

Jesus said to them, "Truly, truly, I say to you, before Abraham was, I AM."

Therefore they took up stones to cast at him, but Jesus hid himself and went out of the temple.

And passing by, he saw a man blind from birth. And his disciples asked him, saying, "Rabbi, who sinned, this man or his parents, that he should be born blind?"

Jesus answered, "Neither did this man sin, nor his parents, but that the works of God should be made visible in him. We must be working the works of him who sent me while it is day. Night is coming, when no one can work. While I am in the world, I am the Light of the World."

Having said these things, he spat on the ground and made mud with the saliva and spread the mud on his eyes and said to him, "Go, wash in the pool of Siloam"—which means "Sent".

He therefore went and washed, and came back seeing. Therefore the neighbors and those who observed him before that he was a beggar, said, "Isn't this the one who sits and begs?" Some said, "It is he." Others said, "No, but he looks like him."

He said, "I am he!"

They therefore said to him, "How then were your eyes opened?"

He answered, "The man called Jesus made mud and spread it on my eyes and said to me, 'Go to Siloam and wash.' Going and washing, I received sight."

And they said to him, "Where is he?"

He said, "I don't know."

They brought to the Pharisees him who had been blind. Now it was a Sabbath on the day Jesus made the mud and opened his eyes. Again therefore the Pharisees also asked him how he received his sight. So he said to them, "He put mud on my eyes and I washed and I see."

Therefore some of the Pharisees said, "This man is not from God, because he doesn't keep the Sabbath." But others said, "How can a man who is a sinner do such signs?" So there was a schism among them. Therefore they said to the blind man again, "What do you say about him, since he opened your eyes?"

So he said, "He is a prophet."

The Jews therefore did not believe about him, that he had been blind and had received his sight, until they called the parents of him who had received his sight and asked them, "Is this your son, whom you say was born blind? How then does he now see?"

His parents answered and said, "We know that this is our son and that he was born blind, but how he now sees we don't know, or who opened his eyes we don't know. Ask him! He's of age, he shall speak for himself." His parents said these things because they feared the Jews, for the Jews had already agreed that if anyone would profess him as Christ, they would be put out of the synagogue. For this reason his parents said, "He's of age, ask him."

So they called a second time the man who was blind and said to him, "Give glory to God. We know that this man is a sinner."

He therefore answered, "Whether he is a sinner, I don't know. One thing I know: that being blind, now I see."

They therefore said to him, "What did he do to you? How did he open your eyes?"

He answered them, "I told you already and you didn't listen! Why do you want to hear it again? Don't you also want to become his disciples?"

And they ridiculed him and said, "You are his disciple, but we are disciples of Moses. We know that God has spoken to Moses, but as for this man, we don't know where he's from."

The man answered and said to them, "Why, this is amazing that you don't know where he is from yet he opened my eyes. We know that God doesn't hear sinners, but if anyone is God-fearing and does his will, he hears him. Since the world began it has never been heard of that anyone opened the eyes of someone born blind. If this man were not from God, he couldn't do anything."

They answered and said to him, "You were born entirely in sins and you teach us?" And they expelled him out.

Jesus heard that they had expelled him out, and finding him, he said, "Do you believe in the Son of Man?"

He answered and said, "And who is he, Lord, that I may believe in him?"

Jesus said to him, "You have watched him, and the one speaking with you is he."

So he declared, "I believe, Lord." And he worshiped him.

And Jesus said, "For judgment I came into this world, that those not seeing may see, and those seeing may become blind."

Those of the Pharisees who were with him heard these things and said to him, "Are we also blind?"

Jesus said to them, "If you were blind, you would have no sin. But since you say, 'We see,' your sin remains. Truly, truly, I say to you, the one not entering in by the gate into the sheep pen but climbs up some other way, that one is a thief and a bandit. But the one entering in by the gate is the shepherd of the sheep. To this one the gatekeeper opens, and the sheep listen to his voice; and he calls his own sheep by name and leads them out. When he brings out all his own, he goes before them and the sheep follow him, for they know his voice. And a stranger they shall certainly not follow, but shall flee from him, for they do not know the voice of strangers." This allegory Jesus said to them, but they did not know what he spoke to them.

Jesus therefore said to them again, "Truly, truly, I say to you, I am the Gate of the Sheep. All who came before me are thieves and bandits, but the sheep did not hear them. I am the Gate; through me if anyone enters in, he shall be saved and shall go in and go out and shall find pasture. The thief does not come but that he may steal and kill and destroy. I came that they may have life and may have it abundantly.

"I am the Good Shepherd. The Good Shepherd lays down his life for the sheep. But the hired hand, not being the shepherd, who does not own the sheep, observes the wolf coming and leaves the sheep and flees, and the wolf snatches them and scatters them. He flees because he is a hired hand and cares not about the sheep. I am the Good Shepherd, and I know my own and I am known by my own, just as the Father knows me and I know the Father, and I lay down my life for the sheep. And I have other sheep, which are not of this pen. Them I must bring also, and they shall hear my voice, and they shall become one flock, one shepherd. For this reason the Father loves me, because I lay down my life, that I may receive it again. No one takes it away from me, but I lay it down of myself. I have authority to lay it down, and I have authority to receive it again. This commandment I received from my Father."

There again arose a schism among the Jews because of these words. Now many of them said, "He has a demon and is crazy! Why do you listen to him?" Others said, "These are not the sayings of one possessed by a demon. Is a demon able to open the eyes of the blind?"

Then came the Feast of the Dedication at Jerusalem. It was winter, and Jesus was walking in the temple in the colonnade of Solomon. The Jews therefore surrounded him and said to him, "How long will you aggravate us? If you are the Christ, tell us openly."

Jesus answered them, "I told you and you do not believe. The works that I do in my Father's name, these bear witness about me. But you do not believe because you are not of my sheep, as I told you. My sheep hear my voice, and I know them, and they follow me. And I give them eternal life, and they shall forever not perish, and never shall anyone snatch them out of my hand. What my Father has given to me is greater than all, and no one is able to snatch it out of my Father's hand. I and the Father are one."

Therefore the Jews took up stones again to stone him. Jesus answered them, "Many good works I have shown you from my Father. For which of those works do you stone me?"

The Jews answered him, "For a good work we don't stone you, but for blasphemy and because you, being a man, make yourself God!"

Jesus answered them, "Is it not written in your Law, 'I said, you are gods?' If he called them gods to whom the word of God came—and the Scripture cannot be broken—do you say of him whom the Father sanctified and sent into the world, 'You are blaspheming,' because I said, 'I am the Son of God?' If I do not do the works of my Father, do not believe me. But if I do them, though you do not believe me, believe the works, that you may know and believe that the Father is in me, and I in the Father."

They therefore sought again to arrest him, but he escaped from their hand.

And again he went away beyond the Jordan to the place where John was first baptizing, and he stayed there. And many came to him and said, "John indeed did no sign, but everything that John said about this man was true." And many believed in him there.

Now a certain man was sick, Lazarus of Bethany, from the village of Mary and her sister Martha. And it was that Mary who had anointed the Lord with fragrant oil and wiped his feet with her hair whose brother Lazarus was sick. The sisters therefore sent to him, saying, "Lord, look! He whom you love is sick."

But hearing this Jesus said, "This sickness is not to death, but for the glory of God, that Son of God may be glorified by it."

Now Jesus loved Martha and her sister and Lazarus. Therefore when he heard that he was sick, he stayed two more days in the place where he was. Then after this he said to the disciples, "Let's go into Judea again."

The disciples said to him, "Rabbi, the Jews were just now seeking to stone you, and you go there again?"

Jesus answered, "Are there not twelve hours in the day? If someone walks in the day, he does not stumble, because he sees the light of this world. But if someone walks in the night, he stumbles, because the light is not in him."

These things he said, and after this he said to them, "Our friend Lazarus has fallen asleep, but I go that I may awaken him."

The disciples therefore said to him, "Lord, if he has fallen asleep, he will be saved."

Now Jesus had spoken of his death, but they thought that he talked about taking rest in sleep. Therefore then Jesus said to them plainly, "Lazarus has died, and I rejoice for your sakes that I was not there, in order that you may believe. Nevertheless, let us go to him."

Therefore Thomas, who is called Didymus, said to his fellow disciples, "Let's go also, that we may die with him."

So having come, Jesus found that he had been in the tomb four days already. Now Bethany was near Jerusalem, about two miles away, so many of the Jews had come to Martha and Mary to console them about their brother. Therefore Martha, when she heard that Jesus was coming, went out to meet him; but Mary was sitting in the house. Therefore Martha said to Jesus, "Lord, if you had been here, my brother wouldn't have died. And even now I know that whatever you request of God, God will give you."

Jesus said to her, "Your brother will rise."

Martha said to him, "I know that he will rise in the resurrection at the last day."

Jesus said to her, "I am the Resurrection and the Life. The one believing in me, though he dies, he shall live; and everyone living and believing in me shall forever not die. Do you believe this?"

She said to him, "Yes, Lord, I have believed that you are the Christ, the Son of God, the one who comes into the world."

And having said this, she went away and called Mary her sister privately, saying, "The Teacher is here and calls you."

So when she heard this, she arose quickly and went to him. Now Jesus had not yet come into the village, but was still in the place where Martha met him. Then the Jews who were with her in the house and consoling her, seeing that Mary got up quickly and went out, followed her supposing that she was going to the tomb to weep there. Mary therefore, when she came to where Jesus was, seeing him, fell down at his feet, saying to him, "Lord, if you had been here, my brother wouldn't have died!"

Therefore when Jesus saw her weeping, and the Jews who came with her weeping, he raged in spirit and troubled himself and said, "Where have you laid him?"

They said to him, "Lord, come and see."

Jesus wept.

The Jews therefore were saying, "See how he loved him!" But some of them said, "Couldn't this man who opened the eyes of the blind man have also kept this one from dying?"

Jesus therefore, again raging in himself, came to the tomb. Now it was a cave, and a stone lay against it. Jesus said, "Take away the stone."

Martha, the sister of him who was dead, said to him, "Lord, by now it smells, for it has been four days."

Jesus said to her, "Did I not say to you that if you believed, you would see the glory of God?"

Then they took away the stone. Now Jesus lifted up his eyes and said, "Father, I thank you that you have heard me. And I knew that you always hear me; but because of the crowd standing around I said this, that they may believe that you sent me."

And having said these things, he shouted with a loud voice, "Lazarus, come out!"

The one who was dead came out, bound hand and foot with strips of linen, and his face was wrapped with a cloth.

Jesus said to them, "Unbind him and let him go."

Therefore many of the Jews, coming to Mary and gazing upon what he did, believed in him. But some of them went away to the Pharisees and told them what Jesus had done.

Therefore the chief priests and the Pharisees gathered a council and said, "What are we doing? For this man does many signs. If we leave him alone like this, all will believe in him, and the Romans will come and take away both our place and our nation."

But a certain one of them, Caiaphas, being high priest that year, said to them, "You know nothing at all, nor do you reckon that it is better for you that one man should die for the people, and that the whole nation not perish."

Now this he did not say on his own, but being high priest that year, he foretold that Jesus was about to die for the nation, and not for the nation only, but that he might also gather together into one the children of God who are scattered abroad.

So from that day forth they took counsel that they might put him to death. Jesus therefore walked openly no more among the Jews, but went from there into the region near the wilderness to a town called Ephraim, and there he stayed with the disciples.

Now Jesus came into the villages of the district of Caesarea Philippi. And it came to pass, as he was praying alone, the disciples were with him, and he asked them, "Who do men say that the Son of Man is?"

So they told him, saying, "Some, John the Baptist; others, Elijah; and still others, Jeremiah or a prophet, one of the ancients, had risen."

And he asked them, "But who do you say that I am?"

So answering Simon Peter said, "You are the Christ, the Son of the living God."

Now responding Jesus said to him, "Blessed are you, Simon son of Jonah, for flesh and blood has not revealed it to you, but my Father who is in heaven. So I also say to you that you are Peter, and upon this rock I shall build my church, and the gates of Hades shall not prevail against it. I shall give to you the keys of the Kingdom of Heaven, and whatever you bind on earth shall be bound in heaven, and whatever you release on earth shall be released in heaven."

Then he charged the disciples that they should tell no one that he was the Christ, saying, "The Son of Man must go to Jerusalem and suffer many things and be rejected by the elders and chief priests and scribes and be killed, and the third day be raised." And he spoke the word plainly.

And having taken him aside, Peter began to rebuke him, saying, "Be it far from you, Lord! Not ever will this be done to you."

But turning around and seeing his disciples, he rebuked Peter and said, "Get behind me, Satan! You are a stumbling block to me, for you have in mind not the things of God, but the things of men."

Now he said to all, "If anyone desires to come after me, let him deny himself and take up his cross every day and follow me. For whoever desires to save his life shall lose it, but whoever shall lose his life for my sake and the Good News shall save it. For what shall it profit a man if he gains the whole world but forfeits his life? Or what shall a man give in exchange for his life? For whoever shall be ashamed of me and of my words in this adulterous and sinful generation, the Son of Man also shall be ashamed of him when he comes in the glory of his Father with the holy angels, and then he shall repay to each according to their deeds. Truly I say to you, there are some of those standing here who shall not taste of death till they see the Son of Man coming in his kingdom."

Now it came to pass, six days after these words, that Jesus took with him Peter and John and James and went up on the high mountain to pray by themselves.

And as he was praying, he was transfigured before them, and the appearance of his face was altered so that it shone like the sun, and his clothing became as lightning, gleaming exceedingly white such as no launderer on earth can bleach them.

And behold, two men were conversing with him, who were Moses and Elijah, who appeared in glory, and spoke of his exodus which he was about to fulfill in Jerusalem.

Now Peter and those who were with him were weighed down with sleep; but fully awakening, they saw his glory, and the two men who stood with him.

And it came to pass, as they were parting from him, Peter said to Jesus, "Rabbi, it's good for us to be here, and if you desire, let's make three tents: one for you and one for Moses and one for Elijah,"—not knowing what he was saying, for they were very terrified.

Now as he was saying these things, behold, a bright cloud came and overshadowed them, and they feared as they entered into the cloud. And a voice came out of the cloud, saying, THIS IS MY BELOVED SON, THE ONE I HAVE CHOSEN, IN WHOM I AM WELL PLEASED. HEAR HIM.

And hearing it, the disciples fell on their faces and were exceedingly afraid. And Jesus coming to them and touching them said, "Arise, and be not afraid."

But lifting up their eyes, they saw no one, except Jesus alone.

And as they were coming down from the mountain, Jesus commanded them, saying, "Tell the vision to no one, till the Son of Man is raised from the dead."

And they were silent, and informed no one in those days any of the things which they had watched. And they kept this word to themselves, contending about what the rising up from the dead should mean.

And his disciples asked him, saying, "Why do the scribes say that Elijah must come first?"

So he declared to them, "Elijah indeed, coming first, restores all things. And how is it written of the Son of Man, that he should suffer many things and be treated with contempt? But I say to you that Elijah has also come, and they did not recognize him, and they have also done to him whatever they desired, just as it is written about him."

Then the disciples understood that he spoke to them of John the Baptist.

Now it came to pass, on the next day, coming to the disciples, they saw a great crowd around them and scribes arguing with them. And straightaway all the crowd, seeing Jesus, were greatly amazed; and running to him, greeted him.

And he asked them, "What are you arguing about with them?"

And behold, there came to him a man from the crowd, kneeling to him and saying, "Teacher, I plead with you to look at my son, for he is my only child. And behold, a mute spirit takes him, and whenever it overwhelms him he suddenly cries out and it throws him down and it convulses him so that he foams and grinds his teeth, bruising him severely. And he becomes stiff and it hardly leaves him. I pleaded with your disciples to expel it and they couldn't!"

So responding Jesus said, "O faithless and perverse generation, how long shall I be with you? How long shall I bear with you? Bring him here to me."

And they brought him to him. And seeing him, straightaway the spirit threw him into convulsions, and falling on the ground, he rolled about, foaming at the mouth.

And he asked his father, "How long a time is it since this has come to him?"

So he said, "From childhood. And often it has cast him both into the fire and into the waters to destroy him. But if you can do anything, have compassion on us and help us!"

So Jesus said to him, " 'If you can'? All things are possible to the one who believes."

Straightaway crying out, the father of the child said, "I believe! Help my unbelief."

Now when Jesus saw that a crowd came running together, he rebuked the unclean spirit, saying to it, "You mute and deaf spirit, I command you, come out of him and no more enter into him!"

And crying out and throwing him into many convulsions, it came out; and he became like a corpse, so that many said, "He's dead!"

But Jesus took him by the hand and raised him up, and he got up; so Jesus gave him back to his father. Now they were all astonished at the majesty of God.

Then having entered into a house, his disciples asked Jesus privately, "Why couldn't we expel it?"

So he said to them, "Because of your little faith, for truly I say to you, if you have faith as a grain of mustard, you shall say to this mountain, 'Move from here to there,' and it shall move; and nothing shall be impossible to you." And he said to them, "This kind can come out by nothing, except by prayer."

Going forth from there, they passed through Galilee, and he did not desire that anyone should know it. For he was teaching his disciples, and he said to them, "Let these words sink into your ears, for the Son of Man is being delivered into the hands of men and they shall kill him; and when he is killed, on the third day he shall rise up."

But they did not understand this saying, and it was concealed from them, that they should not apprehend it. And they were grieved exceedingly, and they were afraid to ask him about this saying.

Now when they had come to Capernaum, those who collected the two-drachma temple tax came to Peter and said, "Your teacher pays the two-drachma, doesn't he?"

He said, "Yes."

And when he came into the house, Jesus anticipated him, saying, "What do you think, Simon? The kings of the earth, from whom do they receive levy or tax? From their sons or from strangers?"

So when he said, "From strangers," Jesus declared to him, "Therefore the sons are exempt. But lest we give offense to them, going to the sea, cast a hook and take up the first fish coming up; and opening its mouth, you will find a four-drachma coin. Taking that, give to them for me and you."

In that hour a dispute came up among them as to which of them was the greatest. And when Jesus was in the house he asked them, "What were you reasoning about on the way?" But they were silent.

So sitting down, he called the Twelve, and knowing the reasoning of their hearts, said to them, "If anyone desires to be first, he shall be last of all and servant of all."

And taking a little child, he set him in the midst of them; and embracing him, he said to them, "Truly I say to you, unless you turn and become as little children, you shall not enter into the Kingdom of Heaven. And therefore whoever shall humble himself as this little child, he is the greatest in the Kingdom of Heaven.

"And whoever shall receive one such little child in my name receives me, and whoever receives me receives not me but the one who sent me. For the one who is least among all of you, this one is great."

John declared to him, "Teacher, we saw someone expelling demons in your name, and we forbade him because he wasn't following us."

But Jesus said, "Forbid him not, for there is no one who shall do a mighty work in my name and be able quickly to speak evil of me. For whoever is not against us is for us. For whoever shall give you a cup of water to drink because in name you are Christ's, truly I say to you, he shall certainly not lose his reward.

"And whoever shall cause one of these little ones who believe in me to stumble, it would be better for him if a huge millstone were hung around his neck and he were sunk in the depths of the sea. Woe to the world for stumbling blocks! For it must be that the stumbling blocks come, yet woe to that person through whom the stumbling block comes!

"So if your hand causes you to stumble, cut it off and cast it from you; it is good for you to enter into life maimed, rather than having your two hands to go into hell, into the unquenchable fire. And if your foot causes you to stumble, cut it off and cast it from you; it is good for you to enter into life lame, rather than having your two feet to be cast into hell. And if your eye causes you to stumble, tear it out and cast it out from you; it is good for you to enter into the Kingdom of God with one eye, rather than having two eyes to be cast into hell, where their worm does not die, and the fire is not quenched. For everyone shall be salted with fire. Salt is good, but if the salt becomes unsalty, with what shall you season it? Have salt in yourselves, and be at peace with one another.

"Watch that you not despise one of these little ones, for I say to you that in heaven their angels always look upon the face of my Father who is in heaven. What do you think? If any man has a hundred sheep, and one of them has gone astray, does he not leave the ninety-nine on the hills and go and seek that which has gone astray? And if he should find it, truly I say to you, he rejoices over it more than over the ninety-nine which have not gone astray. Thus it is not the will of your Father who is in heaven that one of these little ones should perish.

"Now if your brother sins against you, go show him his fault between you and him alone; if he hears you, you have gained your brother. But if he does not hear, take with you one or two more, that at the mouth of two witnesses or three every statement may stand. Now if he refuses to hear them, tell it to the church; but if he refuses to hear the church also, let him be to you as a Gentile or a tax collector.

"Truly I say to you, whatever things you bind on earth shall be bound in heaven, and whatever things you release on earth shall be released in heaven. Again I say to you, that if two of you shall agree on earth concerning anything, whatever they may request, it shall be done for them by my Father who is in heaven. For where two or three are gathered together in my name, there am I in the midst of them."

Then coming to him Peter said, "Lord, how many times will my brother sin against me and I forgive him? Until seven times?"

Jesus said to him, "I do not say to you till seven times, but till seventy-seven times. For this reason the Kingdom of Heaven has become like a man, a king, who wished to settle accounts with his slaves. Now when he had begun to settle, one was brought to him who owed him ten thousand silver talents. But he not having means to repay, his lord ordered him to be sold, and his wife and children and all that he had, and payment to be made. So falling down, the slave bowed to him, saying, 'Lord, have patience with me and I will repay you all!' Now being moved with compassion, the lord of that slave dismissed him and forgave him the loan.

"But going out, that slave found one of his fellow slaves who owed him one hundred denarii, and seizing him, he choked him, saying, 'Repay what you owe!' So falling down, his fellow slave begged him, saying, 'Have patience with me and I will repay you!' But he would not, yet going away, cast him into prison, till he should repay that which was owed.

"Therefore when his fellow slaves saw what happened, they were grieved exceedingly; and having come, explained in detail to their lord all that happened. Then having summoned him in, his lord said to him, 'You evil slave! I forgave you all that debt since you begged me. Was it not necessary for you also to have mercy on your fellow slave, just as I had mercy on you?' And becoming enraged, his lord delivered him to the tormentors, till he should repay all that was owed to him. So shall my heavenly Father also do unto you if you each do not forgive your brother from your heart."

Now it came to pass, when the days approaching his ascension were fulfilled, he resolutely set his face to go to Jerusalem, and sent messengers before his face. And having gone, they entered into a village of the Samaritans so as to prepare for him. And they did not receive him, because his face was set toward Jerusalem. So seeing it, his disciples James and John said, "Lord, do you want us to call fire down from heaven and consume them?"

But turning he rebuked them. And they went to another village.

And as they were going along the way, a scribe said to him, "Teacher, I will follow you wherever you go."

And Jesus said to him, "The foxes have holes, and the birds of the sky have nests, but the Son of Man has no place to lay his head."

Now he said to another of his disciples, "Follow me!"

But he said, "Lord, permit me first to go and bury my father."

So Jesus said to him, "Leave the dead to bury their own dead, but you go and herald the Kingdom of God."

Now another also said, "I will follow you, Lord, but first permit me to say farewell to those at my home."

But Jesus said to him, "No one who puts his hand to the plow and looks back is fit for the Kingdom of God."

Now after these things, the Lord appointed seventy-two others, and sent them two by two before his face into every town and place where he himself was about to come. So he said to them, "The harvest is indeed plentiful, but the laborers are few. Therefore pray to the Lord of the harvest, that he send forth laborers into his harvest. Go your ways; behold, I send you as lambs in the midst of wolves. Carry no money pouch nor bag nor sandals, and greet no one on the way. And into whatever house you enter, first say, 'Peace to this house.' And if a son of peace is there, your peace shall rest upon him; but if not, it shall come back to you. Now stay in that same house, eating and drinking what is provided by them, for the laborer is worthy of his wages. Do not move from house to house. And into whatever town you enter and they receive you, eat the things that are set before you, and heal the sick who are in it, and say to them, 'The Kingdom of God has drawn near to you.' But into whatever town you enter and they do not receive you, going out into its streets, say, 'Even the dust from your town that clings to our feet, we wipe off against you. Yet know this, that the Kingdom of God has drawn near to you.' I say to you, it shall be more tolerable in that day for Sodom than for that town.

"Woe to you, Chorazin! Woe to you, Bethsaida! For if in Tyre and Sidon the mighty works had been done that were done in you, they would have repented long ago, sitting in sackcloth and ashes. Even so for Tyre and Sidon it shall be more tolerable in the judgment than for you. And you, Capernaum, shall you be exalted to heaven? You shall be brought down to Hades.

"The one hearing you hears me, and the one rejecting you rejects me; but the one rejecting me rejects him who sent me."

Now the seventy-two returned with joy, saying, "Lord, even the demons are subject to us in your name!"

But he said to them, "I observed Satan like lightning from heaven falling. Behold, I have given you authority to tread upon serpents and scorpions and over all the power of the enemy, and nothing shall in any way harm you. Yet in this do not rejoice, that the spirits are subject to you, but rejoice that your names are written in heaven."

In that same hour he was jubilant in the Holy Spirit and said, "I thank you, Father, Lord of heaven and earth, that you have hidden these things from the wise and knowledgeable, and revealed them to infants. Yes, Father, for so it was well-pleasing in your sight. All things have been delivered to me by my Father; and no one knows who the Son is, except the Father, and who the Father is, except the Son, and he to whomever the Son wishes to reveal him."

And turning to the disciples he said privately, "Blessed are the eyes that are looking upon the things which you look upon, for I say to you that many prophets and kings desired to see the things which you look upon and did not see them, and to hear the things which you hear and did not hear them."

And behold, a certain expert on the Law of Moses stood up, testing him, saying, "Teacher, what shall I do to inherit eternal life?"

So he said to him, "What is written in the Law? How do you read it?"

And answering he said, "You shall love the Lord your God with all your heart and with all your soul and with all your strength and with all your mind, and your neighbor as yourself.

So he said to him, "You have answered rightly. Do this, and you shall live."

But desiring to justify himself, he said to Jesus, "Who is my neighbor?"

So replying Jesus said, "A certain man was going down from Jerusalem to Jericho, and he fell among bandits who, both stripping him and beating him, went away, leaving him half dead. Now by chance a certain priest was going down that way, and seeing him, he passed by on the other side. Now in the same way a Levite, also being at the place, coming and seeing him, passed by on the other side. But a certain Samaritan traveling came by him, and seeing him, was moved with compassion; and coming to him, bound up his wounds, pouring on them oil and wine. Now setting him on his own animal, he brought him to an inn and took care of him. And on the next day, taking out two denarii, he gave them to the innkeeper and said to him, 'Take care of him, and whatever more you spend, on my return I will repay you.' Which of these three do you think proved to be a neighbor to him who fell among the bandits?"

And he said, "The one who showed mercy toward him."

So Jesus said to him, "Go and do likewise."

Now as they went on their way, he entered into a certain village, and a certain woman named Martha received him into her house. And she had a sister called Mary, who also sat at Jesus' feet and heard his word. But Martha was distracted with much serving, so coming up to him she said, "Lord, don't you care that my sister left me to serve alone? Therefore tell to her that she should help me."

But answering Jesus said to her, "Martha, Martha, you are anxious and troubled about many things, but one thing is necessary. For Mary has chosen the good part, which shall not be taken away from her."

And it came to pass, he was in a certain place praying. When he ceased, one of his disciples said to him, "Lord, teach us to pray, just as John also taught his disciples."

So he said to them, "When you pray, say,

"Father, hallowed be your name,
your Kingdom come.
Give us each day our ceaseless bread;
and forgive us our sins,
for we ourselves also forgive everyone indebted to us;
and bring us not into temptation."

And he said to them, "Which of you shall have a friend and shall go to him at midnight and say to him, 'Friend, lend me three loaves, since a friend of mine has come to me from a journey and I have nothing to set before him,' and he answering from within shall say, 'Don't bother me! The door is already locked, and my children are with me in bed. I can't get up and give it to you'? I say to you, though he shall not get up and give it to him because he is his friend, yet because of his shamelessness, he shall arise and give him as many as he needs.

"And I say to you, request, and it shall be given to you; seek, and you shall find; knock, and it shall be opened to you. For everyone requesting receives, and the one seeking finds, and to the one knocking it shall be opened.

"Now what father among you, if his son requests a fish, instead of a fish shall give him a serpent? Or if he requests an egg, shall give him a scorpion? If you then, being evil, know how to give good gifts to your children, how much more shall the Father from heaven give the Holy Spirit to those requesting of him?"

Jesus was expelling a demon, and it was mute; now it came to pass, when the demon had gone out, the mute man spoke, and the crowds marveled. But some of them said, "By Beelzebul, the prince of the demons, he expels demons." So others, testing him, were seeking from him a sign from heaven.

But he, knowing their thoughts, said to them, "Every kingdom divided against itself is brought to desolation, and a house divided against itself falls. So if Satan also is divided against himself, how shall his kingdom stand? For you say that I expel demons by Beelzebul; but if

I expel demons by Beelzebul, by whom do your sons expel them? For this reason they shall be your judges. But if I by the finger of God expel demons, then the Kingdom of God has come upon you.

"When the strong man, fully armed, guards his own estate, his goods are in peace. But when someone stronger than he comes upon him and overcomes him, he takes from him his whole armor in which he trusted and divides his plunder. The one not with me is against me, and the one not gathering with me scatters.

"The unclean spirit, when he has gone out of the man, passes through arid places, seeking rest; and finding none, it says, 'I will turn back to my house from which I came out.' And having come, it finds it swept and put in order. Then it goes and takes seven other spirits more evil than itself; and entering in, they dwell there. And the last state of that man becomes worse than the first."

Now it came to pass, as he said these things, a certain woman out of the crowd, lifting up her voice, said to him, "Blessed is the womb that bore you and the breasts which nursed you!"

But he said, "Rather, blessed are those hearing the word of God and keeping it."

Now when the crowds were gathering together to him, he began to say, "This generation is an evil generation; it seeks after a sign, and a sign shall not be given to it but the sign of Jonah. For just as Jonah became a sign to the Ninevites, so shall the Son of Man also be to this generation. The Queen of the South shall rise up in the judgment with the men of this generation and shall condemn them; for she came from the ends of the earth to hear the wisdom of Solomon, and behold, something greater than Solomon is here. The men of Nineveh shall stand up in the judgment with this generation and shall condemn it; for they repented at the preaching of Jonah, and behold, something greater than Jonah is here.

"No one, having lit a lamp, places it in a cellar nor under the basket, but upon the lampstand, that those who enter in may see the light. The lamp of the body is your eye. When your eye is sincere, your whole body is also full of light; but when it is evil, your body is also full of darkness. Take care then, lest the light that is in you be darkness. If therefore your whole body is full of light, with no part having darkness, it shall be wholly full of light, as when the lamp with its bright shining gives you light."

Now as he was speaking, a Pharisee asked him to dine with him; so entering in, he reclined at the table. But the Pharisee, seeing it, marveled that he had not first baptized himself before the brunch.

So the Lord said to him, "Now you Pharisees cleanse the outside of the cup and of the platter, but the inside of you is full of greed and wickedness. Fools, did not the one who made the outside make the inside also? Even so give as alms those things which are within, and behold, all things are clean to you.

"But woe to you Pharisees! For you tithe mint and rue and every herb, and you bypass justice and God's love. But these you ought to have done, and not to neglect the others. Woe to you Pharisees! For you love the foremost seats in the synagogues, and the greetings in the marketplaces. Woe to you! For you are like unmarked graves, and the men walking over them do not know it."

Now responding, one of the experts on the Law of Moses said to him, "Teacher, in saying this you also insult us!"

But he said, "Woe to you lawyers also! For you load men with oppressive burdens, and you yourselves do not touch those burdens with one of your fingers. Woe to you! For you build the tombs of the prophets, but your fathers killed them. So you are witnesses and approve of the works of your fathers. For they killed them, but you build their tombs. For this reason also the wisdom of God said, 'I will send to them prophets and apostles; and some of them they shall kill and persecute,' that the blood of all the prophets, which was poured out since the foundation of the world, may be required of this generation, from the blood of Abel to the blood of Zachariah, who perished between the altar and the sanctuary. Yes, I say to you, it shall be required of this generation. Woe to you lawyers! For you took away the key of knowledge. You did not enter in yourselves, and those who were entering in, you hindered."

Having gone forth from there, the scribes and the Pharisees began to fiercely oppose him, and to interrogate him about many things, lying in wait for him, to trap him in something out of his mouth.

In these circumstances, when the many thousands of the crowd had gathered together so that they stepped on one another, he began to say to his disciples first of all, "Yourselves beware of the yeast of the Pharisees, which is hypocrisy. But there is nothing concealed that shall not be revealed, and hidden that shall not be known, because whatever you have said in the darkness shall be heard in the light, and what you have spoken in the ear in the inner rooms shall be proclaimed on the housetops.

"So I say to you, my friends, be not afraid of those who kill the body and after that have no more that they can do. But I will show you whom you should fear: Fear him who, after he has killed, has power to cast into hell. Yes, I say to you, fear him. Are not five sparrows sold for two cents? And not one of them is forgotten before God. But the very hairs of your head are all counted. Fear not, you are of more value than many sparrows.

"So I say to you, everyone who shall profess in me before men, the Son of Man shall also profess in him before the angels of God; but the one who denies me in the presence of men shall be denied in the presence of the angels of God. And everyone who shall speak a word against the Son of Man, it shall be forgiven him; but the one who blasphemes against the Holy Spirit shall not be forgiven. So when they bring you before the synagogues and the rulers and the authorities, be not anxious how or what you shall reply in defense or what you shall say; for the Holy Spirit shall teach you in that same hour what you must say."

Now one of the crowd said to him, "Teacher, tell my brother to divide the inheritance with me."

But he said to him, "Man, who appointed me a judge or an arbitrator over you?" So he said to them, "Watch out, and keep yourselves from all covetousness, for one's life does not consist of the abundance of the things which he possesses."

Now he spoke a parable to them, saying, "The ground of a certain rich man brought forth plentifully, and he reasoned within himself, saying, 'What will I do, because I have no where to store my crops?' And he said, 'This is what I will do: I will tear down my barns and build bigger ones, and there I will store all my grain and my goods. And I will tell my soul, "Soul, you have many goods laid up for many years, take your rest; eat, drink, be merry." '

"But God said to him, 'Fool, this night your soul is demanded of you! So the things which you have prepared, whose shall they be?' Thus is the one laying up treasure for himself and is not rich toward God."

So he said to his disciples, "For this reason I say to you, be not anxious for your life, what you shall eat, nor yet for your body, what you shall wear. For life is more than food, and the body more than clothing. Perceive the ravens, that they do not sow nor reap, which have no storehouse or barn, and God feeds them. How much more valuable are you than birds?

"Now which of you by being anxious can add a foot to his height? If then not even the least you are able to do, why are you anxious about the rest? Perceive the lilies, how they grow; they do not toil nor spin. But I say to you, even Solomon in all his glory was not clothed like one of these. So if God dresses in this way the grass in the field, which is here today and tomorrow is cast into the oven, how much more shall he clothe you, you of little faith?

"And seek not what you shall eat or what you shall drink, and do not be worried. For all these things the Gentile world seeks after, but your Father knows that you need these things. Even so seek his kingdom, and these things shall be added to you. Fear not, little flock, for it is your Father's good pleasure to give you the kingdom. Sell what you possess and give alms. Make for yourselves money pouches which do not grow old, an unfailing treasure in heaven, where no thief draws near nor moth destroys. For where your treasure is, there shall your heart be also.

"Let your waists be girded and the lamps burning, and you be as men waiting for their lord, whenever he shall return from the wedding feast, that coming and knocking, they may straightaway open to him. Blessed are those slaves whom the lord, having come, shall find being vigilant. Truly I say to you, that he shall gird himself and make them recline at the table, and having come, shall serve them. And if in the second or in the third watch he comes and finds them so, blessed are those slaves. But know this, that if the master of the house had known in what hour the thief was coming, he would not have allowed his house to be broken into. You also be ready, for in an hour that you do not think, the Son of Man comes."

Now Peter said to him, "Lord, do you speak this parable to us, or to all as well?"

And the Lord said, "Who then is the faithful and wise steward whom his lord shall set over his servants, to give them their portion of food in due season? Blessed is that slave whom his lord, having come, shall find doing so. Surely I say to you that he shall set him over all that he possesses. But if that slave should say in his heart, 'My lord delays to come,' and should begin to strike the menservants and the maidservants, and to eat and drink and be drunk, then the lord of that slave shall arrive in a day when he does not expect and in an hour that he does not know, and shall cut him in two and place his portion with the unbelievers. So that slave, knowing his lord's will and not having prepared nor having done according to his will, shall be beaten with many lashes. Now the one not knowing, but having done things worthy of lashes, shall be beaten with few lashes. So to whomever has been given much, much shall be required of him; and to whom they have committed much, the more they shall request of him.

"I came to cast fire upon the earth, and what do I desire if it is already kindled? Now I have a baptism to be baptized with, and how pressed I am till it is accomplished! Do you think that I have come to give peace upon the earth? No, I say to you, but rather division. For there shall be from now on five in one house divided, three against two and two against three. They shall be divided father against son and son against father; mother against daughter and daughter against mother; mother-in-law against her daughter-in-law and daughter-in-law against her mother-in-law."

Now he also said to the crowds, "When you see a cloud rising from the west, straightaway you say, 'A shower is coming,' and so it happens. And when a south wind is blowing, you say, 'There will be scorching heat,' and it happens. Hypocrites! You know how to interpret the appearance of the earth and the sky, but how is it that you do not know how to interpret this time? So why even for yourselves do you not judge what is right? For as you are going with your adversary before the magistrate, on the way endeavor to settle with him, lest perhaps he drag you to the judge, and the judge deliver you to the bailiff, and the bailiff cast you into prison. I say to you, you shall not get out of there till you have paid the very last cent."

Now there were some present at that time who informed him about the Galileans whose blood Pilate had mixed with their sacrifices. And responding he said to them, "Do you think that these Galileans were sinners beyond all the Galileans because they suffered such things? No, I say to you, but unless you repent, you shall all likewise perish. Or those eighteen on whom the tower in Siloam fell and killed them, do you think that they were offenders beyond all the men dwelling in Jerusalem? No, I say to you, but unless you repent, you shall all likewise perish."

So he spoke this parable: "A certain man had a fig tree planted in his vineyard, and he came seeking fruit on it, and found none. So he said to the vinedresser, 'Behold, these three years I have come seeking for fruit on this fig tree and found none. Cut it down. Why should it just use up the soil?' But answering he said to him, 'Lord, leave it alone this year also, until I dig around it and fertilize it. And if it bears fruit afterward... But if not, you can cut it down.' "

Now he was teaching in one of the synagogues on the Sabbath day. And behold, there was a woman who had a spirit of infirmity eighteen years, and she was bent over and could not straighten up entirely. So seeing her, Jesus called to her and said to her, "Woman, you are freed from your infirmity." And he laid his hands upon her, and instantly she stood up straight and glorified God.

Now responding the ruler of the synagogue, indignant because Jesus had healed on the Sabbath, said to the crowd, "There are six days in which men should work. Therefore come on those and be healed and not on the day of the Sabbath!"

But the Lord responded to him and said, "Hypocrites! Does not each one of you on the Sabbath release his ox or donkey from the stall and lead it away to drink? So this one, being a daughter of Abraham whom Satan had bound, behold, eighteen years, should she not be released from this bondage on the Sabbath day?"

And as he said these things, all opposed to him were put to shame and all the crowd rejoiced for all the glorious things that were done by him.

Then he said, "What is the Kingdom of God like, and what shall it become like? It is like a grain of mustard, which having taken, a man cast into his garden; and it grew and became a tree, and the birds of the sky nested in its branches."

And again he said, "What shall the kingdom of God become like? It is like yeast, which having taken, a woman hid in three measures of dough, till it was all leavened."

And he passed through towns and villages, teaching and making his journey toward Jerusalem. Now one said to him, "Lord, are there few who are saved?"

So he said to them, "Strive to enter in by the narrow door, for many, I say to you, shall seek to enter in and will not be able. Once the master of the house has arisen and has shut the door, and you begin to stand outside and to knock at the door, saying, 'Lord, Lord, open to us!' and answering he shall say to you, 'I don't know you or where you are from,' then you shall begin to say, 'We ate and drank in your presence, and you taught in our streets!' And he shall say, 'I tell you, I don't know you or where you are from. Leave from me all you workers of unrighteousness!' There shall be weeping and gnashing of teeth when you watch Abraham and Isaac and Jacob and all the prophets in the Kingdom of God, and yourselves being expelled outside. And they shall arrive from the east and west and north and south, and shall recline at the table in the Kingdom of God. And behold, some are last who shall be first, and some are first who shall be last."

In that same hour came certain Pharisees, saying to him, "Get out and go from here because Herod wants to kill you."

And he said to them, "Go and tell that fox, 'Behold, I expel demons and perform cures today and tomorrow, and the third day I accomplish my mission. Even so I must go on my way today and tomorrow and the next day, for it is not possible for a prophet to perish outside of Jerusalem.'

"Jerusalem, Jerusalem, who kills the prophets and stones those who are sent to her, how often I desired to gather your children together in the way a hen gathers her own brood under her wings, and you were not willing. Behold, your house is left to you desolate. So I say to you, you shall not see me till you say, 'Blessed is the one who comes in the name of the Lord.' "

It came to pass, when he went into the house of one of the rulers of the Pharisees on a Sabbath to eat bread, that they were monitoring him. And behold, a certain man who had dropsy was before him. And responding Jesus spoke to the experts on the Law of Moses and Pharisees, saying, "Is it lawful to heal on the Sabbath or not?"

But they were silent.

And taking hold of him, he cured him and dismissed him. And to them he said, "Which of you shall have a son or an ox fall into a well and will not immediately pull him out on a Sabbath day?"

And they could not give a response to these things.

Now he spoke a parable to those who were invited, noticing how they were choosing the foremost places, saying to them, "When you are invited by anyone to a wedding feast, do not sit in the foremost place, lest perhaps one more honorable than you might be invited by him, and having come, the one who invited you and him should tell you, 'Give this one your place.' And then you shall begin with shame to take the last place. But when you are invited, go and sit in the last place, so that when the one who invited you comes, he should tell you, 'Friend, move up higher.' Then you shall have glory in the presence of all who recline at the table with you. For everyone who exalts himself shall be humbled, and the one who humbles himself shall be exalted."

So he also said to the one who had invited him, "When you make brunch or dinner, do not call your friends nor your brothers nor your relatives nor rich neighbors, lest perhaps they might also invite you in return and a repayment be made to you. But when you make a feast, summon the poor, the maimed, the lame, the blind; and blessed you shall be, because they have nothing to repay you. For you shall be repaid in the resurrection of the righteous."

Now having heard these things, one of those who reclined at the table with him said to him, "Blessed is he who will eat bread in the Kingdom of God!"

But he said to him, "A certain man made a great dinner, and he invited many, and he sent his slave at the supper hour to say to those who were invited, 'Come, for now it's ready!' And they all alike began to excuse themselves. The first said to him, 'I have bought a field, and I must go and see it. I ask you, have me excused.' And another said, 'I have bought five yoke of oxen, and I am going to try them out. I ask you, have me excused.' And another said, 'I have married a wife, and because of this I can't come.'

"And having come, the slave reported to his lord these things. Then becoming enraged, the master of the house said to his slave, 'Go out quickly into the streets and alleys of the city and bring in the poor and maimed and blind and lame.'

"And the slave said, 'Lord, it is done as you commanded, and there is still room.' And the lord said to the slave, 'Go out into the highways and hedges and compel them to come in, that my house may be filled. For I say to you that none of those men who were invited will taste of my dinner.' "

Now going with him were great crowds; and having turned, he said to them, "If anyone comes to me, and does not hate his own father and mother and wife and children and brothers and sisters, yes, and also his own life, he cannot be my disciple. Whoever does not bear his own cross and come after me cannot be my disciple. For which of you, desiring to build a tower, does not first sit down and count the cost, whether he has enough to complete it? Lest perhaps, having laid a foundation, and is not able to finish, all who observe begin to mock him, saying, 'This man began to build and wasn't able to finish!' Or what king, going to engage with another king in war, shall not sit down first and take counsel whether he is able with ten thousand to meet him who comes against him with twenty thousand? And if not, while the other is still far way, sending a delegation, he asks for terms of peace. So therefore whoever of you who does not bid farewell to all that he possesses, he cannot be my disciple. Therefore salt is good, but if even the salt becomes tasteless, with what shall it be seasoned? It is fit neither for the soil nor for the dung heap; it is cast out. He who has ears to hear, let him hear!"

Now drawing near to him were all the tax collectors and sinners to hear him. And both the Pharisees and the scribes murmured, saying, "This one welcomes sinners and eats with them."

So he spoke to them this parable: "Which of you men, having one hundred sheep, and losing one of them, does not leave the ninety-nine in the wilderness and go after the one that was lost till he finds it? And finding it, he lays it upon his shoulders, rejoicing. And coming home, he calls together his friends and his neighbors, saying to them, 'Rejoice with me, for I have found my sheep that was lost!' I say to you, thus there shall be more joy in heaven over one sinner repenting than over ninety-nine righteous people who have no need of repentance.

"Or what woman, having ten drachma coins, if she loses one drachma, does not light a lamp and sweep the house and seek diligently till she finds it? And finding it, she calls together her friends and neighbors, saying, 'Rejoice with me, for I have found the drachma which I had lost!' Thus I say to you, there is joy before the angels of God over one sinner repenting."

And he said, "A certain man had two sons, and the younger of them said to his father, 'Father, give me my share of the property.' So he divided between them his estate. And not many days after, the younger son gathered all of this together and traveled into a far country, and there he squandered his property living wastefully.

"But having spent all, there arose a severe famine in that country, and he began to be in need. And having gone, he joined himself to one of the citizens of that country, and he sent him into his fields to feed pigs. And he was longing to fill his belly with the pods that the pigs were eating, and no one gave to him. But coming to his senses, he declared, 'How many hired servants of my father's have more than enough bread, but I'm dying with hunger! I will get up and go to my father, and will tell him, "Father, I have sinned against heaven and before you; I am no longer worthy to be called your son. Make me as one of your hired hands." '

"And he got up and came to his father. But while he was still far off, his father saw him and was moved with compassion, and running, fell upon his neck and kissed him. But the son said to him, 'Father, I have sinned against heaven and before you; I am no longer worthy to be called your son.'

"But the father said to his slaves, 'Quickly bring out the best robe and put it on him, and give a ring for his hand and sandals for his feet. And bringing the fattened calf, kill it; and eating, let us celebrate. For this son of mine was dead and came to life again; he was lost and is found.' And they began to celebrate.

"Now his elder son was in the field; and coming, as he drew near to the house, he heard music and dancing. And summoning to him one of the servants, he inquired what these things might be. So he said to him, 'Your brother has arrived, and your father has killed the fattened calf because he has received him back safe and sound.' But he was angry, and would not go in. So his father came out and begged him. But responding he said to his father, 'Behold, these many years I have slaved for you and I never disobeyed a commandment of yours and you never gave me a goat, that I might celebrate with my friends. But when this son of yours came, the one who devoured your estate with harlots, you killed the fattened calf for him.'

"So he said to him, 'Child, you are always with me, and all that is mine is yours. But it is necessary to celebrate and rejoice, for this your brother was dead and came to life again; he was lost and is found.' "

Now he also said to his disciples, "There was a certain rich man who had a steward, and claims were brought to him that he was wasting his goods. And having called him, he said to him, 'What is this that I hear about you? Give the account of your stewardship, for you can no longer steward.'

"So the steward said within himself, 'What will I do, seeing that my lord is taking away the stewardship from me? I don't have strength to dig; I'm ashamed to beg. I know what I will do, so that when I am removed from the stewardship they might take me into their houses.' And having summoned to him each one of his lord's debtors, he said to the first, 'How much do you owe to my lord?' So he said, 'A hundred measures of oil.' But he said to him, 'Take your bill, and sit down quickly and write fifty.' Then he said to another, 'How much do you owe?' So he said, 'A hundred measures of wheat.' He said to him, 'Take your bill and write eighty.'

"And the Lord commended the unrighteous steward because he had acted shrewdly. For the sons of this age are shrewder than the sons of the light in dealing with their own generation. And I say to you, make for yourselves friends by means of unrighteous wealth, so that when it fails, they may receive you into the eternal tents. The one who is faithful in a very little is also faithful in much, and the one who is unrighteous in a very little is also unrighteous in much. If therefore you have not been faithful in the unrighteous wealth, who will commit to your trust the true? And if you have not been faithful in that which is another's, who will give you that which is your own? No servant can serve two masters; for either he shall hate the one and love the other, or else he shall hold to one and despise the other. You cannot serve God and wealth."

Now the Pharisees, being lovers of money, were listening to all these things and were sneering at him. And he said to them, "You are those who justify yourselves before men, but God knows your hearts. For that which is exalted among men is an abomination before God. The Law and the Prophets were till John; from that time the Good News of the Kingdom of God is announced, and everyone is being pressed into it. But it is easier for heaven and earth to pass away than for one dot of the Law to fall out. Everyone who divorces his wife and marries another commits adultery; and he who marries one who is divorced from a husband commits adultery.

"Now there was a certain rich man, and he was clothed in purple and the finest linen, living merrily every day in luxury. But a certain poor man named Lazarus was laid at his gate, being covered in sores and longing to be fed with the scraps that fell from the rich man's table. Yes, even the dogs came and licked his sores. Now it came to pass that the poor man died and was carried away by the angels to the heart of Abraham. So also the rich man died and was buried. And in Hades, lifting up his eyes, being in torment, he watched Abraham from afar and Lazarus at his heart. And calling out he said, 'Father Abraham, have mercy on me and send Lazarus, that he may dip the tip of his finger in water and cool my tongue, for I am in anguish in this flame!'

"But Abraham said, 'Child, remember that you received your good things in your lifetime, and Lazarus in the same way wretched things. So now here he is comforted, and you are in anguish. And besides all this, between us and you a great chasm is fixed, that those desiring to pass from here to you are not able, nor from there to us can they pass.'

"So he said, 'I urge you then, father, that you would send him to my father's house, for I have five brothers, that he may attest to them so that they also won't come to this place of torment.' But Abraham said, 'They have Moses and the Prophets; let them listen to them.'

"So he said, 'No, father Abraham, but if one goes to them from the dead, they will repent.' But he said to him, 'If they don't listen to Moses and the Prophets, neither will they be persuaded if one rises from the dead.' "

Now Jesus said to his disciples, "It is impossible for the stumbling blocks not to come, even so woe to him through whom they come! It were well for him if a millstone were hung around his neck and he were thrown into the sea, rather than that he should cause one of these little ones to stumble. Beware of yourselves. If your brother sins against you, rebuke him, and if he repents, forgive him. And if seven times in the day he sins against you, and seven times returns to you, saying, 'I repent,' you shall forgive him."

And the apostles said to the Lord, "Increase our faith."

So the Lord said, "If you had faith like a grain of mustard, you would say to this sycamore tree, 'Be uprooted and be planted in the sea,' and it would obey you. But which of you, having a slave plowing or tending sheep, the one having come in from the field, shall say to him, 'Come immediately and recline at the table,' and shall not rather say to him, 'Prepare my supper and gird yourself to serve me while I eat and drink, and afterward you shall eat and drink'? Does he show favor to the slave because he did the things that were instructed? Thus you also, when you have done all the things that are instructed to you, say, 'We are unworthy slaves; we have done what was our duty.' "

It came to pass, on the way to Jerusalem, he was passing between Samaria and Galilee. And on entering into a certain village, there met him ten men who were lepers, who stood at a distance. And they lifted up their voices, saying, "Jesus, Master, have mercy on us!"

And seeing them, he said to them, "Go and show yourselves to the priests." And it came to pass, as they went, they were cleansed. So one of them, seeing that he was cured, returned with a loud voice glorifying God. And he fell on his face at his feet, giving thanks to him; and he was a Samaritan. But responding Jesus said, "Were not the ten cleansed? So where are the nine? Were there none found who returned to give glory to God, except this foreigner?" And he said to him, "Get up and go forth. Your faith has saved you."

Now having been asked by the Pharisees when the Kingdom of God is coming, he answered them and said, "The Kingdom of God does not come amid observation; nor shall they say, 'Behold, here!' or, 'There!' For behold, the Kingdom of God is among you."

So he said to the disciples, "The days shall come when you shall long to see one of the days of the Son of Man, and you shall not watch it. And they shall say to you, 'Behold, here! Behold, there!' Do not go forth or pursue. For as the lightning flashing from one end of the sky to the other shines, so shall the Son of Man be in his day. But first he must suffer many things and be rejected by this generation.

"And as it came to pass in the days of Noah, thus it shall also be in the days of the Son of Man: they ate, they drank, they married, they were given in marriage, till the day that Noah entered into the ark and the flood came and destroyed all. Likewise, just as it came to pass in the days of Lot: they ate, they drank, they bought, they sold, they planted, they built; but in the day that Lot went out from Sodom it rained fire and sulfur from heaven and destroyed all. So shall it be in the day that the Son of Man is revealed. In that day, he who shall be on the housetop and his goods in the house, let him not go down to take them away; and likewise the one in the field, let him not turn back. Remember Lot's wife. Whoever seeks to gain his life shall lose it, but whoever loses it shall preserve it. I say to you, in that night there shall be two in one bed;

one shall be taken and the other shall be left. There shall be two women grinding grain at the same place; one shall be taken and the other shall be left."

And responding they said to him, "Where, Lord?"

So he said to them, "Where the body is, there also the vultures shall be gathered together."

And he spoke a parable to them about how it is necessary for them always to pray and not to lose heart, saying, "There was a certain judge in a certain city who did not fear God and did not respect man. But there was a widow in that city, and she was coming to him, saying, 'Avenge me against my adversary!' And he would not for a while, but afterward he said within himself, 'Even if I do not fear God or respect man, yet because this widow pesters me I will avenge her, or by her constant coming she will give me a blackeye.' "

So the Lord said, "Hear what the unrighteous judge says. So shall not God bring vengeance for his chosen ones, crying out to him day and night, and yet he waits patiently for them? I say to you that he shall bring vengeance to them quickly. Even so, when the Son of Man comes, will he find faith on the earth?"

Now he also spoke this parable to some who trusted in themselves, that they were righteous, and who disdained the rest: "Two men went up into the temple to pray, the one a Pharisee and the other a tax collector. The Pharisee, standing by himself, was praying thus, 'God, I thank you that I am not like the rest of men: extortionists, unrighteous, adulterers, or even like this tax collector. I fast twice a week; I give tithes of all things, whatever I get.' But the tax collector, standing far away, was not desiring to even lift up his eyes to heaven, but was beating his chest, saying, 'God, make atonement for me, the sinner!' I say to you, this one went down to his house justified rather than the other. For everyone who exalts himself shall be humbled, but the one who humbles himself shall be exalted."

It came to pass, when Jesus had finished these words, he came into the region of Judea and beyond the Jordan. And again great crowds came together to him and followed him, and he healed them there. And as was his practice, he again was teaching them.

And coming to him, the Pharisees asked him, "Is it lawful for a man to divorce his wife for any cause?"—testing him.

Now answering he said to them, "What did Moses command you?"

So they said, "Moses permitted a note of divorce to be written and to divorce her."

But Jesus said to them, "Because of your hardness of heart he wrote you this commandment, but have you not read that the one who made them from the beginning of the creation made them male and female, and said, 'For this cause shall a man leave his father and mother, and shall be joined to his wife, and the two shall become one flesh'? Therefore what God has yoked together, let no man divide."

And in the house, again his disciples asked him about the same thing. And he said to them, "Whoever shall divorce his wife, except for fornication, and marry another commits adultery against her; and if she herself shall divorce her husband and marry another, she commits adultery."

His disciples said to him, "If this is the case of the man with his wife, it's better not to marry."

So he said to them, "Not all men can accommodate these words, but those to whom it is given. For there are eunuchs who were so born from their mother's womb, and there are eunuchs who were made eunuchs by men, and there are eunuchs who made themselves eunuchs for the sake of the Kingdom of Heaven. He who is able to accommodate it, let him accommodate it."

Then little children were brought to him, that he should lay his hands on them and pray, but the disciples rebuked them.

Now seeing it, Jesus was indignant and said to them, "Allow the little children to come to me, and forbid them not, for to such as these belongs the Kingdom of God. Truly I say to you, whoever shall not receive the Kingdom of God like a little child, he shall certainly not enter into it."

And embracing them, he blessed them, laying his hands on them.

And proceeding on his way, behold, a certain ruler running up and kneeling before him asked him, "Good Teacher, what should I do that I may inherit eternal life?"

But Jesus said to him, "Why do you ask me about what is good? There is only one who is good—God. But if you desire to enter into life, keep the commandments: Do not murder, do not commit adultery, do not steal, do not bear false witness, do not defraud, honor your father and mother, and you shall love your neighbor as yourself."

So the young man declared to him, "Teacher, all these things I have kept from my youth. What do I lack yet?"

Now Jesus, looking upon him, loved him and said to him, "If you desire to be perfect, go, sell all things, whatever you have, and distribute to the poor, and you shall have treasure in heaven. And come, follow me."

But when the young man heard these words, his face fell, and he went away exceedingly sorrowful, for he was very rich.

So looking around, Jesus said to his disciples, "How difficult it is to enter into the Kingdom of God!"

Now the disciples were amazed at his words. So Jesus responding again said to them, "Children, how hard it is for those who trust in riches to enter into the Kingdom of God! It is easier for a camel to go through an eye of a needle than for a rich man to enter into the Kingdom of God."

So even more were the disciples astonished, saying among themselves, "Then who can be saved?"

Peering at them Jesus said, "With men it is impossible, but not with God. For all things are possible with God."

Then responding Peter said, "Behold, we have left everything and followed you. What then will we have?"

So Jesus said to them, "Truly I say to you, that you who have followed me, in the re-creation when the Son of Man shall sit on the his glorious throne, you also shall sit upon twelve thrones, judging the twelve tribes of Israel. And there is no one who has left house or brothers or sisters or father or mother or wife or children or land, for my sake and for the sake of the Good News, who shall not receive a hundredfold more now in this time—houses and brothers and sisters and mothers and children and land, with persecutions—and in the age to come, eternal life. But many who are first shall be last, and the last shall be first."

"For the Kingdom of Heaven is like a man, a master of a house, who went out early in the morning to hire laborers for his vineyard. So agreeing with the laborers for a denarius a day, he sent them into his vineyard. And going out about the third hour, he saw others standing in the marketplace idle, and he said to them, 'You also go into the vineyard, and whatever is right I will give you.' So they went. Again going out about the sixth and the ninth hour, he did likewise. Now going out about the eleventh hour, he found others standing, and he said to them, 'Why have you stood here idle all day?' They said to him, 'Because no one has hired us.' He said to them, 'You also go into the vineyard.'

"Now when evening came, the lord of the vineyard said to his foreman, 'Call the laborers and pay them their wages, beginning from the last to the first.' And when those came who were hired about the eleventh hour, they each received a denarius. And when the first came, they supposed that they would receive more; and they also each received a denarius. So when they received it, they murmured against the master of the house, saying, 'These last laborers have worked one hour, and you have made them equal to us who have borne the burden of the day and the scorching heat!'

"But responding he said to one of them, 'Comrade, I do you no wrong; did you not agree with me for a denarius? Take that which is yours and go your way; it is my desire to give to this last laborer just as much as to you. Is it not lawful for me to do what I desire to with what I own? Or is your eye evil because I am good?' So the last shall be first, and the first shall be last."

Now they were on the way, going up to Jerusalem. And Jesus was going ahead of them, and they were amazed, but those who followed were afraid. And again taking the Twelve, he began to tell them the things about to happen to him, saying, "Behold, we go up to Jerusalem and all the things that are written through the prophets about the Son of Man shall be accomplished. For the Son of Man shall be delivered to the chief priests and the scribes and they shall condemn him to death and shall deliver him to the Gentiles, and they shall mock him and shall spit on him and shall scourge him and shall kill him, and on the third day he shall rise up."

And they understood none of these things, and this saying was hidden from them and they did not know the things that were said.

Then the mother of James and John the sons of Zebedee came to him with her sons, bowing, and requesting a certain thing of him, saying to him, "Teacher, we desire that whatever we request of you, you would do for us."

So he said to them, "What do you desire me to do for you?"

She said to him, "Speak that these my two sons may sit, one at your right hand and one at your left hand, in your kingdom."

But answering Jesus said to them, "You do not know what you are requesting. Are you able to drink the cup that I drink? Or to be baptized with the baptism with which I am baptized?"

So they said to him, "We are able."

Now Jesus said to them, "The cup that I drink you shall indeed drink, and with the baptism that I am baptized with you shall be baptized; but to sit at my right hand and at my left hand is not mine to give, but it is for those whom it has been prepared by my Father."

And when the ten heard this, they were indignant about James and John.

So Jesus, having summoned them to him, said, "You know that the rulers of the Gentiles exercise lordship over them, and their great ones exercise authority over them. But it is not so among you; rather whoever desires to become great among you shall be your servant, and whoever among you desires to become first shall be slave of all. For the Son of Man also came not to be served but to serve, and to give his life as a ransom for many."

Now it came to pass, as he was drawing near to Jericho with his disciples and a considerable crowd, behold, the son of Timaeus, Bartimaeus, a blind beggar, was sitting by the wayside. And hearing a crowd going by, he inquired what this might be. So they informed him, "Jesus of Nazareth is passing by."

And he began to cry out and say, "Son of David, Jesus, have mercy on me!"

And many rebuked him, telling him that he should be quiet, but he cried out all the more, "Son of David, have mercy on me!"

So coming to a halt, Jesus ordered him to be brought to him, saying, "Call him."

And they called the blind man, saying to him, "Take courage! Get up, he's calling you!"

So casting away his cloak, springing up, he came to Jesus; and drawing near, Jesus asked him, "What do you desire me to do for you?"

So the blind man said to him, "Rabboni, that I may receive my sight."

Now being moved with compassion, Jesus said to him, "Receive your sight. Go, your faith has saved you." And Jesus touched his eyes, and instantly he received his sight and followed him, glorifying God. And all the people, seeing it, gave praise to God.

And he entered and was passing through Jericho. And behold, a man named Zacchaeus, and he was a chief tax collector, and he was rich. And he was seeking to see Jesus, who he was, and could not because of the crowd, since he was small in stature; and having run ahead, he climbed up into a sycamore tree to see him, for he was about to pass that way. And when Jesus came to the place, looking up, he said to him, "Zacchaeus, hurry and come down, for today I must stay at your house."

And hurrying, he came down and received him rejoicing. And seeing it, they all murmured, saying, "He has gone in to lodge with a sinful man!"

But Zacchaeus stood and said to the Lord, "Behold, half of my goods, Lord, I give to the poor. And if I have extorted anything of anyone, I repay four times as much."

So Jesus said to him, "Today salvation has come to this house, because he also is a son of Abraham. For the Son of Man came to seek and to save that which was lost."

Now while they were hearing these things, he proceeded to speak a parable, because he was near Jerusalem and they supposed that the Kingdom of God was about to appear at once. Therefore he said, "A certain nobleman went into a far country to receive for himself a kingdom and to return. So calling ten slaves of his, he gave them ten mina coins and said to them, 'Conduct business till I come.' But his citizens hated him, and sent a delegation after him, saying, 'We don't want this man to reign over us.'

"And it came to pass, on his return, having received the kingdom, he told to be called to him these slaves to whom he had given the silver, that he might know what they had gained by doing business.

"So the first came before him, saying, 'Lord, your mina has made ten more minas.' And he said to him, 'Well done, good slave! Because you were found faithful with very little, you are to have authority over ten cities.'

"And the second came, saying, 'Your mina, Lord, has made five minas.' So he said to him also, 'And you are to be over five cities.'

"And the other came, saying, 'Lord, behold, your mina, which I kept laid away in a handkerchief, for I feared you because you're a severe man. You take up that which you didn't lay down, and reap that which you didn't sow.'

"He said to him, 'Out of your own mouth I will judge you, evil slave! You knew that I am a severe man, taking up that which I didn't lay down, and reaping that which I didn't sow. Then why didn't you give my money to the bank, and at my coming I might have collected it with interest?' And to those standing by he said, 'Take from him the mina and give it to him who has the ten minas.'

"And they said to him, 'Lord, he has ten minas!' 'I say to you that to everyone who has, will be given; but from him who doesn't have, even that which he has will be taken away from him. Even so these enemies of mine, those not wanting me to reign over them, bring here and slay them before me.' "

And having said these things, he went on ahead, going up to Jerusalem.

Now the Passover of the Jews was at hand, and many went up to Jerusalem from the country before the Passover to purify themselves. Therefore they were seeking Jesus, and were talking amongst one another as they stood in the temple, "What do you think? That he will not come to the feast?"

Now the chief priests and the Pharisees had given a command that if anyone knew where he was, he should disclose it, that they might arrest him.

Six days before the Passover Jesus came to Bethany, where Lazarus was, whom Jesus raised from the dead. Therefore they made him a supper there in the house of Simon the leper, and Martha served, so Lazarus was one of those sitting at the table with him.

Then Mary, taking an alabaster jar of a pound of fragrant oil of pure nard, very precious, came to Jesus, and breaking the jar, she poured it upon his head as he reclined at the table, and she anointed the feet of Jesus and wiped his feet with her hair, so the house was filled with the aroma of the oil.

But there were some who were indignant among themselves, and they chastised her, and Judas Iscariot, one of his disciples, who was about to betray him, said, "Why this waste? For this oil could have been sold for over three hundred denarii and given to the poor." Now this he said not because he cared for the poor, but because he was a thief, and having the money bag, what was put into it he pilfered.

Jesus therefore said, "Why do you trouble the women? For she has done a good work to me. Leave her alone, for she has kept it for the day of my burial. For the poor you always have with you, and whenever you desire you can do them good; but me you do not always have. She has done what she could; she has anointed my body beforehand for the burial of me. Truly I say to you, wherever the Good News shall be proclaimed throughout the whole world, what this woman has done shall also be spoken of for a memorial of her."

The great crowd of the Jews therefore learned that he was there, and they came not for Jesus only, but that they might see Lazarus also, whom he had raised from the dead. So the chief priests took counsel to put Lazarus to death also, because on account of him many of the Jews went away and believed in Jesus.

On the next day a great crowd coming to the feast, hearing that Jesus was coming to Jerusalem, took the branches of the palm trees and went forth to meet him and were shouting out, "Hosanna! Blessed is the one coming in the name of the Lord, even the King of Israel!"

And when they drew near to Jerusalem, and came to Bethsphage at the Mount of Olives, then Jesus sent two disciples, saying to them, "Go into the village that is opposite you, and straightaway you will find a donkey tied, and a colt with her on which no man has yet sat. Untie them and bring them to me. And if anyone asks you, 'Why are you doing this?' say, 'The Lord has need of them, and he will send them back here immediately,' and straightaway he will send them."

So the disciples, going and doing as Jesus appointed them, found a colt tied at the door outside in the open street, just as he had said to them. But as they were untying the colt, its owners said to them, "What are you doing, untying the colt?"

So they said, "The Lord needs it." And they allowed them.

And they brought the donkey and the colt to Jesus and put on them their cloaks, and sat Jesus upon them.

Now this came to pass that it might be fulfilled which was spoken through the prophet, saying,

"Tell the daughter of Zion:
    behold, your King comes to you,
gentle, and riding on a donkey,
    and upon a colt, the foal of a beast of burden.' "

These things his disciples did not understand at first, but when Jesus was glorified, then they remembered that these things were written of him and that they had done these things to him.

Therefore the crowd that was with him when he called Lazarus out of the tomb and raised him from the dead bore witness. On account of this also the crowd went and met him, for they heard that he had done this sign.

Now a very great crowd spread their cloaks on the road, and others cut branches from the trees in the fields and spread them on the road. And the crowds going in front of him and those following cried out, saying, "Hosanna! Blessed is the one coming in the name of the Lord! Blessed is the coming kingdom of our father David! Hosanna in the highest!"

And as he was now drawing near, at the descent of the Mount of Olives, the whole multitude of the disciples began to rejoice and praise

God with a loud voice for all the mighty works which they had seen, saying, "Blessed is the King coming in the name of the Lord! Peace in heaven and glory in the highest!"

And some of the Pharisees from the crowd said to him, "Teacher, rebuke your disciples!"

And responding he said, "I say to you, if these were silent, the stones would cry out."

And as he drew near, seeing the city, he wept over it, saying, "If you had known in this day, even you, the things that make for peace! But now they are hidden from your eyes. For the days shall arrive upon you, when your enemies shall cast up a barricade around you and surround you and press you in on every side and smash you to the ground, and your children within you. And they shall not leave one stone upon another within you, because you did not know the time of your visitation."

And when he had come into Jerusalem, the whole city trembled, saying, "Who is this?"

And the crowds said, "This is the prophet Jesus, from Nazareth of Galilee!"

The Pharisees therefore said among themselves, "See how you achieve nothing? Look! The world has gone after him."

Now there were certain Greeks among those coming up to worship at the feast. These then came to Philip, who was from Bethsaida of Galilee, and asked him, saying, "Sir, we want to see Jesus." Philip went and told Andrew; Andrew and Philip went and they told Jesus.

But Jesus responded to them, saying, "The hour has come that the Son of Man should be glorified. Truly, truly, I say to you, unless a grain of wheat falls into the earth and dies, it remains by itself alone; but if it dies, it bears much fruit. The one who loves his life loses it, and the one who hates his life in this world shall keep it to eternal life. If anyone serves me, let him follow me, and where I am, there also shall my servant be. If anyone serves me, him shall the Father honor.

"Now my soul has been troubled, and what shall I say—'Father, save me from this hour'? But for this reason I came to this hour. Father, glorify your name!"

Then came a voice from heaven:

I HAVE BOTH GLORIFIED IT AND WILL GLORIFY IT AGAIN

Therefore the crowd that stood by and heard it said that it had thundered. Others said, "An angel has spoken to him."

Jesus responded and said, "This voice has not come for my sake, but for your sakes. Now is the judgment of this world; now shall the prince of this world be expelled. And I, if I am lifted up from the earth, shall draw all to myself." So this he said signifying by what manner of death he was about to die.

The crowd therefore answered him, "We have heard from the Law that the Christ remains forever. How do you say, 'The Son of Man must be lifted up?' Who is this Son of Man?"

Jesus therefore said to them, "Yet a little while the light is with you. Walk while you have the light, that darkness does not overwhelm you. And the one walking in the darkness does not know where he goes. While you have the light, believe in the light, that you may become sons of light."

These things Jesus spoke, and going away, he was hidden from them. But though he had done so many signs before them, they did not believe in him, that the word of Isaiah the prophet might be fulfilled, which he said,

"Lord, who has believed our message,
and to whom has the arm of the Lord been revealed?"

For this cause they could not believe, for Isaiah said again,

"He has blinded their eyes
and has hardened their heart;
lest they should see with their eyes,
and comprehend with their heart,
and should return,
and I should cure them."

These things Isaiah said when he saw his glory, and spoke of him. Nevertheless even many of the leaders believed in him, but because of the Pharisees they did not profess it, lest they be put out of the synagogue, for they loved the glory of men more than the glory of God.

Now Jesus cried out and said, "The one believing in me believes not in me, but in the one who sent me. The one observing me observes the one who sent me. I have come as a light into the world, that whoever believes in me may not remain in the darkness. And if anyone hears my sayings and does not keep them, I do not judge them. For I came not to judge the world, but to save the world. The one rejecting me and not receiving my sayings has one judging him: the word that I spoke, that shall judge him in the last day. For I did not speak from myself, but the Father who sent me, he gave me a commandment, what I should say and what I should speak. And I know that his commandment is eternal life. Therefore the things which I speak, just as the Father has said to me, so I speak."

And he entered into the temple; and having looked around at everything, the hour already being late, he went out to Bethany with the Twelve.

Now on the next day, returning in the morning to the city from Bethany, Jesus hungered. And seeing a fig tree from afar having leaves, he came if perhaps he might find anything on it; and coming to it, he found nothing but leaves, for it was not the season for figs. And responding he said to it, "No more may any eat fruit from you forever!" And his disciples heard it.

And they came to Jerusalem; and entering into the temple, he began to expel those selling and those buying in the temple, and flipped over the tables of the money changers and the seats of those selling the doves, and he would not allow anyone to carry a container through the temple; and he taught and said to them, "Is it not written, 'My house shall be called a house of prayer for all the nations?' But you have made it a den of rebels!"

And he was teaching daily in the temple, but the chief priests and the scribes and the foremost of the people were seeking to destroy him, for they feared him. And they could not find anything that they might do, for all the people were astonished at his teaching and hung upon him, listening.

And the blind and the lame came to him in the temple, and he healed them. So when the chief priests and the scribes saw the wonderous things that he did, and the children who were crying in the temple and saying, "Hosanna to the Son of David!" they were indignant and said to him, "Do you hear what these are saying?"

So Jesus said to them, "Yes, did you never read,

'Out of the mouth of infants and nursing babies,
you have readied praise'?"

And when evening came, leaving them, he went forth out of the city into Bethany, and passed the night there.

Passing by in the morning, they saw the fig tree withered away from the roots. And having remembered, Peter said to him, "Rabbi, look! The fig tree which you cursed has withered away!"

So responding Jesus said to them, "Have faith in God. Truly I say to you, whoever may say to this mountain, 'Be taken up and cast into the sea,' and does not doubt in his heart, but believes that what he says comes to pass, it shall be done for him. For this reason I say to you, all things, whatever you pray and request, believe that you receive, and they shall be yours. And whenever you stand praying, forgive, if you have anything against anyone, that also your Father who is in heaven may forgive you your trespasses."

And they came again to Jerusalem. And as he was teaching the people in the temple and announcing the Good News, the priests and scribes came to him with the elders of the people, and they spoke, saying, "Tell us, by what authority do you do these things? Or who gave you this authority to do these things?"

But answering he said to them, "I also will ask you one question; answer me and I will tell you by what authority I do these things. The baptism of John, was it from heaven or from men? Answer me."

So they reasoned among themselves, saying, "If we should say, 'From heaven,' he will say to us, 'Why then didn't you believe him? But if we say, 'From men,' all the people will stone us, for they are persuaded that John was a prophet."

So answering Jesus they said, "We don't know."

He declared to them also, "Neither do I tell you by what authority I do these things. But what do you think? A man had two sons, and coming to the first he said, 'Son, go work today in the vineyard.' And responding he said, 'I will not,' but afterward, regretting, he went. Now coming to the second, he said likewise. And responding he said, 'I will, sir,' but he went not. Which of the two did the will of his father?"

They said, "The first."

Jesus said to them, "Truly I say to you, that the tax collectors and the prostitutes go ahead of you into the Kingdom of God. For John came to you in the way of righteousness and you did not believe him, but the tax collectors and the prostitutes believed him. And having seen it, you did not even regret afterward, that you might believe him.

"Hear another parable: There was a certain man, a master of a house, who planted a vineyard and put a fence around it, and dug a pit for a winepress in it and built a tower, and rented it to farmers and went to another country for a long time. Now when the season for the fruit drew near, he sent to the farmers a slave, that from the farmers he might receive his share of the fruit of the vineyard. But the farmers, having beaten him, sent him away empty-handed. And again he sent to them another slave; and him they struck in the head and treated shamefully, and they sent him away empty-handed. And he sent yet a third, but having wounded him, they expelled him. And another he sent, and him they killed, and many others, beating some and killing some.

"So the lord of the vineyard said, 'What should I do? I will send my beloved son. Maybe they will respect him.' But seeing him, those farmers reasoned among themselves, saying, 'This is the heir. Come, let's kill him and the inheritance will be ours!' So taking him, they expelled him from the vineyard and killed him. Therefore when the lord of the vineyard shall come, what shall he do to those farmers?"

They said to him, "Wretched men! He will wretchedly destroy them and will rent out the vineyard to other farmers who will pay him the fruit in its season."

Now peering at them Jesus said, "Did you never read in the Scriptures,

'The stone which the builders rejected,
this became the cornerstone.
This was from the Lord,
and it is marvelous in our eyes.'?

For this reason I say to you, the Kingdom of God shall be taken away from you and shall be given to a people bringing forth its fruit. And everyone who falls upon this stone shall be shattered, but upon whomever it shall fall, it shall crush him into powder."

And when the chief priests and the Pharisees heard his parables, they knew that he spoke about them. And when they sought to lay hands on him that very hour, they feared the crowds, since they held him to be a prophet.

And responding Jesus spoke again to them in parables, saying, "The Kingdom of Heaven has become like a certain king who made a wedding feast for his son and sent his slaves to call those who were invited to the wedding feast, yet they would not come. Again he sent other slaves, saying, 'Tell those who are invited: Behold, I have prepared my brunch; my oxen and my fattened cattle are butchered, and all things are ready; come to the wedding feast!' But paying no regard they went their ways, one to his own farm, another to his merchandise, and the rest, seizing his slaves, abused and killed them. So the king was enraged, and sending his armies, he destroyed those murderers and burned their city.

"Then he said to his slaves, 'The wedding is ready, but those who were invited were not worthy. Therefore go to the intersections of the roads, and as many as you may find, invite to the wedding feast.' And going out to the roads, those slaves brought together all, as many as they found, both bad and good, and the wedding was filled with dining guests.

"But when the king entered in to gaze upon those dining, he saw there a man not wearing wedding attire. And he said to him, 'Comrade, how did you enter in here not having wedding attire?' But he was speechless. Then the king said to the servants, 'Binding him hand and foot, expel him into the darkness outside where there shall be weeping and gnashing of teeth.' For many are called, but few chosen."

Then having gone, the Pharisees took counsel how they might ensnare him in his words. And monitoring him, they sent to him their disciples, along with the Herodians, as spies who pretended to be righteous, saying, "Teacher, we know that you say and teach rightly, and you defer to no one, indeed you are not partial to appearance, but in truth teach the way of God. Therefore tell us, what do you think? Is it lawful to pay taxes to Caesar or not? Pay, or not pay?"

But knowing their wickedness Jesus said, "Why do you test me, hypocrites? Show me the coin for the tax."

So they brought to him a denarius.

And he said to them, "Whose is this image and inscription?"

So they said to him, "Caesar's."

Now Jesus said to them, "Then pay back the things of Caesar to Caesar, and the things of God to God."

And they were not able to catch him in his statement before the people. And marveling at his answer, they were silent; and leaving him, they went away.

On that day there came to him Sadducees, who deny that there is a resurrection, and they asked him, saying, "Teacher, Moses wrote for us that if a man's brother dies and leaves behind a wife and leaves no child, his brother should take his wife and raise up seed for his brother. Now there were seven brothers, and the first took a wife, and dying, left no seed. And the second took her, and died, leaving behind no seed, and the third likewise; and the seven left no seed. Last of all the woman also died. In the resurrection, when they rise up, whose wife will she be, for the seven had her as a wife?"

But answering Jesus declared to them, "You go astray, not knowing the Scriptures nor the power of God. The sons of this age marry and are given in marriage, but those who are deemed worthy to attain to that age, and rise up in the resurrection from the dead, neither marry nor are given in marriage. For they cannot die anymore, for they are equal to the angels, and are sons of God, being sons of the resurrection.

"Now about the dead, that they rise, have you not read in the book of Moses, at the bush, how God spoke to him, saying, 'I am the God of Abraham and the God of Isaac and the God of Jacob'? He is not the God of the dead, but of the living, for all live to him. Greatly you go astray."

Now hearing this, the crowds were astonished at his teaching. And responding some of the scribes said, "Teacher, you have spoken well."

Now the Pharisees, having heard that Jesus had silenced the Sadducees, gathered themselves together. And one of them, a scribe—an expert on the Law of Moses—seeing that he had answered them well, asked him, testing him: "Teacher, which commandment in the Law is the first of all?"

So Jesus declared to him, "The great and first commandment is, 'Hear, Israel: The Lord our God, the Lord is one; and you shall love the Lord your God from all your heart and from all your soul and from all your mind and from all your strength.' The second is like it: 'You shall love your neighbor as yourself.' There is no other commandment greater than these. On these two commandments hang all the Law and the Prophets."

And the scribe said to him, "Right, Teacher, in truth you have said that he is one and there is none other but he, and to love him from all the heart and from all the understanding and from all the soul and from all the strength, and to love one's neighbor as oneself, is more than all the burnt offerings and sacrifices."

And Jesus, seeing that he answered wisely, said to him, "You are not far from the Kingdom of God."

And after that no one dared to ask him any question.

Now while the Pharisees were gathered together, Jesus questioned them, saying, "What do you think of the Christ? Whose son is he?"

They said to him, "Of David."

He said to them, "How then does David in the Holy Spirit call him Lord, saying,

> 'The Lord said to my Lord:
> "Sit at my right hand,
> till I place your enemies as a footstool of your feet." '?

If then David calls him Lord, how is he his son?"

And no one was able to answer him a word. And the great crowd heard him gladly.

Now within the hearing of all the people, he said to his disciples, "Beware of the scribes and the Pharisees. They sit on Moses' seat; therefore all things, whatever they say, you do and keep; but do not do according to their works, for they say and do not do. For they bind heavy burdens and lay them on men's shoulders, but they themselves are not willing to move them with their finger. But all their works they do to be gazed upon by men. For they make broad their phylacteries and enlarge the fringes of their garments and desire to walk in long robes, and love the foremost places at the banquets and the foremost seats in the synagogues and the greetings in the marketplaces and to be called 'Rabbi' by men, who devour widows' houses and as a pretense make long prayers. These shall receive greater condemnation.

"But you shall not be called 'Rabbi', for you have one teacher, and all of you are brothers. And call no one on the earth your father, for you have one Father, who is in heaven. Nor be called 'instructor', for you have one instructor, the Christ. But the greatest among you shall be your servant; and whoever exalts himself shall be humbled, and whoever humbles himself shall be exalted.

“But woe to you scribes and Pharisees, hypocrites, for you shut the Kingdom of Heaven before men. For you do not enter in yourselves, nor do you allow those who are entering in to enter.

“Woe to you scribes and Pharisees, hypocrites, for you travel around by sea and land to make one convert, and when he becomes so, you make him twice as much a son of hell than yourselves.

“Woe to you blind guides who say, ‘Whoever swears by the temple, it is nothing; but whoever swears by the gold of the temple, he is bound by his oath.’ Blind fools! For which is greater, the gold or the temple that sanctifies the gold? And ‘Whoever swears by the altar, it is nothing; but whoever swears by the gift that is on it, he is bound by his oath.’ You blind! For which is greater, the gift or the altar that sanctifies the gift? Therefore the one who swears by the altar, swears by it and by everything on it. And the one who swears by the temple, swears by it and by him who dwells in it. And the one who swears by heaven, swears by the throne of God and by him who sits on it.

“Woe to you scribes and Pharisees, hypocrites, for you tithe mint and dill and cumin, and have neglected the weightier matters of the Law: justice and mercy and faith. But these you need to have done, without neglecting the others. You blind guides that strain out the gnat and swallow the camel!

“Woe to you scribes and Pharisees, hypocrites, for you clean the outside of the cup and of the dish, but within they are full of greed and self-indulgence. Blind Pharisee, first clean the inside of the cup and of the dish, that the outside of them may become clean also.

“Woe to you scribes and Pharisees, hypocrites, for you are like whitewashed tombs, which outwardly appear to be flourishing, but inwardly are full of bones of the dead and of every impurity. Thus you also outwardly appear righteous to men, but inwardly you are full of hypocrisy and lawlessness.

“Woe to you scribes and Pharisees, hypocrites, for you build the tombs of the prophets and adorn the monuments of the righteous and say, ‘If we had lived in the days of our fathers, we would not have been partners with them in the bloodshed of the prophets.’ Therefore you bear witness to yourselves that you are children of those who murdered the prophets. Fill up, then, the measure of your fathers. Serpents, offspring of vipers, how shall you flee the judgment of hell? For this reason, behold, I send to you prophets and wise men and scribes. Some of them you shall kill and crucify, and some of them you shall scourge in your synagogues and persecute from city to city, that upon you may come all the righteous blood poured out upon the earth, from the blood of righteous Abel to the blood of Zachariah son of Barachiah, whom you murdered between the temple and the altar. Truly I say to you, all these things shall arrive upon this generation.

"Jerusalem, Jerusalem, who kills the prophets and stones those who are sent to her, how often I desired to gather your children together in the way a hen gathers her chicks under her wings, and you were not willing. Behold, your house is left to you desolate. For I say to you, you shall not see me from now till you say, 'Blessed is the one who comes in the name of the Lord.' "

Now sitting down opposite the treasury, he observed how the crowd cast money into the treasury; and many who were rich were casting in much. But he saw a certain poor, needy widow cast in two tiny coins worth a few cents. And summoning his disciples, he said to them, "Truly I say to you, this poor widow cast in more than all those who are casting into the treasury. For they all cast out of their abundance, but she out of her poverty cast in all, as much as she had, her whole livelihood."

And as Jesus went forth out of the temple, some were talking about the temple, how it was adorned with lovely stones and consecrated offerings. And his disciples came to him to show him the buildings of the temple, and one of his disciples said to him, "Teacher, look! What stones and what buildings!"

But responding he said to them, "Do you see these great buildings? Do you not see all of these things? Truly I say to you, there shall not be left here one stone upon another that shall not be thrown down."

Now as he was sitting on the Mount of Olives opposite the temple, Peter and James and John and Andrew asked him privately, "Teacher, tell us, when will these things be? And what will be the sign that these things are all about to happen? And what is the sign of your coming, and of the end of the age?"

So Jesus began to say to them, "Look out that no one leads you astray. For many shall come in my name, saying, 'I am the Christ!' and, 'The time draws near!' and shall lead many astray. Do not go after them. So when you hear of wars and uprisings and rumors of wars, do not be scared, for it is necessary that all these things first come to pass, but the end is not yet. For nation shall rise against nation, and kingdom against kingdom; and there shall be great earthquakes and in various places famines and plagues; and there shall be terrors and great signs from heaven. But all these things are the beginning of birth pains.

"So look out for yourselves; before all these things, they shall lay their hands upon you and persecute you, delivering you up to councils, and in synagogues and prisons you shall be beaten, and before rulers and kings and governors you shall stand for my sake, for a testimony to them. And to all the nations the Good News must first be proclaimed. And when they lead you away, delivering you up, it shall be your chance to bear witness; be not anxious beforehand what you shall speak, but settle it in your hearts not to prepare in advance a defense, for I shall give you a mouth and wisdom which all opposed to you shall not be able to resist or to deny. Therefore whatever shall be given you in that hour, speak that; for it is not you who speak, but the Holy Spirit.

"And then many shall stumble and shall deliver up one another and shall hate one another, and brother shall deliver up brother to death, and the father his child, and children shall rise up against parents and cause them to be put to death. So you shall be delivered up to tribulation even by parents and brothers and relatives and friends; and some of you they shall put to death. And you shall be hated by all men for my name's sake. And many false prophets shall arise and shall lead many astray. And because lawlessness shall be multiplied, the love of many shall grow cold. Yet not a hair of your head shall perish; by your endurance you shall obtain your souls. So the one enduring to the end, this one shall be saved. And this Good News of the Kingdom shall be proclaimed in all the world as a testimony to all the nations, and then the end shall arrive.

"But when you see Jerusalem surrounded by armies, then know that her desolation is at hand. Therefore when you see the abomination of desolation, which was spoken of through Daniel the prophet, standing in the holy place where it should not be, then let those who are in Judea flee to the mountains, and let those who are in the midst of her escape; but let not those who are in the country enter into her and the one who is on the housetop, let him not go down, nor enter in, to take anything out of his house, and the one who is in the field let him not turn back to take his cloak. For these are days of vengeance, that all things that are written may be fulfilled.

"But woe to those who are pregnant and to those nursing in those days! So pray that your flight may not be in the winter nor on a Sabbath, for there shall be great distress upon the land and wrath to this people and they shall fall by the edge of the sword and shall be led captive into all the nations; and Jerusalem shall be trampled down by the Gentiles, till the times of the Gentiles are fulfilled. There shall be great tribulation such as there has not been the like from the beginning of the creation which God created till now, no, nor ever shall be. And unless the Lord had shortened those days, no flesh would have been saved; but for the sake of the chosen ones, whom he chose, he has shortened those days.

"Then if anyone says to you, 'Look! Here is the Christ!' or, 'Look! There!' do not believe. For there shall arise false christs and false prophets, and they shall give great signs and wonders so as to lead astray, if possible, even the chosen ones. So you look out, I have foretold to you all things. Therefore if they shall say to you, 'Behold, he is in the wilderness!' do not go forth; or 'Behold, he is in the inner rooms!' do not believe. For as the lightning flashes from the east and is seen even to the west, so shall be the coming of the Son of Man. Wherever the carcass is, there the vultures gather.

"But in those days, immediately after that tribulation, the sun shall be darkened and the moon shall not give its light and the stars shall fall from the sky, and upon the earth dismay of nations in confusion, roaring of the sea and surging waves, men fainting for fear and for expectation of the things which are coming on the world; for the powers of the heavens shall be shaken.

"And then the sign of the Son of Man shall appear in the sky, and then shall all the tribes of the earth mourn, and they shall watch the Son of Man coming on the clouds of the sky with power and great glory. And then he shall send his angels with a great sound of a trumpet, and they shall gather together his chosen ones from the four winds, from the end of the earth to the end of heaven.

"But when these things begin to come to pass, stand up straight and raise your heads, because your redemption draws near. So from the fig tree learn this parable: When its branch has already become tender and puts forth its leaves, seeing it for yourselves, you know that the summer is already near, even at the doors. Thus you also, when you see these things coming to pass, know that the Kingdom of God is near. Truly I say to you, this generation shall certainly not pass away till all these things come to pass. Heaven and earth shall pass away, but my words shall certainly not pass away.

"But of that day and that hour no one knows, not even the angels of heaven, nor the Son, but the Father only. And as the days of Noah, so shall be the coming of the Son of Man. For as in the days which were before the flood they were feeding and drinking, marrying and giving in marriage, till the day that Noah entered into the ark, and they did not know till the flood came and took them all away, so shall be the coming of the Son of Man. Then shall two men be in the field: one shall be taken and one is left. Two women shall be grinding at the mill: one shall be taken and one is left.

"So yourselves beware, lest your hearts be weighed down with carousing and drunkenness and cares of this life, and that day come upon you suddenly like a snare. For it shall come upon all those sitting upon the face of all the earth. So be alert in every season, praying that you may have strength to escape all these things that are about to come to pass, and to stand before the Son of Man.

"Therefore be vigilant, for you do not know on what day your Lord comes. But know this, that if the master of the house had known in what time of the night the thief was coming, he would have been vigilant and would not have allowed his house to be broken into. For this reason you also be ready, for in an hour that you do not think, the Son of Man comes.

"Look out, be alert, for you do not know when the time is. It is like a man going on a journey, having left his house and given authority to his slaves, to each one his work, and commanded the doorkeeper to be vigilant. Be vigilant therefore, for you do not know when the lord of the house comes, whether at evening or at midnight or when the rooster crows or in the morning, lest coming suddenly he should find you sleeping. So what I say to you, I say to all: be vigilant."

"Who then is the faithful and wise slave, whom his lord has set over his household, to give them their food in due season? Blessed is that slave whom his lord, when he comes, shall find doing so. Truly I say to you, that he shall set him over all that he possesses. But if that wretched slave should say in his heart, 'My lord is delayed,' and begins to strike his fellow slaves and eat and drink with the drunkards, the lord of that slave shall arrive in a day when he does not expect and in an hour when he does not know, and shall cut him in two and place his portion with the hypocrites; in that place there shall be weeping and gnashing of teeth.

"Then the Kingdom of Heaven shall become like ten maidens who, having taken their lamps, went forth to meet the bridegroom. Now five of them were foolish, and five were wise. The foolish, who having taken their lamps, took no oil with them, but the wise took oil in their vessels with their lamps. Now while the bridegroom delayed, they all became drowsy and slept. But in the middle of the night came a yell: 'Behold, the bridegroom! Come forth to meet him!' Then all those maidens arose, and trimmed their lamps. Now the foolish said to the wise, 'Give us some of your oil, for our lamps are going out.' But the wise answered, saying, 'No, in case there isn't enough for us and you. You go instead to those who sell, and buy for yourselves.' So while they went away to buy, the bridegroom came, and those who were ready entered in with him to the wedding feast, and the door was shut. Now afterward the other maidens also came, saying, 'Lord, Lord, open to us!' But answering he said, 'Truly I say to you, I don't know you.' Therefore be vigilant, for you do not know the day nor the hour.

"For it is just as when a man, going to another country, called his own slaves and entrusted his possessions to them. And to one he gave five talents of silver, to another two, to another one, to each according to his own ability; and then he went to another country. Having gone, the one who received the five talents traded with them and made another five talents. Likewise, also the one with the two gained another two. But the one who received the one talent, going away, dug in the earth and hid his lord's silver.

"Now after a long time the lord of those slaves came and settled accounts with them. And having come, the one who received the five talents brought another five talents, saying, 'Lord, you entrusted to me five talents. Look! I have gained another five talents.' His lord declared to him, 'Well done, good and faithful slave. You have been faithful over a few things, I will set you over many things; enter into the joy of your lord.'

"Now having come also, the one with the two talents said, 'Lord, you delivered to me two talents. Look! I have gained another two talents.' His lord declared to him, 'Well done, good and faithful slave. You have been faithful over a few things, I will set you over many things; enter into the joy of your lord.'

"Now having come also, the one who had received the one talent said, 'Lord, I knew you, that you're a harsh man, reaping where you didn't sow and gathering where you didn't scatter; and being afraid, going away, I hid your talent in the earth. Look! You have what is yours.'

"But responding his lord said to him, 'You evil and lazy slave, you knew that I reap where I didn't sow and gather where I didn't scatter; therefore it was necessary for you to place my silver with the bankers, and having come I should have received back my own with interest. Therefore take away the talent from him and give it to him who has the ten talents. For to everyone who has, more will be given, and he will have abundance; but from him who does not have, even that which he has shall be taken away. And expel the worthless slave into the darkness outside where there shall be weeping and gnashing of teeth.'

"Now when the Son of Man shall come in his glory, and all the holy angels with him, then shall he sit on the throne of his glory. And before him shall be gathered all the nations, and he shall separate them one from another, as the shepherd separates the sheep from the goats; and he shall set the sheep at his right hand, but the goats at the left. Then shall the King say to those at his right hand, 'Come, you blessed of my Father, inherit the kingdom prepared for you from the foundation of the world. For I was hungry and you gave me food; I was thirsty and you gave me drink; I was a stranger and you took me in; naked, and you clothed me; I was sick and you visited me; I was in prison and you came to me.'

"Then shall the righteous answer him, saying, 'Lord, when did we see you hungry and feed you, or thirsty and give you a drink? And when did we see you as a stranger and take you in, or naked and clothe you? And when did we see you sick or in prison and come to you?' And answering the King shall say to them, 'Truly I say to you, inasmuch as you did it to one of the least of these my brothers, you did it to me.'

"Then shall he say also to those at the left hand, 'Go away from me, you cursed, into the eternal fire that is prepared for the devil and his angels. For I was hungry, and you did not give me food; I was thirsty, and you gave me no drink; I was a stranger, and you did not take me in; naked, and you did not clothe me; sick and in prison, and you did not visit me.'

"Then shall they also answer, saying, 'Lord, when did we see you hungry or thirsty or a stranger or naked or sick or in prison, and didn't serve you?' Then shall he answer them, saying, 'Truly I say to you, inasmuch as you did not do it to one of the least of these, you did not do it to me.' And these shall go away into eternal punishment, but the righteous into eternal life."

And it came to pass, when Jesus had finished all these words, he said to his disciples, "You know that after two days the Passover takes place, and the Son of Man is delivered up to be crucified."

Now during the day he was teaching in the temple, but going out in the evening, he would pass the night on the mountain that is called the Mount of Olives. And all the people came early in the morning to him in the temple to hear him.

Now it was two days until the Passover and the Feast of Unleavened Bread, and the chief priests and the scribes and the elders of the people were gathered together in the courtyard of the high priest, who was called Caiaphas. And they took counsel together that they might seize Jesus by deceit and put him to death, but they said, "Not during the feast, in case there will be an uproar among the people."

Then Satan entered into Judas, who was also called Iscariot, who was counted with the Twelve. And having gone away, he conferred with the chief priests and officers, saying, "What are you willing to give me if I deliver him to you?"

So hearing it, they rejoiced, and weighed out for him thirty pieces of silver. And he promised, and from that time he sought an opportunity to conveniently deliver Jesus to them away from the crowd.

Now on the first day of the Festival of Unleavened Bread, when the Passover lamb must be sacrificed, Jesus sent Peter and John, saying, "Go and prepare the Passover for us, that we may eat."

So they said to him, "Where do you want us to prepare?"

So he said to them, "Behold, when you have entered into the city, you will meet a man carrying a pitcher of water. Follow him into the house which he goes in. And you will say to the master of the house, 'The Teacher says: My time is at hand; at your house I shall keep the Passover with my disciples. Where is the guest room where I may eat the Passover?' And he will show you a large upper room furnished and ready, and there make preparations for us."

So going forth, the disciples did as Jesus appointed them, and they came into the city and found as he had told them. And they prepared the Passover.

Now when evening had come, he sat down, and the twelve apostles with him. So Jesus, knowing that his hour had come, that he should depart from this world to the Father, having loved his own who were in the world, he loved them to the end. And he said to them, "I have fervently desired to eat this Passover with you before I suffer, for I say to you, I shall not eat it till it is fulfilled in the Kingdom of God." And having received a cup, having given thanks, he said, "Take this and share it among yourselves, for truly I say to you, hereafter I shall no more, not ever, drink of the fruit of the vine till that day when I drink it new with you in the Kingdom of God."

And as they were reclining at the table and were eating, knowing that the Father had given all things into his hands and that he came from God and was going to God, having taken bread, and having given a blessing, Jesus broke it; and giving it to the disciples, he said, "Take, eat; this is my body which is given for you. Do this in remembrance of me."

And likewise having taken the cup after supper, and having given thanks, he gave to them, and they all drank of it, and he said to them, "Drink of it, all of you, for this cup is the new covenant in my blood, which is poured out for many for the forgiveness of sins. Do this, as often as you drink it, in remembrance of me.

"Yet behold, the hand of him betraying me is with me on the table. Truly I say to you, one of you will betray me, he who is eating with me."

And they began to contend among themselves about which of them it was who would do this thing. And grieving exceedingly, each one began to say to him, "Is it me, Lord?"

So answering he said, "It is one of the Twelve, the one dipping with me in the dish, this one will betray me. For the Son of Man indeed goes as it has been ordained, yet woe to that man through whom the Son of Man is betrayed! Better it were for him if that man had not been born."

Now responding Judas, who was betraying him, said, "Is it me, Rabbi?"

He said to him, "You have said it."

Now there was also a dispute among them, which of them was considered to be greatest. So he said to them, "The kings of the Gentiles exercise lordship over them, and those who have authority over them are called Benefactors. But not so with you. Rather the greatest among you, let him become as the youngest; and the one leading, as the one serving. For who is greater, the one sitting at the table, or the one serving? Is it not the one sitting? But I am in your midst as the one serving. But you are those who have remained with me in my temptations. And I bestow to you, even as my Father bestowed to me, a kingdom, that you may eat and drink at my table in my kingdom; and you shall sit on thrones, judging the twelve tribes of Israel."

And Jesus arose from supper and laid aside his outer garments; and taking a towel, he tied it around his waist. Then he poured water into the basin and began to wash the disciples' feet and to wipe them with the towel that was tied around him.

So he came to Simon Peter. He said to him, "Lord, do you wash my feet?"

Jesus answered and said to him, "What I do you do not know now, but you shall understand hereafter."

Peter said to him, "You will forever not wash my feet!"

Jesus answered him, "If I do not wash you, you have no part with me."

Simon Peter said to him, "Lord, not my feet only, but also my hands and my head!"

Jesus said to him, "The one who has bathed has no need except to wash his feet, but is entirely clean. And you are clean, but not all of you." For he knew the one who was betraying him; because of this he said, "You are not all clean."

Therefore when he had washed their feet and taken his outer garments, and having sat down again, he said to them, "Do you know what I have done to you? You call me, 'Teacher' and 'Lord' and you say so rightly, for so I am. If I, then, the Lord and the Teacher, have washed your feet, you also ought to wash one another's feet. For I have given you an example, that you also should do as I have done to you. Truly, truly, I say to you, a slave is not greater than his lord, nor a messenger greater than the one who sent him. If you know these things, blessed are you if you do them.

"I do not speak of all of you. I know whom I have chosen, but that the Scripture may be fulfilled, 'The one feeding on my bread lifted up his heel against me.' From this time I tell you before it comes to pass, that when it comes to pass, you may believe that I am he. Truly, truly, I say to you, the one receiving whomever I send receives me, but the one receiving me receives the one who sent me."

Having said these things, Jesus was troubled in spirit and bore witness and said, "Truly, truly, I say to you, that one of you will betray me."

The disciples looked at one another, being confounded about whom he spoke. There was one of his disciples reclining at the heart of Jesus, whom Jesus loved. Therefore Simon Peter beckoned to him and said to him, "Ask who it is of whom he speaks."

Therefore he, leaning back thus on the chest of Jesus, said to him, "Lord, who is it?"

Jesus therefore answered, "It is he to whom I will dip this piece of bread and give it to him." Then dipping the piece of bread himself, he took it and gave it to Judas, son of Simon Iscariot. And after the piece of bread, then Satan entered into him.

Therefore Jesus said to him, "What you do, do quickly."

Now nobody reclining at the table knew why he said this to him. For some thought, since Judas had the moneybag, that Jesus was saying to him, "Buy what things we need for the feast," or that he should give something to the poor.

Therefore having received the piece of bread, he went out immediately. And it was night.

Then when he had gone out, Jesus said, "Now the Son of Man is glorified, and God is glorified in him; if God is glorified in him, God shall also glorify him in himself, and immediately shall glorify him. Little children, yet a little while I am with you. You shall seek me, and as I said to the Jews, 'Where I go, you cannot come,' so now I say to you. A new commandment I give to you, that you love one another; as I have loved you, so also you love one another. By this all shall know that you are my disciples, if you have love for one another."

Simon Peter said to him, "Lord, where are you going?"

Jesus answered, "Simon, Simon, behold, Satan demanded to have you, that he might sift you as wheat, but I prayed for you, that your faith would not fail. And you, when you have returned, strengthen your brothers. Where I go, you cannot follow me now, but you shall follow afterward."

But Peter said to him, "Lord, I am ready to go with you both to prison and to death! Why can't I follow you now? I will lay down my life for you."

Jesus answered, "Will you lay down your life for me? Truly, truly, I say to you, Peter, the rooster will not crow this day till three times you deny that you know me."

And he said to them, "When I sent you without money pouch and bag and sandals, did you lack anything?"

So they said, "Nothing."

So he said to them, "But now the one who has a money pouch, let him take it, and likewise a bag; and the one who does not have, let him sell his cloak and buy a sword. For I say to you that this which is written must still be accomplished by me: 'And he was reckoned with transgressors.' For that which concerns me has an end."

So they said, "Lord, behold, here are two swords."

But he said to them, "That's enough! Let not your heart be troubled. Believe in God; believe also in me. In my Father's house are many dwellings. Now if it were not so, would I tell you that I go to prepare a place for you? And if I go and prepare a place for you, I am coming again and shall receive you to myself, that where I am, also you may be. And where I go, you know the way."

Thomas said to him, "Lord, we don't know where you're going. How can we know the way?"

Jesus said to him, "I am the Way and the Truth and the Life. No one comes to the Father except through me. If you have known me, you will know my Father also. Assuredly you know him and have watched him."

Philip said to him, "Lord, show us the Father, and that is enough for us."

Jesus said to him, "Have I been with you so long a time, and you do not know me Philip? The one who has watched me has watched the Father; how do you say, 'Show us the Father?' Do you not believe that I am in the Father, and the Father in me? The sayings that I speak to you, I speak not from myself; but the Father remaining in me does his works. Believe me that I am in the Father, and the Father in me; but if not, for the very works themselves believe.

"Truly, truly, I say to you, the one who believes in me, the works that I do also he shall do, and greater than these shall he do, because I am going to my Father. And whatever you shall request in my name, that shall I do, that the Father may be glorified in the Son; if you shall request of me anything in my name, that shall I do.

"If you love me, you will keep my commandments. And I shall ask the Father, and he shall give you another Helper, that he may be with you forever; the Spirit of truth, whom the world cannot receive, for it does not observe him nor know him. You know him, for he remains with you and shall be in you.

"I will not leave you as orphans; I am coming to you. Yet a little while, and the world will observe me no more; but you will observe me. Because I live, you also shall live. In that day you shall know that I am in my Father, and you in me, and I in you. The one who has my commandments and keeps them, he is the one who loves me; so the one who loves me shall be loved by my Father, and I shall love him and shall manifest myself to him."

Judas—not Iscariot—said to him, "Lord, what has happened that you are about to manifest yourself to us and not to the world?"

Jesus answered and said to him, "If anyone loves me, he will keep my word; and my Father shall love him, and we shall come to him and shall make our dwelling with him. The one who does not love me does not keep my words; and the word that you hear is not mine, but the

Father's who sent me. These things I have said to you while remaining with you. But the Helper, the Holy Spirit, whom the Father shall send in my name, he shall teach you all things and shall remind you of all that I said to you.

"Peace I bestow to you; my peace I give to you, not as the world gives do I give to you. Let not your heart be troubled, nor let it fear. You heard how I said to you, 'I am going away, and I am coming to you.' If you loved me you would have rejoiced because I am going to my Father, for the Father is greater than I. And now I have told you before it comes to pass, that when it shall come to pass, you may believe. I will no longer speak much with you, for the prince of the world comes, and in me he has nothing. But that the world may know that I love the Father, and as the Father commanded me, so I do. Arise, let's go from here.

"I am the True Vine, and my Father is the farmer. Every branch in me not bearing fruit, he takes it away; and every branch bearing fruit, he cleanses it, that it may bear more fruit. Already you are clean because of the word that I have spoken to you. Remain in me, and I in you. As the branch cannot bear fruit by itself unless it remains in the vine, so neither can you unless you remain in me. I am the vine, you are the branches. The one who remains in me and I in him, this one bears much fruit, for apart from me you can not do anything. If anyone does not remain in me, he is cast forth as the branch and is withered; and they gather them and cast them into the fire and they are burned. If you remain in me, and my words remain in you, whatever you desire you shall request, and it shall be done for you. In this my Father is glorified, that you bear much fruit, and so shall you be my disciples.

"Just as the Father has loved me, I also have loved you. Remain in my love. If you keep my commandments, you shall remain in my love, just as I have kept my Father's commandments and remain in his love. These things I have spoken to you, that my joy may be in you, and that your joy may be full. This is my commandment, that you love one another, just as I have loved you. Greater love than this no one has, that someone lay down his life for his friends. You are my friends if you do what I command you. No longer do I call you slaves, for the slave does not know what his lord does. But I have called you friends, for all things that I heard from my Father I have made known to you. You did not choose me, but I chose you and appointed you, that you should go and bear fruit and that your fruit should remain, that whatever you shall request of the Father in my name, he may give it to you. These things I command you, that you may love one another.

"If the world hates you, you know that it has hated me first before it hated you. If you were of the world, the world would love its own. But because you are not of the world, yet I chose you out of the world, for this reason the world hates you. Remember the word that I said to you: 'A slave is not greater than his lord.' If they persecuted me, they shall also persecute you; if they kept my word, they shall also keep yours. But all these things they shall do to you for my name's sake, because they do not know him who sent me. If I had not come and spoken to them, they would not have had sin; but now they have no excuse for their sin. The one hating me also hates my Father. If I had not done the works among them that no other has done, they would not have had sin; but now they have both watched and hated both me and my Father. But so that the word may be fulfilled which was written in their Law, 'They hated me without cause.'

"When the Helper has come, whom I shall send to you from the Father, the Spirit of truth who proceeds from the Father, he shall bear witness about me. So also you shall bear witness, because from the beginning you have been with me.

"These things I have spoken to you so that you might not be caused to stumble. They shall put you out of the synagogues; indeed an hour is coming when whoever kills you shall think that he offers service to God. And these things they shall do because they have not known the Father, nor me. But these things I have spoken to you, that when their hour comes, you may remember them, how I said them to you. Now these things I did not say to you from the beginning, because I was with you. But now I go to him who sent me, and none of you asks me, 'Where are you going?' But because I have spoken these things to you, sorrow has filled your heart.

"Nevertheless I say to you the truth: it is better for you that I go away. For if I do not go away, the Helper shall not come to you; but if I go, I shall send him to you. And having come, he shall convict the world concerning sin and concerning righteousness and concerning judgment: concerning sin, because they do not believe in me; concerning righteousness, because I go to the Father and you observe me no more; concerning judgment, because the prince of this world has been judged.

"I have yet many things to say to you, but you cannot bear them now. But when he comes, the Spirit of truth, he shall guide you in all truth. For he shall not speak from himself, but whatever he may hear, he shall speak, and the coming things he shall report to you. He shall glorify me, for he shall take that which is mine and shall report it to you. All things, whatever the Father has, are mine; for this reason I said that he shall take that which is mine and shall report it to you.

"A little while, and no more do you observe me; and again a little while, and you will watch me."

Therefore some of his disciples said to one another, "What's this that he says to us, 'A little while, and you don't observe me, and again a little while, and you'll watch me;' and, 'Because I go to the Father'?" Therefore they said, "What's this that he says, 'A little while'? We don't know what he speaks."

Jesus knew that they desired to ask him and he said to them, "About this do you inquire among one another, that I said, 'A little while, and you do not observe me; and again a little while, and you will watch me'? Truly, truly, I say to you, that you will weep and lament, but the world will rejoice. You will be sorrowful, but your sorrow will be turned into joy. When the woman gives birth, she has sorrow because her hour has come. But when she has delivered the child, she no longer remembers the anguish, for the joy that a person is born into the world. And therefore you now have sorrow, but I will see you again and your heart will rejoice, and no one will take your joy away from you.

"And in that day you will not ask of me anything. Truly, truly, I say to you, whatever you may request of the Father in my name, he shall give it to you. Till now you have not requested anything in my name. Request and you shall receive, that your joy may be filled.

"These things I have spoken to you in allegories. An hour is coming when I shall no more speak to you in allegories, but about the Father I shall plainly report to you. In that day you shall request in my name, and I do not say to you that I shall ask the Father concerning you, for the Father himself loves you because you have loved me and have believed that I came forth from God. I came forth from the Father and have come into the world; again I leave the world and go to the Father."

His disciples said, "Look! Now you speak plainly and speak no allegories. Now we know that you know all things and don't need anyone to ask you. By this we believe that you came forth from God."

Jesus answered them, "Do you now believe? Behold, an hour is coming, and has come, that you will be scattered, each to his own place, and you will leave me all alone. Yet I am not alone, because the Father is with me. These things I have spoken to you, that in me you may have peace. In the world you have tribulation; but take courage, I have overcome the world."

These things Jesus spoke. And lifting up his eyes to heaven he said, "Father, the hour has come. Glorify your Son, that the Son may also glorify you, just as you gave him authority over all flesh, that to all whom you have given him, he should give eternal life. Now this is eternal life, that they should know you, the only true God, and him whom you sent, Jesus Christ. I glorified you on the earth, having accomplished the work which you have given me to do. And now Father, glorify me with your own self with the glory that I had with you before the world existed.

"I made your name visible to the people whom you have given me out of the world; they were yours, and you gave them to me, and they have kept your word. Now they know that all things, whatever you have given me, are from you, for the sayings that you have given me I have given to them, and they received them and have come to know for sure that I came forth from you, and they believed that you sent me. Concerning them I ask; not concerning the world do I ask, but concerning those whom you have given me, for they are yours. And all things that are mine are yours, and yours are mine, and I am glorified in them. And I am no longer in the world, but they are in the world, and I come to you.

"Holy Father, keep them in your name which you have given me, that they may be one, just as we are. While I was with them, I kept them in your name which you have given me; and I guarded them, and none of them was destroyed except the son of destruction, that the Scripture might be fulfilled. But now I am coming to you, and these things I speak in the world, that they may have my joy filled within them. I have given them your word, and the world hated them because they are not of the world, just as I am not of the world. I do not ask that you would take them from the world, but that you would keep them from the evil one. They are not of the world, just as I am not of the world. Sanctify them in the truth; your word is truth. Just as you sent me into the world, I also sent them into the world. And for their sakes I sanctify myself, that they themselves also may be sanctified in truth.

"Now not concerning these only do I ask, but also concerning those who shall believe in me through their word, that they may all be one; just as you, Father, are in me, and I in you, that also they may be one in us, that the world may believe that you sent me. And the glory that you have given me I have given to them, that they may be one, just as we are one; I in them, and you in me, that they may be made completely into one, that the world may know that you sent me and loved them just as you loved me.

"Father, those whom you have given me, I desire that where I am they also may be with me, that they may observe my glory, which you have given me, for you loved me before the foundation of the world. Righteous Father, the world did not know you, but I knew you; and these knew that you sent me, and I made known to them your name and shall make it known, that the love with which you loved me may be in them, and I in them."

Having said these things, and having sung a hymn, he went as was his custom to the Mount of Olives; so his disciples also followed him.

Then Jesus said to them, "All of you shall fall away because of me tonight, for it is written,

'I shall strike the shepherd,
and the sheep shall be scattered.'

But after I have risen, I shall go before you into Galilee."

But responding Peter said to him, "If all will fall away because of you, I will never fall away."

Jesus declared to him, "Truly I say to you, that you today, this night, before the rooster crows, will deny me three times."

But all the more Peter spoke, "Even if I must die with you, I will not deny you!" And all of the disciples said so as well.

Then Jesus went forth with his disciples across the stream of Kidron, where there was a garden named Gethsemane, into which he and his disciples entered. And he said to his disciples, "Sit here while I go there and pray."

And taking with him Peter and James and John the two sons of Zebedee, he began to be grieved and distressed. Then he said to them,

"My soul is exceedingly sorrowful, even to death. Stay here and be vigilant with me; pray that you do not enter into temptation."

And going forward a little, he was drawn away from them about a stone's throw, and falling on his knees, he prayed, saying, "Abba, My Father, all things are possible to you; if you are willing let this cup pass away from me. Yet not as I desire, but as you desire."

Now there appeared to him an angel from heaven, strengthening him. And being steeled for battle, he prayed more resolutely, and his sweat became like great drops of blood falling down upon the ground.

And having got up from his prayer, he came to the disciples and found them sleeping and he said to Peter, "Simon, are you sleeping? What, could you not be vigilant with me for one hour? Be vigilant and pray, that you may not enter into temptation; indeed the spirit is willing, but the flesh is weak."

Again a second time, having gone away, he prayed, saying, "My Father, if this cannot pass unless I drink it, your will be done."

And again returning, he found them sleeping, for their eyes were very heavy, and they did not know what to answer him.

And leaving them again, having gone away, he prayed a third time, saying the same word again.

Then he came to his disciples and said to them, "Are you still sleeping and resting? Is it far off? Behold, the hour has come, and the Son of Man is betrayed into the hands of sinners. Arise, let's go. Behold, the one betraying me is at hand!"

Straightaway while he was still speaking, behold, a great crowd, and he who was called Judas, one of the Twelve, was going ahead of them. Now Judas also knew the place for Jesus often gathered there with his disciples. Judas then, having procured the unit of soldiers and guards from the chief priests and the Pharisees and elders of the people, came there with lanterns and torches and swords and clubs.

Jesus therefore, knowing all the things that were coming upon him, went forth and said to them, "Whom do you seek?"

They answered him, "Jesus the Nazarene."

Jesus said to them, "I am he."

When therefore he said to them, "I am he," they went backward and fell to the ground.

Again therefore he asked them, "Whom do you seek?"

So they said, "Jesus the Nazarene."

Jesus answered, "I told you that I am he. Therefore if you seek me, let these men go their way,"—that might be fulfilled the word which he had spoken, "Of those whom you have given me, I lost not any of them."

Now the one betraying him had given them a sign, saying, "Whomever I will kiss, it's him. Seize him and lead him away safely." And straightaway coming to Jesus, he said, "Greetings, Rabbi" and kissed him.

So Jesus said to him, "Judas, do you betray the Son of Man with a kiss? Comrade, do what you came for."

Now those around him, seeing what was about to happen, said to him, "Lord, should we strike with the sword?"

Then coming to him, the soldiers laid hands on Jesus and seized him. And behold, Simon Peter, having a sword, drew it and struck the high priest's slave and cut off his right ear. Now the slave's name was Malchus.

But responding Jesus said, "No more of this!" And touching his ear, he healed him.

Therefore Jesus said to Peter, "Put the sword into the sheath, for all those who take the sword shall die by the sword. Or do you think that I cannot call on my Father and he shall even now send me more than twelve legions of angels? How then would the Scriptures be fulfilled that say it must be so? The cup which the Father has given me, shall I not drink it?"

Now Jesus said to those who had come against him, the chief priests and officers of the temple and elders, "Have you come out as against a bandit with swords and clubs to apprehend me? Every day I was with you in the temple teaching and you did not reach out your hands against me. Now all this has come to pass that the Scriptures of the prophets might be fulfilled, but this is your hour and the dominion of darkness."

So the unit and the commander and the guards of the Jews apprehended Jesus and bound him.

Then the disciples, all leaving him, fled. And a certain young man followed him, having a linen cloth thrown around himself over his naked body. And they seized him, but leaving behind the linen cloth, he fled naked.

Now those who had taken Jesus led him to Annas first, for he was father-in-law to Caiaphas, who was high priest that year. Now Caiaphas was the one who gave counsel to the Jews that it was better that one man should die for the people.

But following Jesus from afar were Simon Peter and the other disciple. Now that disciple was known to the high priest and entered in with Jesus into the courtyard of the high priest, but Peter stood at the door outside. So the other disciple, who was known to the high priest, went out and spoke to the doorkeeper, and brought in Peter.

Then the servant girl, the doorkeeper, staring at Peter, said to him, "You were with the Nazarene, Jesus. Aren't you also one of this man's disciples?"

But he denied it before them all, saying, "I am not. I don't know what you're talking about. I don't know him, woman."

Now the slaves and the guards were standing there, having made a charcoal fire, for it was cold, and they were warming themselves, so Peter was also with them, standing and warming himself.

Then the high priest asked Jesus about his disciples and about his teaching. Jesus answered him, "I spoke openly to the world. I always taught in the synagogue and in the temple, where the Jews always assemble, and in secret I spoke nothing. Why do you ask me? Ask those who have heard what I spoke to them. Look! They know the things that I said."

Now when he had said this, one of the guards standing by slapped Jesus, saying, "Do you answer the high priest like that?"

Jesus answered him, "If I spoke evil, bear witness of the evil; but if rightly, why do you strike me?"

Therefore Annas sent him bound to Caiaphas, the high priest, and there came together all the chief priests and the elders and the scribes.

Now Simon Peter was standing and warming himself outside in the courtyard. And the servant girl, seeing him, began again to say to those standing by, "This is one of them!" And someone else saw him and said to those who were there, "This man was with Jesus of Nazareth!"

Therefore they said to him, "Aren't you also one of his disciples?"

But Peter denied it with an oath and declared, "I am not! I don't know the man."

And after about one hour had passed one of the slaves of the high priest, being a relative of him whose ear Peter had cut off, said, "Didn't I see you in the garden with him?"

And those standing by insisted, saying to Peter, "Surely you're one of them for you are a Galilean; your accent gives you away."

Then he began to call down curses and to swear an oath, "I don't know the man you're talking about!"

And instantly while he was speaking a rooster crowed. And turning, the Lord peered at Peter, and Peter remembered the statement of the Lord, how he said to him, "Before the rooster crows this day you will deny me three times."

And going out, breaking down, he wept bitterly.

Now in the house of the high priest the chief priests and the whole council sought false witness against Jesus, that they might put him to death; and they did not find any, though many false witnesses were coming forward, and the witnesses were not consistent. But at last, two coming forward said, "This man declared, 'I will destroy this temple of God that is made with hands, and in three days I will build another made without hands.' "

And standing up in the midst, Caiaphas the high priest asked Jesus, saying, "Do you not answer anything? What is it that these men witness against you?"

But Jesus was silent and answered nothing.

Again the high priest said to him, "I demand you under oath by the living God that you tell us whether you are the Christ, the Son of the Blessed!"

Now Jesus said, "You have said it. Even so I say to you, hereafter you shall watch the Son of Man sitting at the right hand of Power and coming on the clouds of heaven."

Then the high priest tore his clothing, saying, "He has spoken blasphemy! What further need do we have for witnesses? Look! Now you have heard the blasphemy. What does it appear to you?"

So answering they all condemned him, saying, "He is deserving of death!"

Then the men who held him mocked him, beating him. And having blindfolded him, they spat in his face and punched him and others slapped him, saying, "Prophesy to us, you Christ! Who is it who hit you?" And they were saying many other blasphemous things against him.

Now when morning came, the assembly of the elders of the people were gathered together, both chief priests and scribes. And they led him away to their council, saying, "If you are the Christ, tell us!"

But he said to them, "If I tell you, you will not believe; and if I ask, you will not answer. But from now on the Son of Man shall be seated at the right hand of the Power of God."

So they all said, "Are you then the Son of God?"

And he declared to them, "You say that I am."

So they said, "What further need have we of witness? For we ourselves have heard from his own mouth!"

And all the chief priests and the elders of the people came to the decision against Jesus, to put him to death. And getting up, they carried him away and delivered him up to Pontius Pilate, the governor.

Then Judas, who betrayed him, seeing that he was condemned, having regret, brought back the thirty pieces of silver to the chief priests and elders, saying, "I have sinned in that I betrayed innocent blood."

But they said, "What is that to us? See to it yourself."

And throwing down the pieces of silver in the sanctuary, he withdrew. Then going away, he hanged himself.

But the chief priests, taking the pieces of silver, said, "It is not lawful to put them into the temple treasury, since it is the price of blood." So having taken counsel, they bought the potter's field with them to bury strangers in. Therefore that field has been called the Field of Blood to this day. Then was fulfilled that which was spoken through Jeremiah the prophet, saying, "And they took the thirty pieces of silver, the price of him upon whom a price had been set, whom the sons of Israel priced, and they gave them for the potter's field, as the Lord appointed me."

Now having bound Jesus, the whole multitude of them led him into the Praetorium. Now it was early, and they themselves did not enter into the Praetorium, that they might not be defiled, but might eat the Passover. Therefore Pilate went out to them and declared, "What accusation do you bring against this man?"

They answered and said to him, "If this man weren't doing evil we wouldn't have delivered him to you." So they began to accuse him, saying, "We found this man perverting the nation, and forbidding to give tribute to Caesar, and saying that he himself is Christ, a king."

Pilate therefore said to them, "Take him yourselves and judge him according to your law."

The Jews said to him, "It's not lawful for us to put anyone to death,"—that the word of Jesus might be fulfilled which he had spoken, signifying by what manner of death he was about to die.

Therefore Pilate entered again into the Praetorium and called Jesus and questioned him, saying, "Are you the King of the Jews?"

Jesus answered, "So you say. From yourself do you say this, or did others say it to you about me?"

Pilate answered, "I'm not a Jew, am I? Your own nation and the chief priests delivered you to me. What have you done?"

Jesus answered, "My kingdom is not of this world. If my kingdom were of this world, then my assistants would fight, that I would not be delivered to the Jews. But now my kingdom is not from here."

Therefore Pilate said to him, "Then you are a king?"

Jesus answered, "You say that I am a king. For this I have been born, and for this I have come into the world, that I should bear witness to the truth. Everyone who is of the truth hears my voice."

Pilate said to him, "What is truth?"

And having said this, he went out again to the Jews and said to them, "I find no guilt in this man."

And the chief priests accused him of many things, and he answered nothing.

So Pilate again asked him, saying, "Do you not answer anything? Look how many things they accuse you of!"

But Jesus gave him no answer, not even to one statement, so that the governor marveled greatly.

Now they were persisting, saying, "He stirs up the people, teaching throughout all Judea, and he has begun from Galilee even to this place."

So hearing this, Pilate asked if the man was a Galilean. And learning that he was from Herod's jurisdiction, he sent him to Herod, he also being in Jerusalem in those days.

Now seeing Jesus, Herod rejoiced greatly, for he had desired to see him for a long time, because he had heard about him and was hoping to see some sign done by him. So he questioned him in many words; but he answered him nothing. So the chief priests and the scribes stood, vehemently accusing him. And humiliating him with his soldiers and mocking him, clothing him in splendid apparel, Herod sent him back to Pilate. Now both Herod and Pilate became friends with each other that same day, for before they had hostility between themselves.

Now Pilate, having called together the chief priests and the rulers and the people, said to them, "You brought to me this man as perverting the people, and behold, having examined him before you, I found in this man nothing guilty regarding that which you accuse him. Neither has Herod, for he sent him back to us. And behold, nothing worthy of death has been done by him. Therefore after flogging him, I will free him."

Now at the feast the governor was accustomed to free to the crowd one prisoner, whomever they desired. And they had then a notable prisoner called Barabbas, bound with his fellow insurgents who in the insurrection in the city had committed murder. So they all screamed together, saying, "Away with this man! But free to us Barabbas! Not this one, but Barabbas!"

But again Pilate called to them, desiring to free Jesus, saying, "Whom do you desire me to free to you? Barabbas, or Jesus, the King of the Jews?"—for he knew that because of envy the chief priests had delivered him up.

Now while he was sitting on the judgment seat, his wife sent to him, saying, "Have nothing to do with that righteous man, for I have suffered many things this day in a dream because of him."

But the chief priests and the elders stirred up the crowd, that he should instead free Barabbas to them and have Jesus destroyed. Now responding the governor said to them, "Which of the two do you desire me to free to you?"

So they said, "Barabbas!"

Pilate said to them, "What then should I do to him whom you call the King of the Jews?"

But they all cried back, "Crucify! Crucify him! Let him be crucified!"

So Pilate declared to them, "Why? What evil has this man done? I have found no guilt in him. Therefore after flogging him, I will free him."

But even more they cried out, saying, "Crucify him! Let him be crucified!"

So they were insistent, with loud voices requesting that he be crucified, and their voices prevailed.

Now Pilate, seeing that he accomplished nothing, but rather that an uproar was starting, took water and washed his hands before the crowd, saying, "I am innocent of the blood of this righteous person. You see to it."

And responding all the people said, "His blood be on us and on our children!"

So wishing to satisfy the crowd, Pilate gave sentence that what they demanded would be done. Then he freed him who had been cast into prison for revolt and murder, whom they requested, but Jesus he delivered up to their will.

So then the soldiers of the governor, taking Jesus into the courtyard, which is the Praetorium, gathered before him the whole unit. And stripping him, scourged him. And the soldiers clothed him in a scarlet robe, and twisting together a crown of thorns, put it on his head and a staff in his right hand. And they came to him and began to greet him, "Hail, King of the Jews!" And spitting on him, they took the staff and kept striking him in the head, and they slapped him, and dropping to their knees, worshiped him.

And Pilate went out again and said to them, "Look! I bring him out to you, that you may know that I find no guilt in him."

Jesus therefore came out wearing the crown of thorns and the scarlet robe. Pilate said to them, "Behold, the man!"

Therefore when the chief priests and the guards saw him, they shouted, saying, "Crucify! Crucify!"

Pilate said to them, "Take him yourselves and crucify him, for I find in him no guilt."

The Jews answered him, "We have a law, and according to the Law he ought to die, because he made himself the Son of God."

Therefore when Pilate heard this word, he was even more afraid, and he entered into the Praetorium again and said to Jesus, "Where are you from?"

But Jesus gave him no answer.

Pilate therefore said to him, "You won't speak to me? Don't you know that I have the authority to free you, and I have the authority to crucify you?"

Jesus answered him, "You would not have any authority against me unless it were given to you from above. For this reason the one who delivered me to you has greater sin."

Upon this Pilate sought to free him, but the Jews shouted, saying, "If you free this man, you aren't a friend of Caesar! Everyone who makes himself a king opposes Caesar!"

Therefore Pilate, having heard these words, brought out Jesus and sat down on the judgment seat at a place called the Pavement, but in Aramaic, Gabbatha. Now it was the Preparation Day of the Passover. And he said to the Jews, "Look, your King!"

They therefore shouted, "Away with him! Away with him! Crucify him!"

Pilate said to them, "Shall I crucify your King?"

The chief priests answered, "We have no king but Caesar!"

So then he delivered him to them to be crucified. And they took the robe off him, and put his own clothes on him, and led him out to crucify him.

And as they led him away, laying hold of one Simon of Cyrene coming from the countryside, they compelled him to go with them, that he might bear his cross, to carry it behind Jesus.

Now there followed him a great multitude of the people, including women who were mourning and lamenting him. But turning to them Jesus said, "Daughters of Jerusalem, do not weep for me, yet weep for yourselves and for your children. For behold, the days are coming in which they shall say, 'Blessed are the barren, and the wombs that never bore, and the breasts that never nursed!' Then they shall begin to say to the mountains, 'Fall on us!' and to the hills, 'Cover us!' For if they do these things in the green tree, what shall happen in the dry?"

Now there were also others, two criminals, led with him to be put to death. And they brought him to the place Golgotha, which is, being interpreted, Place of a Skull. And they gave him wine to drink mixed with gall; and tasting it, he would not drink.

Now they crucified him, and with him the two criminals, one on his right and one on his left, and Jesus in the middle. But Jesus said, "Father, forgive them, for they do not know what they do!"

And Pilate also wrote a title and put it on the cross over his head, and there was written,

THIS IS JESUS OF NAZARETH
THE KING OF THE JEWS

Therefore many of the Jews read this title, for the place where Jesus was crucified was near the city; and it was written in Aramaic, in Latin, in Greek. The chief priests of the Jews therefore said to Pilate, "Don't write, 'The King of the Jews,' but, 'He said, I am King of the Jews.' "

Pilate answered, "What I have written I have written."

Then the soldiers, when they had crucified Jesus, took his clothing and made four parts, to every soldier a part; and also the tunic. Now the tunic was without seam, woven from the top throughout; therefore they said to one another, "Let's not tear it, but cast lots for it, whose will it be," that the Scripture might be fulfilled which says,

"They parted my clothing among them,
and for my apparel they cast lots."

Therefore the soldiers did these things, and sitting down, they kept guard over him there. Now it was the third hour when they crucified him, and the people stood observing.

And those passing by spoke blasphemies at him, shaking their heads and saying, "Ha! You who destroy the temple and build it in three days, save yourself! If you are the Son of God, come down from the cross!"

Likewise also the chief priests, mocking among themselves with the scribes and the elders, sneering at him said, "He saved others, let him save himself if this is the Christ of God, the Chosen One! He's the King of Israel, let him come down from the cross now and we will see and believe in him. He trusts in God, let God deliver him now if he wants him; for he said, 'I am the Son of God.' "

So the soldiers also mocked him, coming near, offering him vinegar and saying, "If you're the King of the Jews, save yourself!"

Now one of the criminals who were hanged blasphemed him, saying, "Aren't you the Christ? Save yourself and us!"

But responding, the other one was rebuking him, declaring, "Don't you even fear God, since you're under the same condemnation? And we indeed justly, for we receive the due reward of what we did, but this man has done nothing wrong." And he said "Jesus, remember me when you come into your kingdom!"

And he said to him, "Truly to you I say, this day you shall be with me in Paradise."

Now standing by the cross of Jesus were his mother, his mother's sister, Mary the wife of Clopas, and Mary Magdalene. Jesus therefore, seeing his mother and the disciple whom he loved standing there, said to his mother, "Woman, look, your son!" Then he said to the disciple, "Look, your mother!" And from that hour the disciple took her to his own home.

Now it was now about the sixth hour, and darkness came over the whole land until the ninth hour, the sun failing.

And about the ninth hour Jesus exclaimed with a loud voice, saying, "Eloi, Eloi, lama sabachthani?" which is, being interpreted, "My God, my God, why have you forsaken me?" After this, knowing that all things were now accomplished, that the Scripture would be completed, Jesus said, "I thirst."

But some of those who were standing there, hearing it, said, "Look! This man calls Elijah."

A vessel full of vinegar had been set there, so straightaway one of them running and taking a sponge, filling it with vinegar and putting it on a hyssop stalk, brought it to his mouth and gave him a drink. But the rest said, "Let him be. Let's see if Elijah comes to save him."

Then when Jesus had received the vinegar, he said, "It is accomplished." And calling out with a loud voice, Jesus said, "Father, into your hands I commit my spirit!"

Now having said this, lowering his head, he breathed his last, and delivered up his spirit.

And behold, the veil of the temple was torn in two from top to bottom, and the earth trembled and the rocks were split and the tombs were opened. And many bodies of the saints who had fallen asleep were raised, and coming out of the tombs after his resurrection, they entered into the holy city and were manifested to many.

So the centurion and those who were with him keeping guard over Jesus, having seen the earthquake and the things that had come to pass, were exceedingly afraid and glorified God, saying, "Certainly this man was righteous!"

And all the crowds that came together to this sight, having observed the things that had come to pass, returned beating their chests.

Now all those who knew him stood afar off, watching these things. And many women were there observing, among whom were both Mary Magdalene and Mary the mother of James the younger and of Joses and the mother of the sons of Zebedee and Salome, who, when he was in Galilee, followed him and served him; and many other women who came up with him to Jerusalem.

Then the Jews, since it was the Preparation Day, that the bodies would not remain on the cross on the Sabbath—for that Sabbath was a special one—urged Pilate that their legs might be broken and that they might be taken away. Therefore the soldiers came and broke the legs of the first and of the other who was crucified with him; but coming to Jesus, since they saw that he was already dead, they did not break his legs. But one of the soldiers pierced his side with a spear, and immediately came out blood and water.

These things came to pass that the Scripture might be fulfilled, "A bone of him shall not be broken." And again another Scripture says, "They shall watch him whom they pierced."

Now when evening came, there came a rich man from Arimathaea named Joseph, a respected council member, a good and righteous man —he had not consented to their plan and deed—who was waiting for the Kingdom of God, and who was himself also discipled by Jesus, but secretly for fear of the Jews. He boldly went in to Pilate and requested that he might take away the body of Jesus. So Pilate marveled that he was already dead; and summoning the centurion, he asked him whether he had been dead long. And learning it from the centurion, he granted the corpse to Joseph.

Now also came Nicodemus—the one who came to Jesus by night at first—bringing a mixture of myrrh and aloes, about seventy-five pounds. So they took the body of Jesus down and bound it in linen cloths with the spices, as the custom of the Jews is to bury. Now in the place where he was crucified there was a garden, and in the garden Joseph had his own new tomb where no one was yet laid, which he had hewn out of the rock. There then, because it was the Preparation Day of the Jews and the Sabbath was approaching, for the tomb was near, they laid Jesus. And rolling a great stone to the entrance of the tomb, Joseph went away.

So having followed after, the women who had come with him out of Galilee gazed upon the tomb, and how his body was laid. Now having returned, they prepared spices and fragrant oil. And on the Sabbath they rested according to the commandment.

Now on the next day, which was after the Preparation Day, the chief priests and the Pharisees were gathered together before Pilate, saying, "Sir, we remember what that deceiver said while he was still alive: 'After three days I will rise.' Therefore order that the tomb be secured until the third day, lest perhaps his disciples come and steal him away and tell the people, 'He is risen from the dead;' and the last deception will be worse than the first."

Pilate declared to them, "Take some troops; go, make it as secure as you know how." So going with the troops, they made the tomb secure, sealing the stone.

Now after the Sabbath, as it began to dawn on the first of the week, Mary Magdalene and Mary the mother of James and Salome bought spices, that they might come and anoint him.

And behold, there was a great earthquake, for an angel of the Lord, having descended out of heaven, and having come, rolled away the stone from the door and was sitting upon it. Now his appearance was like lightning and his clothing white as snow, and for fear of him those keeping guard trembled and became like dead men.

Now Mary Magdalene went early, while it was still dark, to the tomb and saw the stone taken away from the tomb. Therefore she ran and came to Simon Peter and to the other disciple whom Jesus loved and said to them, "They have taken away the Lord out of the tomb, and we don't know where they have laid him!"

Therefore Peter and the other disciple went forth and they went toward the tomb.

Now at early dawn, the other women came to the tomb, bringing the spices which they had prepared; the sun having risen. And they were saying among themselves, "Who will roll away the stone from the door of the tomb for us?" And looking up, they observed that the stone was rolled back—it was extremely large.

So entering in, they did not find the body of the Lord Jesus. And it came to pass, while they were perplexed about this, that behold, two men stood by them in white robes of lightning. So they were greatly amazed and they became frightened and lowered their faces down to the earth.

They said to them, "Why do you seek the living among the dead? Fear not, for I know that you seek Jesus the Nazarene, who has been crucified. He is not here, he is risen! Look! The place where they laid him. Remember how he spoke to you when he was still in Galilee, saying that the Son of Man must be delivered up into the hands of sinful men, and be crucified, and the third day be raised? But going quickly, say to his disciples and Peter, 'He has risen from the dead! And behold, he goes before you into Galilee; there shall you see him, as he said to you.' Behold, I have told you." And they remembered his sayings.

And going forth quickly, they fled from the tomb, for trembling and astonishment had gripped them. And they said nothing to anyone, for they were afraid. And with fear and great joy they ran to inform his disciples.

And behold, Jesus met them, saying, "Greetings!"

So coming to him, they took hold of his feet and worshiped him.

Then Jesus said to them, "Fear not. Go inform my brothers that they go into Galilee, and there they shall see me."

And returning from the tomb, they reported all these things to the Eleven and to all the rest. Now they were Joanna and Mary the mother of James and the rest with them telling the apostles these things. And their sayings appeared before them to be nonsense, and they disbelieved them.

Now while they were going, behold, some of the troops going into the city informed the chief priests of all the things that had happened. And being gathered with the elders and taking counsel, they gave much silver to the soldiers, saying, "Say that his disciples came by night and stole him away while we slept. And if this comes to the governor's ears, we will persuade him and free you of worry."

So taking the silver, they did as they were decreed; and this story is circulated among the Jews to this day.

Now Peter and the other disciple ran together, and the other disciple ran ahead faster than Peter, and came to the tomb first; and stooping down, he saw lying there the linen cloths, yet he did not enter. Then Simon Peter also came, following him, and entered into the tomb, and he observed the linen cloths lying, and the cloth that had been on his head not lying with the linen cloths, but rolled up in a place by itself. So then also the other disciple who came first to the tomb entered, and he saw and believed. For as yet they did not know the Scripture, that he must rise from the dead. So the disciples went away again to their own homes, marveling at what had come to pass.

But Mary stood outside the tomb weeping. Yet as she wept, she stooped and looked into the tomb, and she observed two angels in white sitting, one at the head and one at the feet, where the body of Jesus had lain. And they said to her, "Woman, why do you weep?"

She said to them, "Because they have taken away my Lord and I don't know where they have laid him." When she had said this, she turned around and observed Jesus standing and did not know that it was Jesus.

Jesus said to her, "Woman, why do you weep? Whom do you seek?"

Thinking that it was the gardener, she said to him, "Sir, if you have carried him away, tell me where you have laid him and I will take him away."

Jesus said to her, "Mary!"

She turned and said to him, "Rabboni!" which is to say, "Teacher!"

Jesus said to her, "Do not cling to me, for I have not yet ascended to the Father. But go to my brothers and say to them, 'I am ascending to my Father and your Father, and my God and your God.' "

Mary Magdalene came, informing the disciples, "I have watched the Lord!" and that he had said these things to her.

Now behold, two disciples were going on the same day to a village named Emmaus, which was about seven miles from Jerusalem. And they were talking with each other about all of these things which had taken place. And it came to pass, while they were talking and debating, that Jesus himself, drawing near, went with them; but their eyes were kept from recognizing him. Now he said to them, "What words are these that you exchange with one another as you walk?" And they came to a stop, looking downcast.

So answering the one named Cleopas said to him, "Are you the only one visiting Jerusalem that doesn't know the things that have happened there in these days?"

And he said to them, "What things?"

So they said to him, "The things about Jesus the Nazarene, who was a man, a prophet, mighty in deed and word before God and all the people, and how the chief priests and our rulers delivered him up to be condemned to death and crucified him. But we were hoping that it was he who was about to redeem Israel. And besides all these things, it's now the third day since these things happened, but also some women of ours amazed us, having been early at the tomb; and when they didn't find his body, they came saying that they had also seen a vision of angels, who said that he's alive. And some of those with us went to the tomb and found it just like the women had said, but they didn't see him."

And he said to them, "O foolish and slow of heart to believe in all that the Prophets have spoken! Was it not necessary for the Christ to suffer these things and to enter into his glory?" And beginning from Moses and from all the Prophets, he interpreted to them in all the Scriptures the things concerning himself.

And they drew near to the village where they were going, and he acted as though he was going further. And they compelled him, saying, "Stay with us for it's afternoon and sunset is approaching" And he went in to stay with them.

And it came to pass, as he was reclining at the table with them, having taken the bread, he blessed; and having broken it, he gave it to them. Now their eyes were opened and they recognized him. And he vanished out of their sight.

And they said to one another, "Weren't our hearts burning within us while he spoke to us along the way, while he was opening the Scriptures to us?"

And getting up that same hour, they returned to Jerusalem, and found the Eleven gathered together and those with them, saying, "The Lord is risen really and has appeared to Simon!" And they disclosed the things that happened along the road, and how he was recognized by them in the breaking of the bread.

Then when it was evening on that day, the first of the week, and when the doors were locked where the disciples were for fear of the Jews, Jesus came and stood in their midst and said to them, "Peace to you."

But being afraid and filled with fear, they thought that they observed a spirit.

And he said to them, "Why are you troubled? Why do doubts come up in your hearts? See my hands and my feet, that I am he. Touch me and see, for a spirit does not have flesh and bones as you observe that I have."

And having said this, he showed them his hands and his feet and his side. But while they still disbelieved for the joy and marveled, he said to them, "Have you anything to eat here?"

So they gave him a piece of a broiled fish, and taking it, he ate before them.

Therefore the disciples rejoiced, having seen the Lord. Jesus therefore said to them again, "Peace to you. As the Father has sent me, I also send you." And having said this, he blew and said to them, "Receive the Holy Spirit. If you forgive the sins of anyone, they are forgiven them; if you retain the sins of anyone, they are retained."

But Thomas, one of the Twelve, called Didymus, was not with them when Jesus came. The other disciples therefore said to him, "We have watched the Lord!"

But he said to them, "Unless I see in his hands the print of the nails and put my finger into the print of the nails and put my hand into his side, I will not believe."

And after eight days, again his disciples were inside and Thomas was with them. Jesus came, the doors being locked, and stood in their midst and said, "Peace to you." Then he said to Thomas, "Reach here your finger, and see my hands, and reach your hand and put it into my side; and be not unbelieving, but believing."

Thomas answered and said to him, "My Lord and my God!"

Jesus said to him, "Because you have watched me, you have believed. Blessed are those who have not seen yet have believed."

After these things Jesus made himself visible again to the disciples at the sea of Tiberias. Now he was made visible in this way: There were together Simon Peter and Thomas, called Didymus, and Nathanael of Cana in Galilee and the sons of Zebedee and two others of his disciples. Simon Peter said to them, "I'm going fishing."

They said to him, "We're also coming with you."

They went forth and entered into the boat, and that night they caught nothing.

Now when morning had already come, Jesus stood on the beach, yet the disciples did not know that it was Jesus. Therefore Jesus said to them, "Children, do you have anything to eat?"

They answered him, "No."

So he said to them, "Cast the net on the right side of the boat and you will find some."

Therefore they cast, and now they were not able to draw it in for the multitude of fish. So that disciple whom Jesus loved said to Peter, "It's the Lord!"

Therefore Simon Peter, hearing that it was the Lord, wrapped his coat around himself, for he was naked, and cast himself into the sea. But the other disciples came in the little boat, for they were not far from the land but about one hundred yards away, dragging the net of fish. So when they got out on the land, they saw a charcoal fire there, with fish and bread lying on it.

Jesus said to them, "Bring some of the fish which you have caught now."

Simon Peter therefore went up and drew the net to land, full of large fish, one hundred fifty-three, and though there were so many, the net was not torn.

Jesus said to them, "Come have breakfast."

But none of the disciples dared inquire of him, "Who are you?" knowing that it was the Lord.

Jesus came and took the bread and gave it to them, and the fish likewise. This was now the third time that Jesus was visible to his disciples after being raised from the dead.

So when they had eaten breakfast, Jesus said to Simon Peter, "Simon son of John, do you love me more than these?"

He said to him, "Yes, Lord. You know that I love you."

He said to him, "Feed my lambs." He said to him again a second time, "Simon son of John, do you love me?"

He said to him, "Yes, Lord. You know that I love you."

He said to him, "Shepherd my sheep." He said to him the third time, "Simon son of John, do you love me?"

Peter was grieved because he said to him the third time, "Do you love me?" He said to him, "Lord, you know everything! You know that I love you."

Jesus said to him, "Feed my sheep. Truly, truly, I say to you, when you were young, you tied your belt yourself and walked where you desired, but when you shall be old, you shall reach out your hands, and another shall tie you and carry you where you do not desire."

Now this he said, signifying by what kind of death he would glorify God. And having said this, he said to him, "Follow me."

Turning around, Peter saw the disciple whom Jesus loved following, who had also leaned on his chest at the supper and said, "Lord, who is it who is betraying you?" Therefore seeing him, Peter said to Jesus, "Lord, now what about this man?"

Jesus said to him, "If I desire him to remain till I come, what is that to you? You follow me." Therefore this word went out among the brothers, that this disciple would not die. Yet Jesus did not say to him that he would not die, but, "If I desire him to remain till I come, what is that to you?"

Now the eleven disciples went into Galilee, to the mountain where Jesus had arranged for them. And when they saw him, they worshiped him; but some doubted. And coming to them, Jesus spoke to them, saying, "All authority has been given to me in heaven and on earth. Therefore go disciple all the nations, baptizing them into the name of the Father and of the Son and of the Holy Spirit, teaching them to keep all things, whatever I commanded you. And behold, I am with you all the days, even to the end of the age."

Now Jesus presented himself alive after his suffering by many proofs to the apostles whom he had chosen, appearing to them over a period of forty days. And being assembled together with them, he said to them, "These are my words that I spoke to you while I was still with you, that all things must be fulfilled which are written in the Law of Moses and the Prophets and the Psalms about me."

Then he opened their minds to understand the Scriptures, and said to them, "Thus it is written, that the Christ was to suffer and to rise from the dead the third day, and that repentance and remission of sins should be proclaimed in his name to all the nations. Beginning from Jerusalem, you are witnesses of these things. And behold, I am sending the promise of my Father upon you which you heard from me; for John indeed baptized with water, but you shall be baptized in the Holy Spirit not many days from now. But stay in the city till you are clothed with power from on high."

Therefore when they had come together, they asked him, "Lord, are you now restoring the kingdom to Israel?"

But he said to them, "It is not for you to know times or seasons which the Father has set within his own authority. But you shall receive power when the Holy Spirit has come upon you, and you shall be my witnesses both in Jerusalem and in all Judea and Samaria, and to the ends of the earth."

Now he led them out as far as Bethany. And lifting up his hands, he blessed them. And it came to pass, while he blessed them, he parted from them, and a cloud received him out of their sight, and was carried up into heaven.

While they were staring into the sky as he went, behold, two men stood by them in white apparel, who also said, "You men of Galilee, why do you stand looking into the sky? This Jesus, who was taken up from you into heaven, shall come back in the same way as you gazed upon him going into heaven."

Then they returned to Jerusalem from the Mount of Olives, which is near Jerusalem, a Sabbath day's journey away. And when they had come in, they went up into the upper room where they were staying: Peter and John and James and Andrew, Philip and Thomas, Bartholomew and Matthew, James the son of Alphaeus and Simon the Zealot and Judas the son of James. These all with one accord continued steadfastly in prayer, with the women and Mary the mother of Jesus and with his brothers.

And in these days, standing up in the midst of the brethren—the number of names was about one hundred twenty—Peter said, "Men, brothers, it was necessary that the Scripture should be fulfilled, which the Holy Spirit spoke before by the mouth of David concerning Judas, who was guide to those who took Jesus. For he was counted among us, and was allotted a share in this ministry. For it is written in the book of Psalms,

> 'Let his habitation become desolate,
> and let no one dwell in it;'

and,

> 'Let another take his office.'

Therefore, of the men who have accompanied us all the time that the Lord Jesus went in and out among us, beginning from the baptism of John to the day that he was taken up from us, of these must one become a witness with us of his resurrection."

And they put forward two: Joseph called Barsabbas, who was known as Justus, and Matthias. And praying they said, "You, Lord, who know the hearts of all, show which one of these two you have chosen to take part in this ministry and apostleship from which Judas turned aside to go to his own place."

And they cast lots for them, and the lot fell to Matthias, and he was counted with the eleven apostles.

When the day of Pentecost had arrived, they were all together in one place. And suddenly there came from heaven a sound like the rushing of a mighty wind, and it filled all the house where they were sitting. And there appeared to them tongues like fire, divided and resting upon each one of them; and they were all filled with the Holy Spirit and began to speak with other tongues, as the Spirit gave them utterance.

Now there were dwelling in Jerusalem Jews, devout men from every nation under heaven. So when this sound was heard, the multitude came together and were bewildered because each one heard them speaking in his own language. So they were all amazed and marveled, saying, "Behold, aren't all these who speak Galileans? And how do we hear, each of us in our own native language? Parthians and Medes and Elamites and those living in Mesopotamia, Judea and Cappadocia, in Pontus and Asia, in Phrygia and Pamphylia, in Egypt and the parts of Libya around Cyrene, and visitors from Rome, both Jews and proselytes, Cretans and Arabians—we hear them speaking in our tongues the great works of God!"

So they were all amazed and perplexed, saying to one another, "What does this mean?" But others, mocking, said, "They're full of new wine!"

Now Peter, standing up with the Eleven, lifted up his voice and spoke forth to them, "Men of Judea, and all who dwell in Jerusalem, let this be known to you, and give ear to my words. For these people aren't drunk as you suppose, since it's only the third hour of the day. But this is what was spoken through the prophet Joel:

'And it shall be in the last days, says God,
    I shall pour out my Spirit upon all flesh;
and your sons and your daughters shall prophesy,
    and your young men shall see visions,
    and your old men shall dream dreams.
Yes, and upon my slaves and upon my bondmaids in those days,
    I shall pour out my Spirit, and they shall prophesy;

and I shall show wonders in heaven above,
and signs on the earth beneath:
blood and fire and billows of smoke.
The sun shall be turned into darkness,
and the moon into blood,
before the great and glorious day of the Lord comes.
And it shall be that whoever shall call on the name of the Lord shall be saved.'

"Men of Israel, hear these words! Jesus of Nazareth, a man attested by God to you by mighty works and wonders and signs which God did through him in the midst of you, as you yourselves know, this one, being delivered up by the determined plan and foreknowledge of God, you have crucified and killed by the hand of lawless men; whom God raised up, having released him from the agony of death, because it was not possible that he should be held by it. For David says of him,

'I foresaw the Lord always before me,
for he is at my right hand, that I should not be shaken;
because of this my heart was glad and my tongue was jubilant,
moreover my flesh also will dwell in hope;
because you will not leave my soul to Hades,
nor will you allow your Holy One to see decay.
You made known to me the ways of life,
you will make me full of gladness with your presence.'

"Men, brothers, I can say to you freely of the patriarch David that he both died and was buried, and his tomb is with us to this day. Therefore, being a prophet and knowing that God had sworn with an oath to him that he would set one of his descendants upon his throne, foreseeing this, he spoke about the resurrection of the Christ, that neither was he left in Hades, nor did his flesh see decay. This Jesus God raised up, to which we all are witnesses. Therefore, being exalted to the right hand of God and having received from the Father the promise of the Holy Spirit, he has poured out this which you both see and hear. For David didn't ascend into the heavens, but he says himself,

'The Lord said to my Lord:
"Sit by my right hand,
till I place your enemies as a footstool of your feet." '

Therefore, let all the house of Israel know for certain that God has made him both Lord and Christ, this Jesus whom you crucified."

Now when they heard this, they were cut to the heart and said to Peter and the rest of the apostles, "Men, brothers, what should we do?"

So Peter said to them, "Repent and be baptized, every one of you, in the name of Jesus Christ for the forgiveness of sins, and you will receive the gift of the Holy Spirit. For to you is the promise, and to your children and to all who are far off, as many as the Lord our God will call to himself." And with many other words he testified and exhorted them, saying, "Save yourselves from this crooked generation!"

Then those who received his word were baptized, and there were added that day about three thousand souls.

Now they continued steadfastly in the apostles' teaching and fellowship, in the breaking of bread, and prayers. So fear came upon every soul, and many wonders and signs were done through the apostles. So all who believed were together and had all things in common, and they sold their possessions and goods and distributed them to all, as anyone had need. And every day, continuing steadfastly with one accord in the temple, and breaking bread at home, they partook of food with exultation and sincerity of heart, praising God, and having favor with all the people. So the Lord added to their number every day those who were being saved.

How can I be saved?

The gospels provide a beautiful portrait of the life and ministry of Jesus Christ. We see him healing the sick, treating the downtrodden with love and compassion, and teaching great moral lessons. Yet these were not the primary reasons for his earthly mission. Jesus' ultimate objective was to reconcile us back to God. Because of our sins, both towards God and toward others, we are separated from God, and this separation results in death. Jesus came to free us from sin which will release us from the grip of death: "For God so loved the world that he gave his only begotten Son, that whoever believes in him should not perish, but have eternal life" (John 3:16, page 21).

So how can you be saved and receive eternal life? First, you must admit that you are a sinner in need of forgiveness and repent to God. Second, you must confess that Jesus is Lord, that he died for you, and that he rose from the grave. Third, you must leave your old life of sin behind and begin a new life as a follower of Jesus. When you do these, God will welcome you with open arms, regardless of who you are or what you've done in the past: "There is neither Jew nor Greek, there is neither slave nor free, there is no male and female; for you all are one in Christ Jesus" (Galatians 3:28).

Being a disciple of Jesus Christ is more than merely going to church once a week, celebrating particular holidays, or performing certain rituals. It is first and foremost about doing the will of God, giving him your whole heart, and turning all areas of your life over to him. When you do so, you will find new peace and joy, and receive eternal salvation: "Truly I say to you, there is no one who has left house or wife or brothers or parents or children for the Kingdom of God's sake who shall not receive manifold more in this time, and in the age to come, eternal life" (Luke 18:29-30, page 106).

Who is Jesus?

Throughout his ministry Jesus used a variety of "I Am" sayings to vividly describe who he was and what his relationship was to God and to mankind.

"I am the Bread of Life"
Jesus is the spiritual sustenance that forever satisfies our deepest hunger and provides eternal life.
John 6:35, page 63

"I am the Light of the World"
Jesus is the illumination needed to navigate our world properly and know the will of God.
John 8:12, page 71; John 9:5, page 74

"I am the Gate of the Sheep"
Jesus is the only access to the Kingdom of God and a full, abundant life.
John 10:7, page 76

"I am the Good Shepherd"
Jesus is the loving, selfless leader who knows his followers personally and willingly gives up his own life to spare them from destruction.
John 10:11, page 76

"I am the Resurrection and the Life"
Jesus' resurrection from the dead and return to life ensures that his followers will also be resurrected and live forever.
John 11:25, page 78

"I am the Way and the Truth and the Life"
Jesus is our exclusive path to the Father because he is the ultimate truth and the creator and sustainer of all life.
John 14:6, page 133

"I am the True Vine"
Jesus is the means by which our lives bring forth good fruit.
John 15:1, page 134

What is Christianity?

The four gospels furnish us with a detailed portrayal of Jesus Christ's earthly life, but they don't provide the complete picture of God's plan for us. The rest of the Bible supplies the information necessary to understand why Jesus came to earth, why he died, and why it is so important for us to follow him. This section will provide a basic overview of the Christian faith and explain why it's critical for us to become disciples of Christ. It will also give you the foundation for further study and contemplation.

What is God like?

God is the supreme being who created and rules over the entire universe. God is spirit (John 4:24, page 23) which means he does not have a physical body (Luke 24:39, page 156). He is the one and only God: "I am Jehovah, and there is none else; besides me there is no god" (Isaiah 45:5; "Jehovah" is the personal name of God, often written as "Yahweh"; most Bible translations replace it with "the LORD" following Jewish practice). God has existed forever: "Even from everlasting to everlasting, you are God" (Psalm 90:2). God is not part of the universe: "the highest heavens cannot contain Him" (2 Chronicles 2:6). Yet he is present everywhere: " 'Can any hide himself in secret places so that I shall not see him?' says Jehovah. 'Do I not fill heaven and earth?' " (Jeremiah 23:24).

God does not experience time as we do: "one day is with the Lord as a thousand years, and a thousand years as one day" (2 Peter 3:8). This is because time is part of the universe he created. Rather, God "inhabits eternity" (Isaiah 57:15) so he sees the entire span of history at once just as he is aware of every place in the world at once. This is why we can have free will and God can still know our future.

God is perfect (Matt 5:48, page 29) and everything he does is right: "His work is perfect, for all his ways are justice" (Deuteronomy 32:4). God is love (1 John 4:8) and so he is not distant or detached, merely letting the universe unwind in clockwork fashion. On the contrary, he cares for us deeply: "you, O Lord, are a merciful and gracious God, slow to anger, and abundant in lovingkindness and truth" (Psalm 86:15). Out of this love he provides for us: "Perceive the ravens, that they do not sow nor reap, which have no storehouse or barn, and God feeds them. How much more valuable are you than birds?" (Luke 12:24, page 94).

Psalm 145 beautifully captures his wonderful nature:

Great is Jehovah, and greatly to be praised;
  and his greatness is unsearchable.
Jehovah is good to all;
  and his tender mercies are over all his works.
All your works shall give thanks unto you, O Jehovah;
  and your saints shall bless you.
They shall speak of the glory of your kingdom,
  and talk of your power;

To make known to the sons of men his mighty acts,
and the glory of the majesty of his kingdom.
Your kingdom is an everlasting kingdom,
and your dominion endures throughout all generations.
Jehovah upholds all that fall,
and raises up all those that are bowed down.
The eyes of all wait for you;
and you give them their food in due season.
You open your hand,
and satisfy the desire of every living thing.
Jehovah is righteous in all his ways,
and gracious in all his works.
Jehovah is near unto all them that call upon him,
to all that call upon him in truth.
He will fulfil the desire of them that fear him;
he also will hear their cry and will save them.
(verses 3, 9-19)

What is the Trinity?

One of the greatest truths that God has revealed to us is that while he is one, single, indivisible being, he is nonetheless three distinct persons: the Father, the Son (Jesus), and the Holy Spirit. These three persons share the same essence and have the same will, and they are each fully God with the same attributes. Together they created the universe and carry out their divine plan for us.

This tri-unity, or Trinity, is mystifying. It is so contrary to our expectations that over time many have claimed that it's untrue. Yet it absolutely must be true. This is because, as described previously, one of God's fundamental qualities is that he is loving. Now love is something directed outward toward others, yet who did God have to love before he created anything? The answer is provided by the Trinity: the Father and the Son and the Holy Spirit loved each other, and they have done so for all eternity. If this were not the case, then there would have been a time when God had no love which would mean that love is not actually a trait of God.

For a more thorough explanation and biblical proof of the Trinity, see page 186.

What is Creation?

The first two chapters of the first book of the Bible, Genesis, succinctly lay out how God created the universe and everything in it. This creation was deliberate and orderly, contrary to so many ancient myths where the world and its inhabitants are an accident or the result of a messy process of trial and error. These chapters inform us that the universe was created out of nothing instead of being a rearrangement of existing matter (see also Hebrews 11:3: "the worlds were prepared by the word of God, so that what is seen was not made out of things which are visible").

Further, we see that humanity is the pinnacle of creation. First and foremost, we are made in the image and likeness of God. This doesn't refer to our physical appearance since God does not have a body. Rather, it refers to attributes that God possesses such as intelligence, reason, love, creativity, morality, and authority as well as others. Additionally, God tasked us with ruling over the world, a unique responsibility that solely belongs to people.

Genesis also reveals that the original creation was perfect. God repeatedly declared that what he made was "good", and when he was finished he said that the entire creation was "very good". Since disease, suffering, and death are not good, people and animals were not to experience any of these. We were to live forever in harmony with God, each other, and the animals. Indeed, people and animals were to only eat plants.

What is the Fall?

After God had finished with creation, he placed the first two people, Adam and Eve, in a lush garden where they could live in peace and effortlessly collect all of the food they would need. God gave them only one prohibition, that they did not eat from the Tree of the Knowledge of Good and Evil, and he explicitly told them that if they did eat from it that they would die. Yet, in Genesis chapter 3, we see that this simple command was too much for Adam and Eve to obey, and they ate from the forbidden tree in hopes of having God-like knowledge.

Because of their blatant disobedience of the one who created and provided for them, Adam and Eve were not only banished from the garden, from then on they would have to sufferer from pain, disease, and ultimately death. This is because disobeying God is sin, and "the wages of sin is death" (Romans 6:23). And all people since then have had to bear the same hardship and death because everyone sins: "through one man sin entered into the world, and death through sin; and so death passed unto all men, because all sinned" (Romans 5:12). Each one of us is a "slave of sin" (John 8:34, page 72) and bear the consequences.

Not only was humanity punished directly, but the ground was cursed so that we could no longer live at ease but had to labor arduously just to get food to survive (Genesis 3:17-19). Elsewhere we learn that all of creation is corrupted because of man's sin: "the whole creation groans and travails in pain together until now" (Romans 8:22). This means that the natural disasters and calamities in the world were not part of the original creation but a result of man's disobedience.

The Bible makes clear that the broken, painful world we live in is not how God made it. Hardship, suffering, and death are not natural and God will not allow them to persist forever.

It may be asked why God permitted people to sin in the first place. The reason is that God wanted to have a relationship with us built on love, and love requires free will. If you programmed your computer to say "I love you", this wouldn't be real love at all. Similarly, if people only obeyed God because we had no choice, then we would basically be robots. Since God wanted us to genuinely love him, he allowed us to choose not to do as he commanded.

What are Angels, Demons, and Satan?

Angels are intelligent created spirit beings. They are servants of God who have many duties. They deliver God's message to his people, such as the visits to Mary and Joseph before Jesus' birth. They guard and protect us: "For he shall give his angels charge over you, to keep you in all your ways. They shall bear you up in their hands, lest you dash your foot against a stone" (Psalm 91:11-12).They carry out God's judgements, like when the Assyrian army came to capture Jerusalem: "Jehovah sent an angel, who cut off all the mighty men of valor, and the leaders and captains, in the camp of the king of Assyria" (2 Chronicles 32:21).

Angels have great power: "Bless Jehovah, you his angels, that are mighty in strength, that fulfil his word" (Psalm 103:20). They will also come with Jesus when he returns (Matt 24:30-31, page 124). However, they are not to be worshiped (Colossians 2:18; Revelation 19:10). While they do not have physical bodies, they can take human form. In fact, we may interact with angels and not even realize it: "Do not forget to show love to strangers, for thereby some have entertained angels unawares" (Hebrews 13:2).

Demons are fallen angels who rebelled against God and were expelled from heaven. They are deeply evil, seeking to thwart God's plans and to inflict suffering upon people. Satan, otherwise known as the devil, is the head demon. It was Satan in the form of a serpent who talked Eve into eating from the forbidden tree. Thus he was "a murderer from the beginning" and father of lies (John 8:44, page 73).

Satan and his dark forces shouldn't be blamed for every misfortune that befalls us, but his malevolent works are not to be ignored, either. While he is capable of harming us directly (see the biblical book of Job), more often he achieves his wicked goals by tempting us to indulge in our sinful desires. He persuades us that evil actions are not only okay, but actually good for us. This is exactly how he convinced Eve to disobey God. Satan has also "blinded the minds of the unbelieving, that the light of the gospel of the glory of Christ, who is the image of God, should not dawn upon them" (2 Corinthians 4:4).

Despite his power, Satan is no match for God, and when we rely on God the devil has no hold over us: "Put on the whole armor of God, that you may be able to stand against the schemes of the devil" (Ephesians 6:11); "Be subject therefore to God; but resist the devil, and he will flee from you" (James 4:7). God has judged Satan and the demons (2 Peter 2:4) and will banish them from our world forever (Revelation 20:10).

Who is Christ?

Long after Adam and Eve first sinned, people continued to be disobedient and often horribly wicked. However, God did not give up on humanity. He still loved us and desired to restore our relationship with him. So he chose to reveal himself to the Jewish people and promised them that if they followed him faithfully he would bless them. They would then serve as a role model to all other nations who God would also bless if they turned to him: "I will make of you a great nation, and I will bless you, and make your name great, so you shall be a blessing; and I will bless them that bless you, and him that curses you will I curse; and in you shall all the families of the earth be blessed" (Genesis 12:2-3).

In order to guide his chosen people, God gave them numerous rules to live by so that they would devote themselves to God, treat each other in a loving way, and avoid becoming like the surrounding pagan nations. These rules are referred to as the Law. Yet the Jews did not obey him and continued practicing worldly evils. So God did the most amazing thing in history, he became a man and dwelt among us: "but when the fullness of the time came, God sent forth his Son, born of a woman, born under the Law, that he might redeem them that were under the Law, that we might receive the adoption as sons" (Galatians 4:4-5). This was Jesus of Nazareth.

Jesus was fully God: "for in him dwells all the fullness of the Godhead bodily" (Colossians 2:9). Thus he "is the image of the invisible God" (Colossians 1:15). But at the same time he was fully human. He needed to eat, drink, and sleep. He grew physically and mentally from a helpless baby to a mature adult. He felt hunger, thirst, pain and grief, even crying in anguish. This means he was the perfect mediator between God and humanity: "For there is one God, one mediator also between God and men, himself man, Christ Jesus" (1 Timothy 2:5).

Even though Jesus was tempted just as we are, he never sinned (Hebrews 4:15). Whereas Adam and Eve allowed Satan to talk them into disobeying God despite living in a lush paradise, Jesus resisted Satan's offers while hungering in an empty desert (page 17). Throughout his life he did exactly as God required. This perfect obedience to God set an example for us. Further, by driving out demons from many people he began to break Satan's grip on us. He also provided instruction for us on how we are to live our lives properly: "Take my yoke upon you and learn from me, for I am gentle and lowly in heart, and you shall find rest for your souls. For my yoke is easy and my burden is light" (Matt 11:29, page 42).

But above all, Christ Jesus was our redeemer who brought us back into a right relationship with God, the "Lamb of God, who takes away the sin of the world" (John 1:29, page 18). Therefore, he was the most direct expression of God's love for us: "Herein was the love of God manifested in us, that God has sent his only begotten Son into the world that we might live through him" (1 John 4:9).

Jesus was born around 5 BC and he was most probably crucified in 30 AD or 33 AD, with his ministry lasting about 3 years.

Why did Jesus have to die?

While Jesus' ministry was extremely important, his ultimate objective was to die as a despised criminal on a cross. But why would God have himself killed, let alone in such a cruel fashion? To understand this incredible act, we need to remember two facts: God loves us, and our sin separates us from him resulting in our death.

Since God loves us, he does not wish for us to die, and so he received the punishment for our sins that we deserved and died in our place: "God shows his love for us in that while we were still sinners, Christ died for us" (Romans 5:8). This reversed the judgment on humanity that stemmed from Adam's sin: "Therefore, as one trespass led to condemnation for all men, so one act of righteousness leads to justification and life for all men. For as by the one man's disobedience the many were made sinners, so by the one man's obedience the many will be made righteous" (5:18-19). Because of this, those who follow Jesus are no longer judged by God: "There is therefore now no condemnation for those who are in Christ Jesus" (Romans 8:1).

This reconciles us to God which brings us back into the deep relationship with him that he has desired from the beginning: "All this is from God, who through Christ reconciled us to himself and gave us the ministry of reconciliation; that is, in Christ God was reconciling the world to himself, not counting their trespasses against them, and entrusting to us the message of reconciliation...For our sake he made him to be sin who knew no sin, so that in him we might become the righteousness of God" (2 Corinthians 5:18-19, 21).

Jesus' death was also a defeat of Satan and his dark forces: "through death he might bring to naught him that had the power of death, that is, the devil" (Hebrews 2:14); "He that does sin is of the devil; for the devil sinned from the beginning. To this end was the Son of God manifested, that he might destroy the works of the devil" (1 John 3:8).

This was achieved through Jesus' perfect compliance with the Law which God had commanded the Jews to follow. As we have seen, Satan did not kill Adam directly, rather he got Adam to disobey God and therefore suffer the consequences, which was death. By resisting Satan's temptations to sin yet dying on our behalf, Jesus fulfilled our obligation to follow the Law and so Satan can no longer use the Law to have us condemned: "Christ redeemed us from the curse of the Law, having become a curse for us" (Galatians 3:13); "having blotted out the bond written in ordinances that was against us, which was contrary to us...he has taken it out of the way, nailing it to the cross" (Colossians 2:14).

Not only did Jesus' sacrifice free us from the hold of sin and Satan, it served as an example for us to emulate as well: "Christ also suffered for you, leaving you an example, that you should follow his steps" (1 Peter 5:8). Jesus commanded his disciples to love each other just as he loved them (John 15:12, page 134). He then explained what this kind of loved entailed: "Greater love than this no one has, that someone lay down his life for his friends" (verse 13). Since Jesus was willing to die for others, we must love others so much that we would be willing to do the same. This necessarily means we are to do all other acts of love, too.

Despite Jesus' execution coming at the hands of men with the prompting of Satan, this was not a defeat for God but rather it was part of his plan for us. After Adam and Eve sinned, God declared to Satan that one of Eve's descendants would destroy Satan after being harmed by him: "he shall bruise your head, and you shall bruise his heel" (Genesis 3:15). Later, about 750 years before Jesus' crucifixion, God announced through the prophet Isaiah why Jesus would die:

> Surely he has borne our griefs,
>   and carried our sorrows;
> yet we did esteem him stricken,
>   smitten of God, and afflicted.
> But he was wounded for our transgressions,
>   he was bruised for our iniquities;
> the chastisement of our peace was upon him;
>   and with his stripes we are healed.
> We all like sheep have gone astray;
>   we have turned every one to his own way;
>   and Jehovah has laid on him the iniquity of us all.
> He was oppressed, yet when he was afflicted he opened not his mouth;
>   as a lamb that is led to the slaughter,
> and as a sheep that before its shearers is silent,
>   so he opened not his mouth.
> By oppression and judgment he was taken away;
>   and as for his generation, who considered
> that he was cut off out of the land of the living
>   for the transgression of my people?

And they made his grave with the wicked,
and with a rich man in his death;
although he had done no violence,
neither was any deceit in his mouth.
Yet it pleased Jehovah to bruise him;
he has put him to grief:
when you shall make his soul an offering for sin,
he shall see his seed, he shall prolong his days;
and the pleasure of Jehovah shall prosper in his hand,
he shall see of the travail of his soul, and shall be satisfied;
by his knowledge the just one, my servant, shall justify many,
and he shall bear their iniquities.
Therefore shall I divide him a portion among the many,
and he shall divide the spoil with the numerous;
because he poured out his soul unto death,
and was numbered with the transgressors;
yet he bore the sin of many,
and interceded for their transgressions. (Isaiah 53:4-12)

What was the Resurrection?

Jesus' death was not permanent, but rather he rose from the grave. This was not a purely spiritual event as if he were merely a ghost, rather he had a physical body that people could touch (Luke 24:39, page 156; John 20:27, page 157). He also broke bread (Luke 24:30, page 156), prepared food (John 21:9-13, page 158), and ate (Luke 24:41-43, page 156). So while Jesus could do supernatural acts such as appear and disappear at will, his resurrected body was not a spirit, nor did the disciples merely have a vision or a dream. His resurrected body was also imperishable, and so he continues to live in his resurrected body today and forever.

Jesus' resurrection was not merely a dramatic show that was of no real consequence. On the contrary, our entire salvation depends on it, as the Apostle Paul explained: "if Christ has not been raised, then our preaching is empty; your faith also is empty" (1 Corinthians 15:14). This is because Jesus died on our behalf, and so "we have died with Christ" (Romans 6:8). Thus, if Jesus stayed dead, then when we die we would stay dead as well. But by being resurrected, Jesus ensures that our own death will not be the end. Instead, we too will be resurrected and live again: "For if we have been united with him in a death like his, we shall certainly be united with him in a resurrection like his" (Romans 6:5).

With his resurrection, Jesus grandly proclaims that he will defeat death itself: "For he must reign, till he has put all his enemies under his feet. The last enemy that shall be abolished is death" (1 Corinthians 15:25-26). The raising of Jesus is the greatest victory of all time for which we should celebrate with great joy as it guarantees that all who follow him will have eternal life:

> We shall all be changed in a moment, in the twinkling of an eye, at the last trumpet. For the trumpet shall sound, and the dead shall be raised incorruptible, and we shall be changed. But when this corruptible shall have put on incorruption, and this mortal shall have put on immortality, then shall come to pass the saying that is written, 'Death is swallowed up in victory. O death, where is thy victory? O death, where is thy sting?'...Thanks be to God, who gives us the victory through our Lord Jesus Christ. Wherefore, my beloved brethren, you be steadfast, unmovable, always abounding in the work of the Lord, forasmuch as you know that your labor is not empty in the Lord.
> (1 Corinthians 15:51-55, 57-58)

What will happen when Christ returns?

While Jesus ascended into heaven after his resurrection, we are assured that he will return once more: "This Jesus, who was taken up from you into heaven, shall come back in the same way as you gazed upon him going into heaven" (Acts 1:11, page 161). He will do so in order to judge those who continue to rebel against God and to restore this broken world. As we have seen, the suffering and misery that we experience is not at all what God intends for us and he will set everything right again.

When Jesus comes again it will be a glorious and majestic event that will be awe-inspiring: "For the Lord himself shall descend from heaven, with a shout, with the voice of the archangel, and with the trumpet of God" (1 Thessalonians 4:16). After this, everyone who has died will be resurrected and return to life: "for the hour is coming in which all who are in the tombs shall hear his voice and shall come forth: those who have done good, to the resurrection of life, but those who have done vice, to the resurrection of judgment" (John 5:28-29, page 56). Those who did not follow Jesus will be punished (2 Thessalonians 1:8-9). But the followers of Jesus will not be punished since their sins had already been forgiven.

God will then remake all of creation: "the heavens shall pass away with a great noise, and the elements shall be dissolved with fervent heat, and the earth and the works that are therein shall be burned up…we look for new heavens and a new earth, wherein dwells righteousness" (2 Peter 3:10, 13). Earth will be restored to its original glory, without disease or suffering or death: "the creation itself also shall be delivered from the bondage of corruption into the liberty of the glory of the children of God" (Romans 8:21). We will live in our perfect, resurrected bodies which will never age or decay, and we will be in perfect harmony with God and each other forever:

> I saw a new heaven and a new earth, for the first heaven and the first earth had passed away; and the sea is no more. And I saw the holy city, new Jerusalem, coming down out of heaven from God, made ready as a bride adorned for her husband. And I heard a great voice from the throne saying, "Behold, the tabernacle of God is with men, and he shall dwell with them, and they shall be his peoples, and God himself shall be with them and be their God; and he shall wipe away every tear from their eyes; and death shall be no more; neither shall there be mourning, nor crying, nor pain, any more; the first things have passed away."
> (Revelation 21:1-4)

What does it mean to become a Christian?

Jesus came to earth to save us from sin, Satan, and death. But in order to receive this salvation we must become his disciples: "if you shall confess with your mouth Jesus is Lord, and shall believe in your heart that God raised him from the dead, you shall be saved" (Romans 10:9).When we do so we are no longer judged and shall live forever: "Truly, truly, I say to you, the one who hears my word and believes him who sent me has eternal life and does not come into judgment, but has passed from death into life" (John 5:24, page 56). Because God so deeply loves us, he will enthusiastically accept anyone who comes to him no matter how much they've forsaken him (see the Parable of the Prodigal Son, page 99).

Once we become followers of Christ Jesus we are completely forgiven of all our sins: "though your sins be as scarlet, they shall be as white as snow" (Isaiah 1:18). We then receive the Holy Spirit (Galatians 4:6-7) who begins to remake us into the image of Christ: "But we all, with unveiled face beholding as in a mirror the glory of the Lord, are transformed into the same image from glory to glory, even as from the Lord the Spirit" (2 Corinthians 3:18). As part of this transformation we receive a new heart: "A new heart also will I give you, and a new spirit will I put within you; and I will take away the stony heart out of your flesh, and I will give you a heart of flesh" (Ezekiel 36:26). This new heart produces a new attitude and outlook: "the fruit of the Spirit is love, joy, peace, longsuffering, kindness, goodness, faithfulness, meekness, self-control" (Galatians 5:22-23). This process of becoming more and more like Christ is called 'sanctification' and continues for the rest of our current life.

Being a disciple of Christ isn't merely an intellectual acceptance of who God is. The demons recognize that God is supreme but they aren't saved (James 2:19). To be a disciple and receive salvation we must sincerely repent for our sins: "Therefore repent of this your wickedness, and pray the Lord, if perhaps the thought of your heart shall be forgiven you" (Acts 8:22). We then must actively serve Christ by telling others about him so they can be saved (Luke 24:47, page 159) and working to improve the world with a special regard for the downtrodden (Luke 10:25-37, page 89). Being a disciple means that we are willing to make great sacrifices to serve Jesus: "If anyone desires to come after me, let him deny himself and take up his cross and follow me. For whoever desires to save his life shall lose it, but whoever shall lose his life for my sake shall find it" (Matthew 16:24-25, page 81).

As a disciple of Jesus we are to put an end to our sinful past and turn our mind entirely toward God: "be not fashioned according to this world, but you be transformed by the renewing of your mind, that you may prove what is the good and acceptable and perfect will of God" (Romans 12:2). This complete abandonment of our old life and total commitment to a new one is demonstrated through baptism. Going under the water represents the death of our old life, and coming out of the water symbolizes the birth of our new life in Christ: "We were therefore buried with him through baptism into death, that like as Christ was raised from the dead through the glory of the Father, so we also might walk in newness of life" (Romans 6:4).

What is the Bible?

The Bible is God's written revelation to humanity that explains who he is, what he expects from us, and what he has in store for us. Some portions of the Bible are God's direct words, while most of it is what he inspired certain Jews and Christians to write using their own distinctive voices. The Bible contains a wide variety of different genres, including poetry, songs, letters, and contemplative works of wisdom. However, the backbone of the Bible is straightforward history. It is through this history that we learn how God has involved himself in our world and why things are the way they are. By reading this history we gain a much deeper understanding of what we need to do to be right with God.

The Christian Bible is divided into two major sections which are called the Old Testament and the New Testament. The Old Testament is the collection of inspired books that the Jews have relied upon for thousands of years. Its historical books cover the time period from the creation of the world to the establishment of the Israelite kingdom and beyond. The Old Testament also includes the Psalms, which are a compilation of songs, and Proverbs, which are wisdom sayings. In addition, there are many books by prophets through whom God often expressed his displeasure with the Jews' disobedience and announced what would happen in the future. The Old Testament is the foundation of the Christian faith and it contains many prophecies about Jesus.

The New Testament opens with the four gospels: Matthew, Mark, Luke, and John. The word "gospel" is from the Greek word for "good news" and refers to the life and teachings of Jesus Christ. The names of the gospels refer to their author. Matthew and John were apostles of Jesus. Mark was a close associate of the apostle Peter. Luke was friends with Paul and a diligent historian. The gospels are followed by the book of Acts which covers the first 30 years after Jesus' death. It describes the rise of the early church and the spread of Christ's message throughout the Roman empire. After Acts are numerous letters written by the apostles. These explain who Jesus is and what he demands of us. The final book is Revelation which describes what will happen when Christ returns. Revelation is a challenging book because it uses lots of imagery and numbers that are symbolic and so there is great debate about what they mean. The entire New Testament was completed within 70 years of Jesus' ministry, with most of the letters and likely the first three gospels written within 40 years of his crucifixion.

Now how can we know that the Bible really is reliable? A significant reason is that there are many facts that demonstrate the validity of the Bible's contents. Indeed, archaeology has provided strong support and often refuted claims of error. For instance, for a long time secular scholars insisted that there was never a King David, that he was a myth made up by the Jews. But in 1993 a stone was discovered from a neighboring kingdom during that general time period which referred to the Davidic dynasty. There have been many other finds that match the details mentioned in the Bible.

The most powerful proof of the Bible's reliability comes from the many fulfilled prophecies that it contains. For example, in the book of the prophet Isaiah, which was written around 700 BC, it is foretold that Babylon would conquer the Assyrian empire (which occurred in 612 BC) and the Jewish nation (587 BC), and then Babylon would be destroyed by the Persians under Cyrus the Great (539 BC). The book of Daniel, written before 530 BC, predicts the fall of the Persians at the hands of the Greeks (331 BC), the rise of the Romans as a dominant power (around 200 BC) and the oppression of the Jews by Antiochus IV (175-164 BC).

These prophecies of events that happened decades and even centuries later could only be the result of revelations from God. They are so accurate that skeptics of the divine nature of the Bible have to resort to claiming that they were written after the fact and thus are fake predictions. Yet a review of all the facts shows this assertion to be clearly false and so we can be sure that they are real prophecies. Therefore, we can be certain that the Bible is the Word of God and is completely trustworthy: "Every Scripture is God-breathed and profitable for teaching, for reproof, for correction, for instruction which is in righteousness that the man of God may be complete—furnished completely unto every good work" (2 Timothy 3:16-17).

For a clear explanation of why the Old Testament is so critical to understanding who Jesus is and what he has achieved see *Knowing Jesus Through the Old Testament* by Christopher J.R. Wright.

For a superb rebuttal of secular claims about the authorship and dating of the Old Testament see *A Survey of Old Testament Introduction* by Gleason Archer. For refutations of secular claims about Jesus, the New Testament, and the early church see *Dethroning Jesus* by Darrell L. Bock and *Reinventing Jesus* by Komoszewski, Sawyer, and Wallace.

How can I learn more about Christianity?

There are many resources available today to learn more about the Christian faith, and the following books are great assets for the average person to increase their understanding. However, the best way to truly grasp who God is and what is his plan for us is to read the Bible. And the best way to read the Bible is with a reader's bible which is a book like this one where all chapter and verse numbers and other extraneous distractions are removed, such as *The Books of the Bible* from Zondervan.

A reader's bible should be your primary Bible as it makes reading for long stretches far easier and more enjoyable. It is strongly suggested that you read through the Bible from beginning to end at least once, or at least through the Old Testament history books (Genesis through Kings plus Esther, Daniel, Ezra, and Nehemiah). Doing so will dramatically increase your knowledge of the different people and events in the Bible and help you see how God's plan comes to fruition.

Study Bibles

A study bible is a great resource for both answering questions about specific verses and for deeper learning. They not only feature extensive notes explaining the text, they also include discussions of each book and essays on a range of topics.

The first four study bibles listed are from a Protestant perspective while the fifth is from an Eastern Orthodox viewpoint and the sixth is Catholic. If you only want one, the first is suggested as it is geared toward showing how the Bible can be directly applied to your life. If you want the most thorough version, get either the second or third ones. The last one listed is a wonderful way to experience the insights and teachings of the early, great Christian theologians.

- *Life Application Study Bible*
- *NIV Zondervan Study Bible* (also printed as *Biblical Theology Study Bible* but not to be confused with the *NIV Study Bible* which is also good)
- *ESV Study Bible*
- *CSB Study Bible*
- *The Orthodox Study Bible*
- *Ignatius Catholic Study Bible New Testament*
- *Ancient Faith Study Bible*

History

While much of the Bible is straightforward history and narrative, it may not always be clear where the events take place or how they fit into the big picture. The first book below brings tremendous clarity not only since it provides many maps but because it gives a clear overview of the whole history covered in the Bible as well as the greater context.

The other two books concisely relate the rise and development of Christianity. Learning about this history can provide inspiration for us as wee see how other Christians persevered and lived out the faith. It also forces us to reflect on such important issues as what the relationship between the church and governments should be, when is it appropriate to go to war, and what the proper way is to respond to those with different beliefs, whether Christian or non-Christian.

- *The Historical Atlas of the Bible* by Ian Barnes
- *Zondervan Essential Companion to Christian History* by Stephen Backhouse
- *Church History in Plain Language* by Bruce L. Shelley

Christian Denominations

There are three major branches of Christianity: Catholicism, Eastern Orthodoxy, and Protestantism. All three share the same fundamental beliefs regarding the divinity of Jesus and God's plan for us, yet have significant differences, too. Learning about them allows us to see things from different perspectives which helps us gain a deeper understanding of the faith and grow in mutual respect. The first three books are good introductions, while the others provide further discussion and insight.

- *Waking Up Catholic* by Chad R. Torgerson
- *The Orthodox Church: An Introduction to Eastern Christianity* by Timothy Ware
- *Why We're Protestant: An Introduction to the Five Solas of the Reformation* by Nate Pickowicz
- *The Beauty of the Mass* by Charles S. Johnston
- *Welcome to the Orthodox Church* by Frederica Mathewes-Green
- *Exploring Protestant Traditions* by W. David Buschart
- *Orthodoxy and Heterodoxy: Finding the Way to Christ in a Complicated Religious Landscape* by Andrew Stephen Damick
- *Light from the Christian East* by James R. Payton, Jr.
- *Catholic and Christian: An Explanation of Commonly Misunderstood Catholic Beliefs* by Alan Schreck

The Word and the Trinity

John's gospel opens with a prologue that describes Jesus Christ as the Word and states that the Word was both with God and was God himself. This is extremely profound and yet very mysterious. What does it mean that Jesus is "the Word"?

Throughout the Bible, God's spoken word has great power. It is a means by which he reveals himself to us, such as when he speaks to prophets: "Now the word of Jehovah came unto me" (Jeremiah 1:4). It is a way he carries out his plans: "For as the rain and the snow comes down from heaven, and do not return there but waters the earth, and makes it bring forth and bud, and gives seed to the sower and bread to the eater; so shall my word be that goes forth out of my mouth: it shall not return unto me empty, but it shall accomplish that which I please, and it shall prosper in the thing for which I sent it" (Isaiah 55:11). It delivers judgment: "The voice of Jehovah flashes forth flames of fire. The voice of Jehovah shakes the wilderness; Jehovah shakes the wilderness of Kadesh" (Psalm 29:7-8).

God's word was also the means by which he created the universe. In the first chapter of the first book of the Bible, Genesis, we see that God merely had to speak and all things came into existence. So when Jesus is described as "the Word", we are to think of all of these actions of God. John is clear about this, explaining in the prologue that all things were created by Jesus. Indeed, the first words of the prologue echo the very first words of Genesis: "In the beginning".

Elsewhere in the Bible Jesus is referred to as "the wisdom of God" (1 Corinthians 1:24). John also may very well have had this concept in mind. Wisdom is having the right goals and objectives and knowing the best way to achieve them. This further helps us understand Jesus' relation to God. It also informs us that Jesus has existed forever since there could never have been a time that God lacked wisdom.

Therefore, calling Jesus "the Word" illustrates that he is the supreme wisdom, creator of all things, ultimate revelation, and final judge. It also indicates that he is eternal.

By describing Jesus as both with God and being God himself, John's prologue provides a glimpse of God's fundamental nature. While God is one being, he is three distinct persons: the Father, the Son (Jesus), and the Holy Spirit. We see this tri-unity clearly in the Great Commission of Matthew 28:19 where Jesus commands his followers to "go disciple all the nations, baptizing them into the name of the Father and of the Son and of the Holy Spirit" (page 159). Each person of the Trinity is referred to separately, yet he says to baptize in their "name" rather than "names". This means that the three persons are fundamentally one, and therefore are the same being.

Over the last 2000 years some people and groups have insisted that the Trinity is a false doctrine. One such claim is that the Father, Son, and Holy Spirit are just different forms that God presents himself to us as. This is the heresy known as modalism. The baptism scene depicted in the gospels (page 16) demonstrates this to be false. There we see all three persons of the Trinity at the same time: the Father in heaven speaking, the Son on Earth being baptized, and the Holy Spirit descending to the Son. The many times that Jesus prays to the Father also show that they are separate persons. For instance, at the Last Supper Jesus prays, "Father, the hour has come. Glorify your Son, that the Son may also glorify you" (John 17:1, page 137). In the Garden of Gethsemane he prays: "My Father, if this cannot pass unless I drink it, your will be done" (Matthew 26:42, page 139). These prayers only make sense if the Father and Jesus the Son are distinct persons rather than merely different forms of the same person.

Another claim is that the Father, Son, and Holy Spirit are each different beings and thus three separate gods. This claim sometimes includes the assertion that the Son and Holy Spirit are literal offspring of the Father. God himself has declared in no uncertain terms that he is the one and only God and the sole being to be worshiped: " 'You are my witnesses,' says Jehovah, 'and my servant whom I have chosen; that you may know and believe me, and understand that I am he: before me there was no God formed, neither shall there be after me' " (Isaiah 43:10); "Look unto me, and you be saved, all the ends of the earth; for I am God, and there is none else" (Isaiah 45:22); "I am Jehovah your God, who brought you out of the land of Egypt, out of the house of bondage. You shall have no other gods before me" (Exodus 20-2-3). Jesus said, quoting Deuteronomy 6:4, "Hear, Israel: The Lord our God, the Lord is one" (Mark 12:29, page 119). So there is a single God, which means the Son and Holy Spirit cannot be separate gods.

A different claim is that the Son, Jesus, is not God, but a created, lesser being. Those who believe this often also assert that the Holy Spirit is not a distinct person but the impersonal, active force of God. To demonstrate this view to be untrue, two things must be done. First, it needs to be proven that there is only one God. This was done above. Second, it needs to be shown that the Father, the Son, and the Holy Spirit are each God. We can see that the Father is God since the Apostle Peter wrote, "For he received from God the Father honor and glory" (2 Peter 1:17).

Next, we need to establish that Jesus, the Son, is also God. But first, let us see how God presents himself to us: "Thus says Jehovah, the King of Israel…'I am the first and I am the last; and besides me there is no God'" (Isaiah 44:6); "'I am the Alpha and the Omega,' says the Lord God, 'who is and who was and who is to come, the Almighty'" (Revelation 1:8; alpha and omega are the first and last letters of the Greek alphabet, so this is like saying "from A to Z"). Now let us see how Jesus speaks about himself: "I am the Alpha and the Omega, the first and the last, the beginning and the end…I Jesus have sent my angel to testify unto you these things" (Revelation 22:13, 16). Jesus himself makes it crystal clear that he is the supreme God of the universe, that there is no one else who compares to him.

There are also many instances where the New Testament writers took Old Testament passages that referred to God and applied them to Jesus. One example is in Paul's letter to the Romans, verses 10:11-13:

> Because if you shall confess with your mouth Jesus as Lord, and shall believe in your heart that God raised him from the dead, you shall be saved: for with the heart man believes unto righteousness; and with the mouth confession is made unto salvation. For the scripture says, "Whosoever believes in him shall not be put to shame." For there is no distinction between Jew and Greek: for the same Lord is Lord of all, and is rich unto all that call upon him: for, "Whosoever shall call upon the name of the Lord shall be saved."

In this passage every use of "Lord" refers to Jesus. Yet the last line is a quote from Joel 2:32 about God: "whosoever shall call on the name of Jehovah shall be delivered."

The most explicit proof that Jesus is God occurs when he appeared to the apostles in his resurrected body after his crucifixion. In response the Apostle Thomas said to him "My Lord and my God!" (John 20:28, page 157). Jesus didn't rebuke him for calling him "God", but instead affirmed his declaration, saying: "Because you have watched me, you have believed. Blessed are those who have not seen yet have believed." So Jesus not only admits to being God, but he blesses those who believe it. As he succinctly stated before his death, "I and the Father are one" (John 10:30, page 77). And as we saw earlier, Jesus is God's wisdom which means Jesus is intrinsic to God and thus has always existed rather than being created.

Finally, we must determine that the Holy Spirit is God. We see this when Peter, speaking to someone who had lied to the early church, said, "why has Satan filled your heart to lie to the Holy Spirit…you have not lied to men, but to God" (Acts 5:3-4). Here Peter equates the Holy Spirit with God. Not only that, but this indicates that the Holy Spirit is a person because you can't lie to an impersonal force.

The Holy Spirit also speaks, and he even refers to himself: "And while Peter thought on the vision, the Spirit said to him, 'Behold, three men seek you. But arise, and you go down and go with them, doubting nothing, for I have sent them' " (Acts 10:19-20); "the Holy Spirit said, 'Set apart for me Barnabas and Saul for the work to which I have called them' " (Acts 13:2). An impersonal force can't speak let alone refer to itself. Therefore the Holy Spirit is a person, which is why he can have grief (Isaiah 63:10; Ephesians 4:30), be insulted (Hebrews 10:29), provide instruction (Nehemiah 9:20), have an opinion (Acts 15:28-29), and give testimony (Acts 20:23).

This is why Jesus and the writers of the New Testament always use "he" and "him" to refer to the Holy Spirit, never "it": "But when he comes, the Spirit of truth, he shall guide you in all truth. For he shall not speak from himself, but whatever he may hear, he shall speak, and the coming things he shall report to you" (John 16:13, page 136). This verse, which is a statement by Jesus, also shows how the Holy Spirit relays what he hears in the same manner one person repeats what they are told by another person. Here Jesus does not speak as if the Holy Spirit is merely the voice of someone. And again, the baptismal scene of Jesus provides visual proof that the Father and Holy Spirit are distinct from each other.

Since there is only one God and the Father, the Son, and the Holy Spirit are each God, the reality of the Trinity is firmly established. This Trinitarian nature is evident in Romans 8:9 where the Apostle Paul presents the "Spirit of God" as equivalent to the "Spirit of Christ", and both phrases refer to the Holy Spirit. This shows that God is Christ and Christ is God, and that the Holy Spirit is directly linked with both. Yet in verse 11 he says that the Holy Spirit raised Jesus from the dead and that God raised Christ Jesus, so the Holy Spirit and God are at the very same time distinct from Christ. In addition, in John 2:19-21 (page 20) Jesus declares that he would raise himself from the dead which means the Father, the Son, and the Holy Spirit were each responsible for raising Jesus. This vividly displays how all three are God and are each different persons.

For a thorough examination of the claims made by other religious groups and the criticisms they direct toward mainstream Christianity see *The Kingdom of the Cults* by Walter Martin.

The Trinity is challenging to imagine and so many analogies have been put forward as ways to visualize what it's like. However, all of these analogies have serious flaws which can lead to wrong conclusions. For instance, the common analogy of water's ability to take three different forms (ice, liquid, and steam) promotes the modalism heresy described previously. A similar problem applies to the analogy of a man being simultaneously a father, husband, and son. On the other hand, comparing the Trinity to the parts of an egg (shell, whites, and yolk) overlooks that the Father, Son, and Holy Spirit are made up of the same essence, or substance. The three-leaf clover analogy is misleading because it presents the Father, Son, and Holy Spirit as mere parts of God when in reality they are each fully God.

In the natural realm we run into similar situations where no description can allow us to understand how some things truly work in our world. For example, light behaves like both a stream of solid particles and a spread out wave of energy. It would seem impossible for anything to have both properties and scientists struggle to make sense of this incredible fact. One of the greatest minds of all time, physicist Albert Einstein, wrote, "We are faced with a new kind of difficulty. We have two contradictory pictures of reality; separately neither of them fully explains the phenomena of light, but together they do."

This dual nature actually applies to everything in existence, which means our world and the entire universe are at a fundamental level extraordinarily mysterious and downright bizarre. Now, if the universe we live in is beyond our comprehension, then it should be no surprise that the God who created the universe is beyond our comprehension, too. So while God has revealed his nature to us, we can't come close to fully understanding it, let alone picturing it. That means we should be very careful about using analogies to describe him. At most they can help us describe certain qualities of God, with a collection of analogies explaining a variety of aspects. But in the end, nothing we can think up could truly illustrate what God is like.

This shouldn't be troubling to us because any god that we could comprehend would be a very limited god. So the Almighty God who rules over everything is both the ultimate truth and the greatest mystery, and by embracing this mystery we can more fully appreciate how immense and majestic and special he is.

Sermon on the Mount and the New Covenant

Chapters 5 through 7 of Matthew's gospel contain one of the longest discourses of the ministry of Jesus that appears in any of the gospels (pages 27-32). Since the speech took place on a mountain, it's commonly referred to as "The Sermon on the Mount". While it may not be what Matthew had in mind, this scene of Jesus going up a mountain in order reveal to his disciples the principles they are to abide by is reminiscent of Moses ascending Mt. Sinai to receive the Ten Commandments from God. This is fitting because just as Moses served as a mediator of a covenant between his people and God, Jesus came to bring a new covenant (Luke 22:20, page 129) under which all people are to live, and this sermon lays out the standards and expectations of the new covenant.

The Old Testament describes how God made a covenant (a treaty) with the Jewish people. Under this covenant, if the people devoted themselves fully to God, then God would bless them. Through the prophet Moses, God laid down the rules which the Jews were to follow, including the Ten Commandments. These rules spelled out the actions (moral and ceremonial) that the Jews were to do. God's plan was that by guiding their external behaviors, they not only would act in a moral way, but their internal desires would become righteous as well and their hearts would be devoted to God.

However, the Jews didn't obey the laws God established for them and they fell into great wickedness. And even when they did perform the required rituals, they just went through the motions without giving their hearts to God. The result was that God punished the Jewish people for their defiance and evils by having numerous pagan nations conquer them and rule over them.

For this reason, God made a new covenant. This covenant would be very different from the original (Jeremiah 31:31-34). First, rather than speaking through prophets, God himself came to dwell among his people in order to talk to them directly and personally show by example how they were to live their lives. Second, the standards for obeying the new covenant would have a fundamentally different form from those of the old covenant: instead of a long list of specific actions followers were to do or not do, a few general principles are given that will shape a person's attitude. Under the new covenant, followers are required to radically transform their thoughts and feelings which will then result in their actions becoming more like God demands.

In the Sermon on the Mount, Jesus vividly portrays the expectations of the new covenant. He explains that our inner desires are what ultimately determine our actions, saying that the "good tree brings forth good fruit, but the corrupt tree brings forth evil fruit" (7:17) Therefore, we must focus on changing our lives from the inside out, and he illustrates what this transformation of heart and mind looks like.

Jesus demands that we not only don't murder anyone, but that we don't even harbor any anger towards others (5:22). On the contrary, we must love our enemies (5:44). He says that simply avoiding committing adultery isn't enough, we are not to so much as lust after others (5:28). When mistreated, we are to respond with graciousness rather than retaliate (5:38-41).

The expectations of the new covenant are most succinctly expressed by Jesus' command that "whatever you desire that men should do unto you, thus also you do unto them" (7:12). Many philosophers and theologians from different cultures and religions have made similar statements, and these expressions are called the "Golden Rule". However, most of these statements are made in the negative form: don't do to others what you don't want them to do to you. This may seem like a small difference from Jesus' positive form, but it is actually radically different. Under the negative Golden Rule, a person could be greedy and selfish and still be okay if they simply don't harm another person. Under Jesus' positive Golden Rule, such a person would be condemned because we are called to proactively do good things for others, not just avoid hurting them.

Jesus lucidly demonstrates this with the Parable of the Good Samaritan (Luke 10:27-37, page 89). With this parable he makes clear that we must act compassionately and selflessly toward others, even strangers, rather than be like the priest and the Levite who didn't help the man who had been beaten and robbed. Yet, according to the negative form of the Golden Rule, the priest and the Levite didn't do anything wrong precisely because they did nothing!

In the book *Letter to a Christian Nation*, atheist Sam Harris praises the founder of the Jain religion, saying that he "surpassed the morality of the Bible with a single sentence: 'Do not injure, abuse, oppress, enslave, insult, torment, torture, or kill any creature or living being.' " But as we have seen, Jesus insists on far more than that from us. We are not merely to avoid hurting other people, but to joyfully give ourselves to others. Jesus tells us that the greatest commandment, besides loving God wholeheartedly, is to "love your neighbor as yourself" (Matt 22:38; Mark 12:31, page 105). And as he explained with the Parable of the Good Samaritan, our neighbor is *anyone we come across*. Our duty is immense: we are to act with an overflowing abundance of love towards everyone, including those who persecute us.

So rather than having a very low standard of morality, Christianity has an impossibly high standard. It is so high and so contrary to our nature that no one can achieve it. That is why under the new covenant, our eternal salvation comes only from our acceptance of Jesus as God: "No one comes to the Father except through me" (John 14:6, page 133); "if you will confess with your mouth Jesus as Lord, and will believe in your heart that God raised him from the dead, you will be saved" (Romans 10:9). If it were based on our deeds, then no one would be saved because no one measures up to God's standards of righteousness.

In Luke's gospel there is a similar sermon (6:20-49, pages 38-40) which is said to have taken place on a flat area near or on a mountain, and thus has been called "The Sermon on the Plain." Although it may have been part of a much longer speech, as presented by Luke this sermon is significantly shorter than the Sermon on the Mount and therefore distills Jesus' message even further into its most essential essence. Jesus also places the Golden Rule in the middle of the speech which emphasizes how central it is to the demands of the new covenant. There are some other differences between the two sermons that are worth exploring.

Whereas the Sermon on the Mount opens with eight beatitudes (blessings), the Sermon on the Plain begins with four beatitudes and four corresponding woes. What may be easily missed is that the beatitudes in the Sermon on the Mount are addressed in the third person ("blessed are the/those...") while those in the Sermon on the Plain are in the second person ("blessed are you..."). Thus, in the Sermon on the Mount, Jesus speaks of the beatitudes applying broadly to everyone, while in the Sermon on the Plain he presents the beatitudes as applying directly to his listeners.

Another difference is that where in the Sermon on the Mount Jesus refers to the "poor in spirit", in the Sermon on the Plain he only says "poor". Similarly, he speaks of those who "hunger and thirst for righteousness" in the Sermon on the Mount, while he merely refers to those who "hunger now" in the Sermon on the Plain. Also, whereas Jesus blesses "those who mourn" in the Sermon on the Mount, in the Sermon on the Plain he blesses "you who weep now." Therefore, three of the four beatitudes in the Sermon on the Plain apply directly to the hardships of the impoverished and hurting people in his midst. In contrast, six of the eight beatitudes in the Sermon on the Mount have a very general and more spiritual application.

The distinctions are likely due to the different audiences he was teaching for each speech. In the Sermon on the Mount, he was speaking primarily to his closest disciples who would be carrying out his ministry, some of whom would later be leaders of the church. So he emphasized the deeper and more spiritual dimensions of his lessons. In the Sermon on the Plain, Jesus was speaking before a large group of diverse people so he had a more down to earth message. The form of the four beatitudes and four woes make clear to the poor and downtrodden before him that their suffering was seen by God and that there will be justice for them in the end.

This crafting of the message for the target audience can be seen in the way the metaphor about bad trees not producing good fruit is used. In the Sermon on the Mount it is a warning to the disciples to be on guard against false prophets specifically. This is because the sermon is geared to the future church leaders who needed to be alert for those who could corrupt and undermine the church. In the Sermon on the Plain, it's just a general commentary on how people who are evil on the inside do evil acts on the outside and is connected to Jesus' admonishment of hypocritically criticizing others. That is more applicable to the lay people who were in the audience for that sermon.

Over the last two centuries there have been scores of gospel harmonies produced and almost every one of them treat these two sermons as actually being the very same speech. This is also the accepted view of many biblical scholars. However, this is almost certainly incorrect. These were two separate sermons delivered on different occasions. There are several reasons why this is clear.

First, the order of events preceding the sermons are opposite of each other. With the Sermon on the Mount, Jesus sees the crowds and goes up the mountain (seemingly to get away from them) and then begins teaching his disciples. With the Sermon on the Plain, Jesus prays and selects his twelve disciples on the mountain and then comes down the mountain where he sees the crowds and more disciples, at which point he begins his sermon.

Second, Jesus' delivery is different. During the Sermon on the Mount, Jesus is sitting while he is preaching. During the Sermon on the Plain, he is standing.

Third, as explained above, there are substantial differences between the two sermons in terms of content, wording, and theme. The order of the overlapping content is also quite different, not only in regard to the Golden Rule but many other details as well (see endnote).

The reasons given for viewing them as the same talk are limited and don't demand that the two speeches are the same. One reason is that both occur on or near a mountain (or hill; the Greek word could mean either, or even something as vague as "the hill country"). But a specific mountain isn't mentioned so they could be different ones. And if it is the same place, Jesus could easily have spoken there multiple times.

Another reason given is that in both Matthew and Luke the sermons are followed shortly by the healing of the centurion's servant. However, the event Matthew describes immediately after the Sermon on the Mount is the healing of a man with leprosy. Luke places that incident before the Sermon on the Plain. Furthermore, if the two sermons are viewed as the same, in order to harmonize them Matthew's gospel needs to be cut up and rearranged far more than if they are treated as separate. Specifically, large sections of chapters 8, 9, and 12 must be moved to a position before chapter 5 in order to bring the gospels into agreement. While some parts of Matthew are not chronological, the ordering of the events in the gospels overwhelmingly points to the sermons being separate episodes.

Of course, the biggest reason why they are taken to be the same sermon is because their content is similar. Yet, as we have seen, there are major differences. But even if the words were identical that wouldn't mean they were the same speech. Jesus traveled all over speaking to many different people in lots of different places so he would have naturally repeated his teachings on numerous occasions. Indeed, there are many quotations in Matthew's gospel that are in Luke's gospel which harmonists and scholars have no problem seeing as occurring at different times and places. The Lord's Prayer is a perfect example: it appears in the Sermon on the Mount near the beginning of Jesus' ministry and in Luke 11:2-4 close to the end of his ministry (pages 30 and 90).

Those who maintain that the two sermons were actually the same event try to explain the differences by arguing that Matthew and Luke shaped their presentations of the sermon to suit their intended readers: Jews in the case of Matthew; Gentiles in the case of Luke. Yet, as shown previously, it is much more likely that these were two distinct sermons in front of two different audiences and thus it was Jesus who tailored his words to his listeners. This also explains why he was sitting during the Sermon on the Mount. That is the normal posture for a rabbi or teacher when instructing his students. However, he was standing during the Sermon on the Plain which would be the natural way to address a large gathering of listeners out in the open.

In summary, viewing these sermons as separate events is both heavily supported by the evidence and creates no significant problems. On the other hand, treating them as the same event has minimal affirmative support and produces a host of issues. Therefore, not only is it probable that they were two different sermons, this is clearly the case.

If they were separate speeches, then the issue arises of where to fit them into the harmony. A major clue comes at the conclusion of the Sermon on the Mount, where Matthew states that "the crowds were astonished at his teaching, for he taught them as one having authority, and not as their scribes." Both Mark and Luke have identical or similar comments when Jesus first teaches in the synagogue in Capernaum after being rejected in Nazareth. Since Matthew likely used Mark as a source (or vice versa), this is a strong indicator of when the Sermon on the Mount took place and so this harmony places it shortly before that event. Luke's gospel is highly chronological and the events before the Sermon on the Plain match those in Mark's gospel, which is also largely chronological. So the Sermon on the Plain can be left where it appears in Luke, which is after the selection of the twelve apostles and just before the healing of the centurion's servant.

NOTE

The table at right is a comparison of the two sermons which shows how their content and order are different. The lines indicate verses that are similar and the verses in **bold** are the Golden Rule. Every instance of lines crossing is a mismatch in the order. Most significantly, notice how the Golden Rule is squarely in the middle of the Sermon on the Plain, while in the Sermon on the Mount it comes near the end and serves as a summary of his teachings ("for this is the Law and the Prophets"). Many of the other similar verses have been shifted around a bit as well.

If they were a single sermon then either Matthew or Luke more accurately presents the actual order that Jesus spoke these words. Yet, in *The Expositor's Bible Commentary*, top New Testament scholar D.A. Carson (who believes they are one and the same) admits that "Both make such good sense in their own context that it seems impossible to decide in favor of either" (volume 8, page 183). If that's the case then it strongly suggests that both Matthew and Luke provide the correct order of Jesus' words, which would mean they were spoken on separate occasions and Jesus structured each speech in a highly logical fashion. Note also that nothing from the middle of the Sermon on the Mount (chapter 6 of Matthew) appears in the Sermon on the Plain. Rather, Luke places that content elsewhere in his gospel at totally different times and places, which should make clear that Jesus repeated his teachings, including those in the Sermon on the Mount, throughout his ministry.

Sermon on the Mount	**Sermon on the Plain**
Matt 5:3	Luke 6:20b
Matt 5:4	Luke 6:21a
Matt 5:5	Luke 6:21b
Matt 5:6	Luke 6:22-23
Matt 5:7	Luke 6:24
Matt 5:8	Luke 6:25a
Matt 5:9	Luke 6:25b
Matt 5:10-12	Luke 6:26
Matt 5:13	
Matt 5:14-16	
Matt 5:17-20	
Matt 5:21-26	
Matt 5:27-30	
Matt 5:31-32	
Matt 5:33-37	
Matt 5:38-42	Luke 6:27-28
Matt 5:43-44	Luke 6:29-30
Matt 5:45	**Luke 6:31**
Matt 5:46-47	Luke 6:32-35a
Matt 5:48	Luke 6:35b
Matt 6:1-4	Luke 6:36
Matt 6:5-8	
Matt 6:9-15	
Matt 6:16-18	
Matt 6:19-34	
Matt 7:1-2	Luke 6:37-38
Matt 7:3-5	Luke 6:39-40
Matt 7:6	Luke 6:41-42
Matt 7:7-11	
Matt 7:12	
Matt 7:13-14	
Matt 7:15-16	Luke 6:43
Matt 7:17	Luke 6:44
Matt 7:18-20	Luke 6:45
Matt 7:21	Luke 6:46
Matt 7:22-23	
Matt 7:24-27	Luke 6:47-49

About the Harmony

The four gospels of the Bible each provide a distinct view of Jesus' life and ministry. The specific events, sayings, and details that each author provides as well as how they are presented serve to emphasize certain themes, with each gospel highlighting different aspects. For this reason, studying each gospel individually is very rewarding.

However, each gospel only discusses a small part of Jesus' life which can make it very difficult to understand how a particular incident fits into the bigger picture. Further confusion comes from the fact that some events appear in multiple gospels, while similar but different events and sayings may also appear. This can create uncertainty over whether a certain occurrence in one gospel is the same or different as a similar event in another gospel. This is where a harmony can be very valuable. A harmony is a book that shows how the events in the various gospels relate to each other. Some harmonies place the gospels in columns next to each other for easy comparison. Others, like this one, combine the gospels into one text. Harmonies provide tremendous clarity about how all the different events connect together. This then helps us see how Jesus' life unfolded, which brings greater understanding of when, where, and why he did and said what he did.

This harmony is also presented in a manner that is unlike traditional Bibles. Almost all Bibles have chapter and verse numbers, footnotes, and headings within the text. These and other features common to Bibles like sidebars and commentary serve as great reference tools, but they badly distract from the reading experience. It can be very hard to read normal Bibles from beginning to end like we do with other books because the typical Bible isn't formatted for that purpose. These features also reinforce the all too common approach of treating each verse in isolation without considering the larger context.

The original manuscripts didn't have any chapter or verse numbers. These weren't added to the text until 1551. Similarly, this book appears in a clean, clear format without any distractions in order to allow the reader to become immersed in the story. This makes for a far more enjoyable and powerful experience. It also leads the reader to see how everything ties together rather than viewing each verse, parable, or scene as independent from the surrounding text and overall narrative.

Structure is provided by dividing the account into a few large chapters which clarify the major phases of Jesus' life. Within these chapters significant shifts in the narrative, such as when Jesus travels to a different location, are indicated by a space between paragraphs. This presentation both improves the reading experience and enhances comprehension.

This harmony is not intended to replace the four canonical gospels. Instead, it is a tool to aid in understanding them. For instance, when more than one gospel describes a particular event, they often include different details. By bringing all these details together, the harmony makes it easy to see the complete picture. On the other hand, when the gospels recount multiple events or sayings of Jesus that seem similar to each other but actually occur at different times and places, the harmony makes the different contexts clear which is extremely important for understanding their significance. Throughout his ministry, Jesus would often reuse a particular parable or saying but with varying meanings. In order to understand what Jesus meant, it is necessary to pay attention to the particular context in which he said something. It should not be assumed that when he repeated a saying that he was communicating the same message every time.

For an example of how this harmony helps to enhance the reader's understanding, the Parable of the Persistent Widow (page 104) is a great illustration. In modern Bibles this is placed at the beginning of chapter 18 of Luke's gospel. This creates the impression that this is merely a random comment about the need to continually pray and have hope. In reality, it directly ties into the end of chapter 17.

There we see that Jesus is asked by some Pharisees when the Kingdom of God would come. Jesus answers by telling them it had already arrived. He then turns to his disciples and explains to them how after he is gone they are to persevere in his absence through all trials and tribulations until "the days of the Son of Man". The parable is used to show how their resolve would eventually be rewarded. That is why Jesus follows it with the question "when the Son of Man comes, will he find faith on the earth?"

This isn't the end of the scene, however. Jesus continues his lesson with another parable, this one about two men who go to the temple to pray. One is arrogant and thinks because he lives a seemingly righteous life that he is better than others. The other man, a tax collector, admits to being a sinner and begs God for mercy. Jesus explains that it was the repentant man who was justified in the eyes of God, not the one who was full of himself.

This connects to the preceding comments by Jesus by building on the parable about the widow by making it clear that it is those humble enough to recognize the necessity of relying on God who will ultimately be saved, not those who think they are superior to everyone else. It is also likely a deliberate rebuke of the Pharisees who got this discussion started (and who may still have been listening to him) since the arrogant man in the story was said to be a Pharisee.

It should be now clear how all these sayings fit together and how seeing the connections between them help us understand what Jesus was trying to teach. There are numerous instances in the gospels of similar scenes where someone says or does something and Jesus responds with a lengthy serious of statements and parables that flow together and build upon each other. By removing the chapter and verse numbers as well as the chapter and section headings it becomes much easier to see how the words and actions of Jesus tie together into a coherent whole rather than reading them as isolated pieces.

Over the centuries there have been dozens and dozens of harmonies produced in various formats, often by diligent scholars. However, these routinely have very major errors that seriously undermine their value. This harmony seeks to correct these errors in order to provide a far more accurate chronology of Jesus' life.

One of the most visible mistakes is the conflation of the Sermon on the Mount presented in Matthew's gospel with the Sermon on the Plain which appears in Luke's work. Since these two discourses have a similar setting and content, it is widely presumed that they are the same speech. Yet careful consideration of all the facts makes it clear that these are truly two separate sermons. This isn't a small issue because the purposes of the sermons are significantly different despite their similarities. In addition, treating them as one results in a very different chronology, such as placing the selection of the twelve apostles before the Sermon on the Mount rather than sometime later as was most likely the case. (For a more thorough discussion of these two sermons, see page 192)

A far bigger issue is the way harmonies handle Jesus' final journey to Jerusalem. This is described in detail in Luke 9:51-19:28 and the overlapping sections of Matthew and Mark. As presented in these gospels, this was for the most part a rather direct trek from the far north of Palestine down to Jerusalem for the Passover with Jesus "resolutely" (Luke 9:51, page 87) committed to facing his fate of suffering and death. Now the collection of the temple tax mentioned in Matthew 17:24-27 (page 84) was begun a month before the Passover which means the final trip was undertaken within a few weeks of the Passover at most. Yet other harmonies weave a large section of John (chapters 7 through 11) into this part of the narrative.

That portion of John relates Jesus' appearances in Jerusalem for the Feast of Tabernacles and the Feast of the Dedication as well as the raising of Lazarus from the dead in Bethany near Jerusalem. The consequences of interweaving these events with the travels described in the other gospels are severe. Doing so means that Jesus' "final" journey involves him going to Jerusalem for the Feast of Tabernacles, returning for the Feast of the Dedication, leaving to go beyond the Jordan River, coming back to the vicinity of Jerusalem to revive Lazarus, going up north to the border of Samaria and Galilee, and then once again circling back to Jerusalem for the Passover. If that sounds extremely convoluted and contrary to the notion that Jesus was "resolutely" determined to complete his mission, that's because it is. It also turns his last trip into a six-month long tour which contradicts the timeframe mandated by the reference to the collection of the temple tax. Worse, this is all done despite there not being one single event in common between this section of John and the other three gospels. (For a clear visual of the complete lack of overlap between these sections of John and the other gospels, see pages 225 through 228)

About the only concrete justification for this scheme comes from John 11:1 where it says, "Now a certain man was sick, Lazarus *apo* Bethany, *ek* the village of Mary and her sister Martha" (page 77). Both *apo* and *ek* mean "of" or "from", so this is taken to mean that all three lived in Bethany, which was a couple of miles from Jerusalem. Now in Luke 10:38-39 it says that Jesus "entered into a certain village, and a certain woman named Martha received him into her house. And she had a sister called Mary..." Harmonists assume based on John 11:1 that this village must be Bethany. If that were the case it would place Jesus in the outskirts of Jerusalem well before his arrival for Passover. Such an assumption is most likely incorrect.

John 1:44 has a formulation similar to John 11:1, saying, "Now Philip was *apo* Bethsaida, *ek* the town of Andrew and Peter" (page 19). This cannot mean that Andrew and Peter were living in Bethsaida because Mark 1:29 (page 33) shows that Andrew and Peter had their home in Capernaum. John probably meant that Philip lived in Bethsaida but was originally from the town of Andrew and Peter (Capernaum). Therefore, the likely intention of John 11:1 was to say that Lazarus lived in Bethany and his hometown was the village where Mary and Martha were living, wherever that might be. That would mean that the village mentioned in Luke 10:38 is not Bethany, but more probably a town somewhere in Galilee. This is supported by the fact that there is no indication in that section of Luke that Jesus is anywhere near Jerusalem. Overall, the facts strongly suggest that the events of John chapters 7 through 11 did not occur during Jesus' final journey. Instead, they all took place before then.[1]

The Last Supper is another occasion where harmonies come to questionable conclusions. The standard way to arrange the happenings that occurred that night is to place Jesus' announcement that an apostle would betray him before his institution of the Eucharist (the breaking of bread and drinking of wine). This conflicts with Luke's account which presents the declaration as taking place immediately after Jesus explains the meaning of the Eucharist. It also requires placing the foot washing by Jesus detailed in John before the Eucharist. This would separate the foot washing from Jesus' rebuke of the disciples for arguing about which of them was the greatest (Luke 22:23-30). The foot washing was an extreme lesson on how the apostles needed to be humble and serve each other, and so it must have been in response to their prideful argument. Yet harmonies typically make them appear as if they are unconnected. This not only presents the disciples as completely ignoring Jesus's command, it also makes it seem as if Jesus himself forgot what he just ordered them to do. This is at odds with the way Jesus reacts when his disciples disregard his teachings elsewhere in the gospels. When his disciples didn't do as he instructed, he made his displeasure known.

---

[1] For further discussion, see Robert A. Singer's paper "Rethinking the Harmonization of Luke 9:18-19:28 with John 7:1-11:54" presented to the 2003 Evangelical Theological Society Annual Meeting.

While Matthew and Mark put Jesus' declaration of betrayal before the breaking of bread, the way they are written doesn't require that this be taken as the actual order, they could be arranged thematically. Luke's gospel, on the other hand, demands that the Eucharist happened first. Furthermore, Luke's and John's descriptions of that night align very well with each others. Therefore, the best approach is to use their accounts to guide our reconstruction of how that night unfolded.

When we do this, Jesus' institution of the Eucharist takes on a whole new meaning. By placing it at the beginning of the narrative of the Last Supper as this harmony does, we see that it not only is the demonstration of a ritual Christians are to perform, but it also marks the end of Jesus' earthly ministry. The rest of his teachings that evening were to prepare them for his imminent departure and the challenges that they would face after he was gone. It also set in motion the events that would transpire over the next several hours. By sending Judas out when he did, it ensured that his trial and death would take place the next day as Jesus intended. Thus, the Eucharist wasn't just one of many things that happened that night, it marked the moment when Jesus willfully signed his own death warrant.

One more issue is worth discussing. Chapter 5 of the Gospel of John (pages 55-57) describes Jesus going to Jerusalem for an unnamed feast where he creates a stir by healing a disabled man on the Sabbath. This chapter has no connection with the other gospels and so where it fits in with their narratives is a mystery. Harmonies often place it before the scene where Jesus' disciples are criticized for picking grain on the Sabbath (page 36) and thus shortly before Jesus selects his twelve apostles. There doesn't appear to be any strong reason for this placement, though.

Now John's gospel mentions three Passovers during the ministry of Jesus which means his ministry lasted at least two years. Many scholars believe the unnamed feast in chapter 5 is another Passover, which would make four of them total and therefore add another year to his ministry. This is often a basis for the widely held belief that Jesus' ministry lasted about 3 ½ years.

However, in John chapter 7, when he is in Jerusalem for the Feast of Tabernacles, he is again harshly criticized. He responds by saying "I did one work and you all marvel...are you angry with me because I made a man entirely well on the Sabbath?" (John 7:21, 23, page 70). This clearly is referring to his healing of the disabled man in chapter 5. This would place the feast of chapter 5 somewhat close in time to the Feast of Tabernacles in chapter 7.

If as scholars speculate the feast in chapter 5 is a Passover, it would mean that that the healing of the disabled man took place 18 months before the events of chapter 7 since there is a Passover mentioned in chapter 6. That is a far too long of time for such a simple remark by Jesus. That healing would have been long forgotten, especially since he had done many other dramatic things since then. Another issue is that it would substantially increase the amount of time where nothing is recorded about Jesus' ministry in any of the gospels. Therefore, the unnamed feast was most likely not a Passover. For these reasons, this harmony places John chapter 5 as close to chapter 7 as possible. Further, if it were not a Passover, then it is reasonable to believe that Jesus' ministry lasted around 2 ½ years.[2]

It should now be clear that a proper harmonization of the gospels results in not only a correct order of the various events, it also improves our ability to grasp the meanings of what Jesus taught. In addition, it provides clues as to how long his ministry lasted as well. By significantly improving upon the accuracy of the timeline of Jesus' life, this harmony seeks to greatly enhance the reader's understanding of the most important person ever.

---

[2] See Robert A. Singer's paper "What Was the Duration of Jesus' Public Ministry? Can a Case Be Made for Two and a Half Years?" presented to the 2004 Evangelical Theological Society Annual Meeting.

About the Translation

This book uses a translation of the gospels produced uniquely for this harmony. With the wealth of modern translations available, it may be asked why a new translation would be necessary. Surely others are perfectly good. To answer this we need to consider the three major characteristics of a translation: accuracy, readability, and style.

Accuracy is how well a translation captures the meaning of the original text. Readability is how easy the translation is to understand. Style is how enjoyable the translation is to read. An ideal translation would maximize all three traits. Of course, a perfect translation is impossible; compromises are inevitable. Even still, a translation should strive to be strong in all three areas.

Unfortunately, this isn't the case with most modern, mainstream Bible translations. Modern translations tend to put so much emphasis on readability that accuracy suffers. Worse, there is often little effort put into the stylistic aspects. The books of the Bible are not just bland instruction manuals or textbooks, they are works of literature with great senses for style. Yet this isn't apparent with popular translations because the translation committees are so focused on the clarity of each individual verse they lose sight of the overall literary character of the Bible.

Further, modern translations are meant to be read silently to one's self since that is the standard way people consume reading material today. This means they are written for efficiency, with simple sentences of consistent length and few redundant words. However, ancient books were intended to be read aloud. Back then, not only was reading aloud to others normal, but even if a person was alone they would read out loud. The Biblical books are no exception. They have a rhythm to the phrasings of sentences that create a sense of flow that is apparent when read aloud which present day books lack. This rhythm is lost with modern Bible translations.

The lack of awareness for the literary nature of the Bible is made abundantly clear when one reads almost any article on the methods used to translate Scripture, including those explanations from translation committees that often appear in the front or back of Bibles. Invariably they state that there are two ways to translate the Bible: one is a literal "word-for-word" technique and the other is a looser "thought-for-thought" approach. These articles might use technical terms like "formal equivalence" and "dynamic equivalence". Yet they almost never make any mention of the need to instill a sense of style in the translation. The translators' job is portrayed as a purely clinical task of representing the meaning of individual words and phrases. No one would consider taking such a lifeless approach to other classics of literature, but it's the norm when it comes to the Bible.

This harmony's translation is based on the American Standard Version. The ASV was published in 1901 and is an update to the King James Bible. Since it is a descendant of the King James version, the ASV utilizes a rich, beautiful vocabulary that is very colorful. It is also quite literal in its interpretation. This makes it generally more accurate than many more recent translations, and it pleasantly captures the rhythm of the original books. The downside is that the ASV uses lots of outdated words and often has stilted phrasing, both of which badly hurt its readability.

The goal of this translation was to update the ASV so that it is highly readable while maintaining its strong literary qualities. In the process, its accuracy was enhanced further so that it does an even better job of relating the proper meaning of the original texts. The end result is intended to be both very enjoyable to read and be more accurate than popular translations.

To learn more about the literary virtues of the King James Bible, which also apply to this translation, see Robert Alter's article "Beyond King James" at:
www.commentarymagazine.com/articles/beyond-king-james/.

For an extremely thorough examination of the issues concerning the accuracy of modern translations, see Michael Marlowe's article "Against the Theory of 'Dynamic Equivalence' " at:
www.bible-researcher.com/dynamic-equivalence.html.

It is worth discussing some of the word choices used by this translation. The first noteworthy decision is in John's prologue (page 3). Verse 1:14 is usually translated along the lines of "the Word...dwelt among us". The Greek word translated as "dwelt" refers more specifically to setting up a tent. John uses that word in order to evoke the imagery of the tabernacle which was the tent used by the Israelites for all their religious rituals, including sacrifices, before the temple was built. Therefore, John is saying that Jesus is the new tabernacle. So this has been translated as "pitched his tent among us".

Throughout his ministry, Jesus cured many people of their afflictions. When he did so, he often told them what he did for them (such as with the women who had been bleeding for years; page 51). Usually his words are rendered as "healed" or "made whole". However, the word he said normally means "saved" and is the same word used in Matthew 1:21 when the angel tells Joseph that Jesus will "save his people from their sins" (page 9). Thus, Jesus was doing more than healing people physically, he was healing them spiritually as well.

In the Lord's Prayer (Matt 6:9-13, page 30; Luke 11:2-4, page 90) Jesus says, "Give us this day our *epiousios* bread". This is the only use of the word *epiousios* in any document so it is unknown what it means. Numerous suggestions have been made over the centuries with "daily" being only one of them. Kenneth E. Bailey in his book *Jesus Through Middle Eastern Eyes* notes that there is a translation of the gospels from the second century written in Syriac which is a language similar to the Aramaic Jesus likely spoke. That text is one of the earliest translations of the gospels and for *epiousios* it uses a word that means "never-ending" or "perpetual". In that vein, this translation uses the word "ceaseless". This may not be what Jesus meant, but by using a different word than what we are used to it helps to highlight the uncertainty around the word which encourages us to stop and reflect upon the passage.

What may be the most notable word choice relates to the location of Jesus' birth. The popular story everyone is familiar with is that Joseph and Mary were coldly turned away from an inn, forcing them to resort to delivering Jesus in a filthy stable all by themselves. The reason for this is that Luke writes that Mary "laid him in a manger, because there was no room for them in the *katalyma*" (Luke 2:7, page 9). This instance of the word *katalyma* has often been translated as "inn", while it is assumed that a manger must be somewhere away from people such as in a stable, a cave, or in a pasture. Both of these conclusions are most likely wrong.

Luke uses a different word for "inn" in his telling of the Parable of the Good Samaritan (10:34, page 89), while he uses *katalyma* for the location of the Last Supper (22:11, page 129) which clearly was in a private home instead of a commercial inn. So Luke probably meant that the spare room in a house was unavailable, rather than a lack of vacancy at an inn. This makes sense because Joseph was going to a town where he had family to stay with.

To understand why the presence of a manger doesn't mean that they were in a stable, it's necessary to know what a peasant house of that time was like. Such a home typically had a single, large room for the family to live in. It also had a second, smaller guest room for visitors. At one end of the main room was a section where the family's animals (a donkey, cow, and/or sheep) were kept at night that was a few feet lower than the rest of the room. These animals were brought into the house to keep them from being stolen and to warm the home (since there wasn't a fireplace). This meant that the house had a manger inside to feed the animals.

Joseph and Mary most certainly went to a family member's home for their stay in Bethlehem, but had to sleep in the main room of the house with the family because another visitor was already using the spare bedroom. Since there wasn't a crib available, they placed Jesus in the home's manger.

If Jesus had really been born in a stable or cave, Luke most certainly would have mentioned such a stunning fact. That he did not strongly suggests that the birth occurred in a place where people of that time would expect to have their babies, which is in a private home with other women assisting. For this reason, this translation uses "guest room" for *katalyma.*

Jesus and the gospel writers were very thoughtful in their use of words. Sometimes they used a variety of synonyms. This translation attempts to capture this variety by using a different English word for each Greek word when possible. For instance, many different sight words are used and so this translation uses a broad range of similar terms: see, look, behold, watch, peer, observe, gaze. This variety adds color and nuance.

Other times Jesus and the gospel writers repeat a particular word. These repetitions could be done for emphasis, for effect, or to tie different sayings or passages together. This translation tries to be consistent in how it handles particular words in order to bring out these repetitions. An example of this is in those passages where Jesus is warning his disciples that they need to be constantly ready for his return because they won't know when that will be (pages 94 and 125-126). In these warnings he uses forms of a specific word, *gregoreo*, which Bibles typically render with words and phrases such as "watch", "be alert", or "stay awake".

Now the only other time Jesus uses that word is in the Garden of Gethsemane when he is chastising the disciples for falling asleep while he prayed (page 139). By using that particular word, Jesus makes clear that the disciples have already failed to do as he commanded them. So this is a huge wake up call for them, both literally and figuratively. This connection is lost with other translations because they are not consistent in what English word they use for *gregoreo*, and the words they use for *gregoreo* are used elsewhere for different Greek words. This translation always uses "be vigilant" for *gregoreo* and not for any other Greek words which allows the reader to see this key repetition. This manner of consistency is applied to many other words throughout the harmony.

There is one more topic that is of academic interest. The apostle John uses the term *monogenes* to describe Jesus' relation to the Father (John 1:14 and 1:18, page 3; 3:16 and 3:18, page 21). For almost two thousand years this was translated as "only begotten". However, during the 20th century this view fell out of favor and was seen as a major error. In his book *Exegetical Fallacies* D.A. Carson went so far as to call the traditional translation "linguistic nonsense". Now the strong consensus of scholars is that it simply means "only" or "unique". Yet there are very good reasons to believe "only begotten" is correct which is why this translation uses the traditional rendering. In his chapter of *Retrieving Eternal Generation* Lee Irons reports on a comprehensive survey of ancient Greek texts which demonstrates that "only begotten" is a proper translation. It's worth noting that Carson contributes a chapter in that same book wherein he acknowledges that Irons' research reopens the issue. Denny Burk's post "Deep in the Weeds on MONOGENES and Eternal Generation" that is on his blog also provides a quality defense of "only begotten" (see www.dennyburk.com/deep-in-the-weeds-on-monogenes-and-eternal-generation/).

New Testament Timeline

37 BC Roman Senate makes Herod king of Judea
27 Augustus becomes first Roman emperor
5* John the Baptist and Jesus born
4* Magi visit Jesus; his family flees to Egypt
4 King Herod dies; kingdom divided amongst his three sons
3* Jesus' family returns to Nazareth
8 AD* 12-year old Jesus in the temple
14 Tiberius becomes Roman emperor
18 Caiaphas becomes High Priest
26 Pontius Pilate becomes prefect of Judea
27/30 John the Baptist and Jesus begin their ministries
30/33 Jesus' death and resurrection; Holy Spirit at Pentecost
34* Paul encounters risen Jesus and converts (Acts 9:1-30)
36 Caiaphas and Pilate removed from their positions
37 Caligula becomes emperor
39 Herod Antipas is removed as Tetrarch of Galilee by Caligula
41 Claudius becomes emperor
44 Martyrdom of James, son of Zebedee
46-48* Paul's first missionary journey
48-55 Approximate time first New Testament books are written
49 Christians hold council in Jerusalem (Acts 15:1-19)
49-52* Paul's second missionary journey, including to Corinth
52-57 Paul's third missionary journey, including to Ephesus
54 Nero becomes emperor
57 Paul arrested in Jerusalem
58-59 Paul imprisoned in Caesarea
60-62* Paul under house arrest in Rome
62 Martyrdom of James, leader of church in Jerusalem
64 Nero begins persecuting Christians
64-68 Peter and Paul are martyred
66 Jewish war breaks out against Romans
68 Nero dies
69 Vespasian becomes emperor
70 Jerusalem captured and temple destroyed by Romans
81 Domitian becomes emperor
90-99 Last New Testament book (Revelation) probably written

* indicates date is approximate

Glossary

Aaron—The brother of Moses and the first Jewish high priest.

Abba—The Aramaic term for "Father".

Annas—The Jewish high priest from 6 AD to 15 AD. His son-in-law Caiaphas was high priest at the time of Jesus' trial. Annas was removed from his position by the Romans but likely continued to have significant influence which is why both he and Caiaphas are referred to as high priest in the gospels.

Abraham—The first patriarch of the Jewish people, God promised him that his descendants would become a great nation and that through him all nations would be blessed. This promise would be fulfilled in Israel and Jesus, a descendant of Abraham. His son was Isaac and his grandson was Jacob, both of whom are also key figures in Jewish history. Their story is told in the biblical book of Genesis.

Archelaus—Son of Herod the Great. He ruled Judea and Samaria from 4 BC to 6 AD.

Caesar Augustus—Also known as Octavian, he was the ruler of the Roman empire from 31 BC to 14 AD. The Romans had conquered Jerusalem in 63 BC and they dominated the Jewish homeland during the life of Jesus. The Jews rebelled in 66 AD which led to the Romans destroying the temple. The Jews revolted again in 132 AD, ultimately resulting in the Romans crushing the Jewish nation and killing hundreds of thousands of Jews with many more sold into slavery.

Centurion—A commander in the Roman army, he led 80 soldiers.

Christ—Greek word meaning "Anointed One". It is the equivalent of the Jewish term "Messiah" and therefore is a title rather than a name. The Messiah was the prophesized descendant of King David who would bring salvation to Israel. This was Jesus.

clean/unclean—The Jewish religion has the concept that people and objects can become "unclean" as a result of certain acts (such as touching a dead body) and that particular actions need to be performed to make them "clean" again. This concept has nothing to do with hygiene but rather concerns ritual purity. In order for people to approach God they need to be spiritually pure, and this is represented by the actions that make them ritually clean. A person needed to be ritually clean in order to take part in the temple practices. This is why in the gospels when the practices of the Pharisees are described the term "baptized" is used (page 65). This makes clear that they were not doing normal sanitary washing but elaborate ritual cleansing.

David—The second and greatest king of Israel. Famous for his killing of Goliath with a sling and stone as a youth, he conquered Jerusalem, making it the capital of his kingdom. He also wrote many of the songs in the book of Psalms. He is revered for his deep dedication to God who promised that David's kingdom would last forever. This promise was fulfilled through Jesus.

Dispersion—The communities of Jews outside of Palestine scattered throughout the Middle East and around the Mediterranean Sea, also known as the diaspora. At the time of Jesus about 5 million Jews lived outside Palestine compared to 3 million within.

Denarius/Denarii—A denarius was the money a laborer was paid for a day's work. So 300 denarii would be about a year's wage.

Elijah—One of the greatest Jewish prophets, he chastised the Israelites for turning to pagan gods and practices. It was prophesized that Elijah would return and this was fulfilled by John the Baptist. While he was not literally Elijah, John came in "the spirit and power of Elijah" (Luke 1:17, page 5).

Feast of Dedication—Also known as Hanukkah, it is a Jewish holiday celebrating the cleansing of the temple after it had been defiled by Antiochus Epiphanes in 167 BC. It takes place in the winter and lasts eight days.

Feast of Tabernacles—Also known as Sukkot, it is one of the three major Jewish holidays that all Jewish men were required to celebrate in Jerusalem. The people were to make booths (called tabernacles) from tree branches that they were to live in during the eight-day event. This served as a reminder of the temporary shelters the Israelites lived in the desert after their deliverance from slavery in Egypt. This holiday occurred after the fall harvest and so also served as thanksgiving for their crops.

Gentile—A person who is not Jewish. The Jews often abhorred Gentiles because they worshiped other gods and had many evil practices. However, God's blessings were ultimately to be offered to Jews and Gentiles alike. This was achieved through Jesus' death and resurrection.

Herod—Known as Herod the Great, he was the ruler of Palestine when Jesus was born. A great builder, he grandly renovated the temple in Jerusalem. He was also cruel and paranoid to the point that he had two of his sons executed. While he held the title of king, he only ruled with permission of the Romans. When he died in 4 BC his kingdom was divided among his sons Archelaus, Antipas, and Philip.

Herod Antipas—Son of Herod the Great and tetrarch (governor) of Galilee and Peraea during Jesus' ministry. It was this Herod who interrogated Jesus during his trial and had John the Baptist imprisoned and beheaded.

"I AM"—In Exodus 3:14 God tells Moses after he asks for God's name, "I AM WHAT I AM...Thus shall you say to the children of Israel, I AM sent me to you." So in John 8:59 when Jesus says "before Abraham was, I AM" (page 73) he was declaring himself to be God. That is why the Pharisees instantly became furious and tried to stone him.

Jonah—A Jewish prophet who was ordered by God to preach to the Assyrian capital of Nineveh. However, he initially refused to go and fled on a ship. When the crew threw him overboard he was swallowed by a "great fish" (likely a whale) where he miraculously survived for three days. He eventually fulfilled his obligation to proclaim to the people of Nineveh and they repented for a time.

Levite—A member of the Jewish tribe of Levi. They were responsible for carrying out the many tasks at the temple, including playing music, manning the gates, and standing guard.

Manna—Bread that miraculously appeared every day (except on each Sabbath) during the 40 years the Israelites spent in the desert following their escape from Egypt. They were only allowed to collect enough manna for that day's needs (or double on the day before the Sabbath). Any excess collected would spoil.

Moses—The greatest Jewish prophet. He led the Israelites out of slavery in Egypt and during their 40 years of wandering in the desert. It was through him that the Jews received the laws that God required them to live by, most famous of which was the Ten Commandments. His story is told in the books of Exodus through Deuteronomy. Those books along with Genesis were written by him and so are called the Books of Moses (as well as Torah and the Pentateuch by Jews).

Passover—One of the three major Jewish holidays that all Jewish men were required to celebrate in Jerusalem. It commemorates the miraculous deliverance of the Israelites from slavery in Egypt which is described in the biblical book of Exodus. It takes place in the spring.

Pentecost—Also known as Shavuot or Feast of Weeks, it is one of the three major Jewish holidays that all Jewish men were required to celebrate in Jerusalem. It is held 50 days after Passover and is a thanksgiving for the wheat harvest. It was on Pentecost that the disciples received the Holy Spirit and so it is also a Christian holiday.

Pharisees—A religious sect of devout Jews. They not only strictly followed the rules that the Israelites were ordered to obey that are contained within the written Scriptures, they also abided by lots of practices that had accumulated over time and were communicated orally that went far beyond the written Law. These extra rules were intended to ensure that someone didn't even accidently violate God's Law. After the temple was destroyed in 70 AD, Judaism needed to be dramatically reformed because it was no longer possible to carry out the required rituals and sacrifices. The Pharisees had the most influence over the new direction of the religion and the major modern branches of Judaism trace their roots back to them.

Preparation Day—The day before the Sabbath. Since Jews were forbidden to do any work on the Sabbath they would take care ahead of time routine duties like preparing food.

The Prophet—This refers to God's promise in Deuteronomy 18:15-20 to send another prophet like Moses. This prophet was Jesus.

Rachel—Wife of the Jewish patriarch Jacob.

Sabbath—The day of rest that was devoted to God the Jews were commanded to partake in on the last day of every week (now called Saturday). No work was to be done on the Sabbath. However, the written Scriptures did not explain what counted as work and so devout Jews came up with lots of precise standards of what did and did not constitute work and exactly how far someone was allowed to travel on the Sabbath. While some Christians continue to celebrate the Sabbath, most attend worship services on Sunday because that is when Jesus was raised from the dead.

Sadducees—A Jewish sect that sharply disagreed with the Pharisees about doctrine and practices. This included the Sadducees' disbelief in any after life or the future resurrection of humanity. They also were more comfortable with adopting Greek culture and cooperating with the Romans. After the destruction of Jerusalem and the Jewish state by the Romans in 70 AD, the Sadducees cease to exist as a meaningful group.

Samaritans—After the northern kingdom of Israel was conquered by the Assyrians in 722 BC, the Israelites were forcibly exiled from their land and the Assyrians resettled other conquered people in their place. These new inhabitants lived in the region of Samaria and so they were called Samaritans. While they adopted many of the religious beliefs of the Jews, the Samaritans worshiped at Mt. Gerizim rather than the temple in Jerusalem and the two groups were in regular conflict with each other. The Jews despised the Samaritans and avoided them.

Scribes—The primary copyists of Jewish religious texts, they were respected experts on the contents and application of the Jewish Law. Some scribes were Pharisees but most were not.

Scripture—The Jewish holy books which are the authoritative word of God, also called the Tanakh by Jews and the Old Testament by Christians. The Scriptures are divided into three major sections: the Law, the Prophets, and the Writings. When Jesus spoke of "the Law and the Prophets" he was referring to all of Scripture.

Sodom and Gomorrah—Towns destroyed by God because of their great wickedness. The event is described in chapter 19 of Genesis.

Solomon—The third king of Israel and son of King David. He built the original Jewish temple and was known for his great wisdom. He wrote the biblical books of Ecclesiastes, Song of Songs, and most of Proverbs. The Queen of Sheba (referred to as "the Queen of the South" in the gospels) visited him because of his fame and wisdom.

Synagogue—A Jewish place of worship and religious study within a community.

Tax collectors—The Romans relied on locals to collect their taxes. These tax collectors were despised because they would demand from people far more than was owed. The Jews would have especially loathed fellow Jews who collected Roman taxes because they were working for the hated pagan oppressors.

Talent—The largest unit of weight for currency in the ancient world. A single talent of silver weighed around 75 pounds (34 kg). Since silver was worth even more than gold at that time, this was worth a fortune.

Temple—Located in Jerusalem, this was where the major Jewish religious rituals and all the required animal sacrifices were carried out making it central to the Jewish faith. Herod the Great dramatically renovated it over several decades, turning it into a massive, beautiful complex that was an absolute marvel of engineering and opulence. It was destroyed in 70 AD by the Romans during the Jewish rebellion, fulfilling the prophecy of Jesus (page 122). It has never been rebuilt and its site is now occupied by a Muslim mosque. This is not a problem because Jesus is now our temple.

A model of the temple complex in the time of Jesus. The top of the page is north and the temple opens to the east.

Harmony Outline

Gospel Openings

	Matt	Mark	Luke	John	Page
Jesus' Genealogy	1:1-17		3:23b-38		-
Mark's Opening		1:1			1
Luke's Introduction			1:1-4		-
John's Prologue				1:1-18	3

Two Miraculous Births

	Matt	Mark	Luke	John	Page
Jerusalem					
John's birth foretold to Zacharias			1:5-25		5
Nazareth					
Jesus' birth foretold to Mary			1:26-38		6
Hill country of Judea					
Mary's visit to Elizabeth			1:39-45		6
Mary's song of joy			1:46-56		7
Birth of John			1:57-66		7
Zacharias' prophetic song			1:67-79		8
John's growth and early life			1:80		8
Nazareth					
Circumstances of Jesus' birth explained to Joseph	1:18-25				9
Bethlehem					
Birth of Jesus			2:1-7		9
Witness of the shepherds			2:8-20		9
Circumcision of Jesus			2:21		10
Jesus presented to the temple			2:22-38		10
Jesus' family returns to Nazareth			2:39		-
Visit of the Magi	2:1-12				11
Jesus' family flees to Egypt	2:13-18				12
Nazareth					
New home in Nazareth	2:19-23				12
Jesus' growth and early life			2:40		12
Jesus' first Passover in Jerusalem			2:41-50		13
Jesus' adolescence			2:51-52		

Beginning of Jesus' Ministry

	Matt	Mark	Luke	John	Page
Jordan River in Judea					
John the Baptist's ministry launched			3:1-2		15
John's proclamation and baptism	3:1-6	1:2-6	3:3-6		15
John's messages to those who come to him	3:7-10		3:7-14		15
John's description of the Christ	3:11-12	1:7-8	3:15-18		16
Jesus' baptism by John	3:13-17	1:9-11	3:21-23a		16
Jesus' temptation by Satan in the wilderness	4:1-11	1:12-13	4:1-13		17
John's self-identification to the priests and Levites				1:19-28	17
John declares Jesus to be the Lamb and Son of God				1:29-34	18
Jesus' first disciples				1:35-51	18
Cana					
Turning water to wine				2:1-11	19
Visit at Capernaum with his disciples				2:12	20
Jerusalem					
First cleansing of the temple at the Passover				2:13-22	20
Early response to Jesus' miracles				2:23-25	20
Nicodemus' night visit with Jesus				3:1-21	20
Ænon					
John superseded by Jesus				3:22-36	21
John imprisoned			3:19-20		22
Jesus' departure from Judea	4:12	1:14a		4:1-4	22
Sychar					
Discussion with Samaritan women at well				4:5-26	22
Challenge of a spiritual harvest				4:27-38	24
Evangelization of Sychar				4:39-42	24
Arrival in Galilee				4:43-44	24

Jesus' Ministry in Galilee and the Kingdom Explained

Jesus' Ministry in Galilee and the Kingdom Explained
(Continued)

Three Feasts and Two Miraculous Feedings

	Matt	Mark	Luke	John	Page
Jerusalem					
Jesus goes to Jerusalem for a feast				5:1	55
Disabled man healed on the Sabbath				5:2-9	55
Attempt to kill Jesus for violating Sabbath and saying he was equal to God				5:10-18	56
Jesus explains his equality with the Father				5:19-47	56
Galilee					
Shortage of spiritual workers	9:35-38	6:6b			57
Commissioning of the Twelve	10:1-42	6:7-11	9:1-5		57
Twelve Apostles sent out	11:1	6:12-13	9:6		57
Herod Antipas' mistaken identification of Jesus	14:1-2	6:14-16	9:7-9		59
Earlier imprisonment and beheading of John the Baptist	14:3-12	6:17-29			59
Return of the Twelve Apostles		6:30	9:10a		60
Hill country near Bethsaida					
Withdrawal from Galilee	14:13-14	6:31-34	9:10b-11	6:1-3	60
Feeding the five thousand	14:15-21	6:35-44	9:12-17	6:4-13	61
Attempt to make Jesus king	14:22-23	6:45-46		6:14-15	62
Walking on water during storm	14:24-33	6:47-52		6:16-21	62
Galilee					
Healings at Gennesaret	14:34-36	6:53-56			62
Crowd seeks Jesus at Capernaum				6:22-25	63
"I am the Bread of Life"				6:26-59	63
Some disciples desert Jesus				6:60-7:1	64
Conflict over tradition of ceremonial defilement	15:1-20	7:1-23			65
Near Tyre					
Healing Gentile woman's daughter	15:21-28	7:24-30			66
Decapolis					
Healing of deaf man and others	15:29-31	7:31-37			67
Feeding the four thousand	15:32-38	8:1-9			67

Three Feasts and Two Miraculous Feedings
(Continued)

	Matt	Mark	Luke	John	Page
Galilee					
Return to Galilee	15:39	8:10			68
Second request for a sign	16:1-16:4	8:11-12			68
Warning about the Pharisees, Sadducees, and Herodians	16:5-12	8:13-21			68
Healing of blind man at Bethsaida		8:22-26			69
Jesus ridiculed by brothers				7:2-9	69
Jerusalem					
Secret arrival in Jerusalem for Feast of Tabernacles				7:10	69
Mixed reaction to Jesus' teaching and miracles				7:11-31	69
Attempt to arrest Jesus				7:32-52	70
"I am the Light of the World"				8:12-20	71
Call to believe to avoid dying in sins				8:21-30	72
Jesus' relationship to Abraham and attempted stoning				8:31-59	72
Healing of man born blind				9:1-7	74
Reaction of the blind man's neighbors				9:8-12	74
Interrogation and excommunication of blind man by Pharisees				9:13-34	74
Jesus identifies himself to blind man				9:35-38	75
Spiritual blindness of Pharisees				9:39-41	75
"I am the Gate of the Sheep"				10:1-10	76
"I am the Good Shepherd"				10:11-18	76
Division among Jews about Jesus				10:19-21	76
In Jerusalem for Feast of Dedication				10:22	76
Demand that Jesus say if he is the Christ				10:23-30	77
Another attempt to stone and arrest Jesus				10:31-39	77
Withdrawal to wilderness beyond Jordan river				10:40-42	77
Bethany					
Sickness and death of Lazarus				11:1-24	77
"I am the Resurrection and the Life"				11:25-26	78
Jesus raises Lazarus from dead				11:27-44	78
Decision of the Sanhedrin to put Jesus to death				11:45-54	80

Final Journey to Jerusalem

	Matt	Mark	Luke	John	Page
Near Caesarea Philippi					
Peter's identification of Jesus as the Christ	16:13-17	8:27-30	9:18-21		81
Peter told he will be foundation of the church	16:18-20				81
First direct prediction of Jesus' rejection, murder, and resurrection	16:21-26	8:31-37	9:22-25		81
Coming of the Son of Man and judgment	16:27-28	8:38-9:1	9:26-27		81
Near Caesarea Philippi or in Galilee					
Transfiguration	17:1-9	9:2-10	9:28-36		82
Explanation of Elijah, John the Baptist, and the Son of Man's coming	17:10-13	9:11-13			83
Healing of demonized boy and disciples rebuked for lack of faith	17:14-20	9:14-29	9:37-43a		83
Second direct prediction of Jesus' arrest, murder, and resurrection	17:22-23	9:30-32	9:43b-45		84
Capernaum					
Payment of temple tax	17:24-27				84
Disciples argue about which of them is greatest	18:1-5	9:33-37	9:46-48		85
Warning against causing believers to stumble	18:6-14	9:38-50	9:49-50		85
Approach of the church toward sinning member	18:15-35				86
Beginning of final journey			9:51		87
Samaria					
Rejection by Samaritans			9:52-56		87
Complete commitment required of followers	8:19-22		9:57-62		87
Commissioning of seventy-two disciples			10:1-16		87
Return of the seventy-two			10:17-24		88
Parable of the Good Samaritan			10:25-37		89

Final Journey to Jerusalem (Continued)

Final Journey to Jerusalem (Continued)

	Matt	Mark	Luke	John	Page
Peraea across from Judea					
Pharisees challenge Jesus over the legality of divorce	19:1-12	10:1-12			104
Example of little children in relation to the Kingdom	19:13-15	10:13-16	18:15-17		105
Rich ruler's question on how to achieve eternal life	19:16-22	10:17-22	18:18-23		105
Difficulty of the wealthy to enter the Kingdom	19:23-30	10:23-31	18:24-30		106
Parable of the Generous Vineyard Owner	20:1-16				106
Third direct prediction of Jesus' arrest, murder, and resurrection	20:17-19	10:32-34	18:31-34		107
Request that John and James receive the seats of highest honor in the Kingdom	20:20-28	10:35-45			107
Jericho					
Recovering the sight of Bartimaeus and his companion	20:29-34	10:46-52	18:35-43		108
Salvation of Zacchaeus the chief tax collector			19:1-10		109
Parable of the Vengeful King			19:11-28		109
Jerusalem					
Jews wonder if Jesus will risk coming to Jerusalem for Passover				11:55-57	110

Passion Week

	Matt	Mark	Luke	John	Page
Saturday					
Arrival at Bethany				12:1	111
Mary's anointing of Jesus	26:6-13	14:3-9		12:2-11	111
Palm Sunday					
Triumphal entry into Jerusalem	21:1-11	11:1-11a	19:29-44	12:12-19	111
Necessity for the Son of Man to be lifted up				12:20-36a	113
Failure of the crowd to believe and its consequences				12:36b-50	114
Entrance into the temple and return to Bethany		11:11b			115
Monday					
Cursing of fig tree	21:18-19a	11:12-14			115
Second cleansing of the temple	21:12-16	11:15-18	19:45-48		115
Return to Bethany at evening	21:17	11:19			116

Passion Week
(Continued)

Last Supper

Trial and Crucifixion

	Matt	Mark	Luke	John	Page
Good Friday					
Arrest of Jesus	26:47-56	14:43-52	22:47-53	18:2-12	141
First Jewish phase of trial before Annas				18:13-14, 19-24	142
Peter denies knowing Jesus	26:69-75	14:66-72	22:54b-62	18:15-18, 25-27	142
Second Jewish phase of trial before Caiaphas and Sanhedrin	26:57-68	14:53-65	22:54a, 63-65		143
Third Jewish phase of trial before the Sanhedrin	27:1	15:1a	22:66-71		143
Remorse and suicide of Judas	27:3-10				144
First Roman phase before Pontius Pilate	27:2, 11-14	15:1b-5	23:1-5	18:28-38	145
Second Roman Phase before Herod Antipas			23:6-12		146
Third Roman phase before Pilate, scourging of Jesus, and release of Barabbas	27:15-30	15:6-19	23:13-25	18:39-19:16	146
Journey to Golgotha	27:31-34	15:20-23	23:26-33a	19:17	148
Crucified	27:35a, 38	15:24a, 27	23:33b-34a	19:18	149
Inscription above the cross	27:37	15:25-26	23:38	19:19-22	149
Soldiers cast lots over Jesus' clothes	27-35b-36	15:24b	23:34b	19:23-24	149
Bystanders mock Jesus	27:39-43	15:29-32	23:35-37		149
Response of the other crucifixion victims	27:44		23:39-43		150
Jesus gives his mother over to John's care				19:25-27	150
Darkness over the land	27:45	15:33	23:44-45a		150
"My God, my God, why have you forsaken me?"	27:46	15:34			150
Vinegar given to Jesus	27:47-49	15:35-36		19:28-29	150
Death	27:50	15:37	23:46	19:30	150
Miraculous events at Jesus' death	27:51-53	15:38	23:45b		151
Witnesses of Jesus' death	27:54-56	15:39-41	23:47-49		151
Removal of the body	27:57-58	15:42-45	23:50-52	19:31-38	151
Jesus' body placed in tomb	27:59-60	15:46	23:53-54	19:39-42	151
Tomb watched by women and guarded by soldiers	27:61-66	15:47	23:55-56		152

"He is Risen!"

Epilogue

Made in the USA
Middletown, DE
09 December 2020

27057933R00136